Art of
Screenplay Writing
Kuldeep Sinha

Dedicated

to

My mentor **Dr. Vrindavan Lal Varma** , a prominent and celebrated
Indian Author who gave me my first lesson in writing.

Kuldeep Sinha

ACTS

Acknowledgment

XXXXX

'I dream films, I talk films,

I think films, I live films

and I sleep with films.'

-Raj Kapoor

The great showman of India

Kuldeep Sinha

Acknowledgement:

The book '**Art of Screen play writing**' is the culmination of many years of experience I gained in my association with the marvels in various disciplines of film making those included film directors, editors, writers, sound Designers and many more. It has given me an opportunity to imbibe the intricacies of each department during the production of both fiction and non - fiction films. It was my privilege to be associated with them as Producer, Director, writer and Editor for more than three decades.

It is my privilege to pay my tributes to my mentor **Dr.Vrindavan Lal Verma**, an eminent Hindi novelist and playwright who is known for his writing on historical and mythological subjects. He was decorated with *Padma Bhushan* for his literary works; Agra University presented him with *honorary D. Lit*. He received *Soviet Land Nehru Award* and the government of India also awarded him for his novel, *Jhansi Ki Rani*.

Dr.Vrindavan Lal Verma was born into a noble Srivastava Kayasthya family in the year 1889.He was drawn towards mythological and historical narratives from early childhood. His masterpiece, *Mriganayani*, set at the end of the 15th century in Gwalior, tells the legend of Man Singh and his "doe-eyed queen". His first original work was *Mahatma Buddha Ka Jivan Charitra* (1908). His play *Senapati Udal* (1909) was proscribed by the government. He wrote some short stories and essays also.

His **historical novels** are *Gadh Kundar, Virata ki Padmini , Musahibju ,Jhansi ki Rani , Kachnar , Madavji Sindhia , Tute Kante, Mriganayani, Bhuvan Vikram, Ahilya Bai .* **social novels:** *Sangam , Lagan, Pratyagat , Kundali Chakra , Prem ki Bheni ,*

Kabhi na Kabhi Achal Mera Koyi, Rakhi ki Laj , Sona , Amar Bel . **Plays:** include an adaptation of his novel, *Jhansi ki Rani, Hans Mayur, Bans ki Phans, Pile Hath , Purva ki Aur , Kevat , Nilkanth , Mangal Sutra , Birbal ,* and *Lalit Vikram .* He died in the year 1969.

Dr. Vrindavan Lal Varma played a catalyst when I wrote my first novel **'*Udte Panchhi*** (Birds sre flying),' in my teen years and had the honor to narrate it to him. He heard me patiently till I completed thereafter he gave me my first lesson by explaining the significance of ' ***The Cause, Action and Relationship'*** in writing. In these three words he had concise the entire thesis of writing that laid the foundation of my future. I salute Dr Varma for his genius.

I will be failing in my duty if I don't mention my alma mater the **Film and Television Institute of India** which taught me the basics of film making.

Shri Hrishikesh Mukherjee, the veteran Film Editor and director in Indian Cinema, was always my Inspiration who inspired me to be an Editor first and then be a director. I owe my success and achievements as a film maker to this great film veteran of his time.

A book on such a complex subject like ***Screen play writing*** cannot be completed without illustrations and references of outstanding film scenes shot by pioneer directors . I bow to all of them who guided many generations of film makers.

Kuldeep Sinha

The book 'Art of Screenplay writing' is designed to benefit those who have long nurtured a dream to be a writer in cinema. They neither have dearth of imagination nor lack of merit; what they lack is proper guidance to hone their skill and technical knowledge to step out on the path of writing for screen. The book attempts to enlighten budding writers about the genesis, methodology and chronology of screenplay writing from *an Idea to complete screen play*. A peep in to film techniques in the chapter *'Behind the camera'* helps remove technical glitches of a writer who sometime encounters few dark patches while writing script. Similarly, understanding of different *'Sound'* and *'Image'* symbols arms a writer to properly interpret different emotions and expressions. **'Art of Screen play writing'** is a complete learning experience for passionate writers.

XXXXX

Prologue:

Kuldeep sinha with his book '**Art of Screen play writing'** has attempted to fill the technical void in *writing for film and television.* His accomplished journey as writer, director,editor and producer is an evidence of a multi dimensional expression that is unearthed from the deep layers of unknown grounds covering long road of experiences. *Screenplay* is the soul of a film or television creation, it is neither less nor more. The film maker in *Mr. Kuldeep Sinha* not only knows it well but understands it too that prompts his knowledge flow flawlessly to write a book on such a complex subject. Each chapter of the book is a milestone leading to contentment and satisfaction at the end for both the writer and the readers.

While narrating the beginning of cinema with its historical perspectives, the writer is lost when his creativity is seen waiting on the back seat however he quickly moves forward to establish the importance and the genesis of writing script in the rustic form during age of silent cinema. The content, the process of film writing, basics of a story, development of a plot and sub-topics Join hands to discover a formula to write a story. It is a clear reflection of his writing experience and skills. The problems to *'outline'* a story to the *'Theme'* that includes management of screen time to integrate the scenes and the dialogues have been technically simplified with appropriate illustrations. A peephole view of the techniques of cinematography and film editing helps a newcomer to understand the fundamentals of film technology that are essential for a writer to cross some technical hurdles. Similarly, the impact of *'sound'* and *'dialogues'* as a means of effective expression and communication has also been explained in simple words. While the book **'Art of Screen play writing'** would attract ever growing bunch of film and television professionals, it would also invite scholars to analyze it for the ***benefits of cinema students and critics.***

Anubha Sharma,
Author & Poet
(Honored in Limca book of Records)
Mumbai.

XXXXX

About the Author:

Kuldeep Sinha is a *National and International award winner,* author and film maker who has won considerable professional place for his thought provoking films and writings. He has Three anthologies of original *short stories* to his credit: **Kashish**, **Siskiyaan** and **Dastak** a book on Personality Development **'Galion se Chaurahe Tak',** His trilogy (in Hindi) on Film making 'Patkatha Lekhan ke Tatva', **'Film Nirdeshan and 'Film Sampadan'**are equally popular with students of cinema. He is conferred the **Rajbhasha shree** and the **Saraswat Samman** at the *Ashirwad awards , Hindi Sahitya Samman* by the Government of India and few others for his exemplary work in Hindi language.

His work in English includes Novels '**Darkness in the arc',** '**Neither: The Birth of Transgender'**, 'Behind the moving **Images',** a trilogy (in English) **'Art of Screenplay writing', 'Film & TV.: A Director's guide', 'Elements of film Editing',** and **'Mohammad Rafi: The Melody man'.**

He has written and directed more than hundred short films on a wide variety of subjects from Agriculture to Arts, from Music to Science and from News and current affairs to Educational films. His films have begged several National and International

Honors. He is honored with **'Scroll of Honor'** for outstanding services towards the welfare & growth of Hindi Talkie Cinema by Indian Organization of Mass Communication & School of Broadcasting & Communication, Mumbai , and the **'Life Time Achievement Award'** for contribution in the growth and promotion of Documentary Films by International Centre for Cultural Relations, Mumbai and many more.

An Honors graduate from the University of Pune, he has also graduated in cinema from the Film and Television Institute of India with a rare flair in Hindi and English equally .He later studied Journalism, Press relations and Management.

XXXXX

Expressions:

Everyday a new television channel, every day a new film release, everyday a new soap, ever expanding world of cinema, encroachment of film and television in every home, craze and crave of children for entertainment, young and old, men and women for small and big screen entertainment, Indian cinema at the door of Oscars, has all diminished the distance between Cinema and Television. TV soaps have become an extension of film entertainment. Popularity of television has given a new dimension to film promotion and exhibition. Film stars too are not left behind the glamour of small screen who jump on the very first opportunity to be seen on small screen to promote them. Film and television complement each other's existence. Ever growing number of television channels has spurred the demand for more films and more television productions. It has created a need for writers who could integrate and assimilate both the visual media and attract more eyeballs. It is the golden period for those creative people who want to earn their bread and cheese in writing for films and television.

Contrary to the film which has always been considered a visual medium, the television has taken its form from 'Sound Broadcasting' or the Radio. Cinema amalgamates all other art forms in its production and presentation technology. It spread its roots much before the television came to its existence therefore while discussing the nuances of *screenplay writing* in this book, we take **'Cinema'** as a base without losing the track for television writing. We can now call television an offshoot of cinema in its present form that is technically similar in it's production design and technology so writers for cinema not only will be equally benefitted by the explanations in this book but will also be equally confident to write for television.

The book **'Art of Screen play writing'** is a boon for those who have long been nourishing dreams to be a film writer. They neither have dearth of imagination nor lack of merit. What they lack is proper guidance to hone their skills, technical knowledge and chronology to move them forward on the path of screen writing systematically. A brief introduction about film technique in the chapter *'Behind the Camera'* helps remove technical glitches of a writer who sometime encounters few dark spots while writing a script. Similarly, understanding of different 'sound' and 'Image symbols' arm a writer to properly interpret different emotions and *expressions.*

The Book in its previous incarnation in Hindi language titled **'Patkatha Lekhan Ke Tatva'** has earned the honor of a *'Reference Book'* for the students of Media awarded by *SNDT women's University, Mumbai* that serves its purpose. It has also received high accolades from those who matter in the field of cinema. The book **'Art of Screen play writing'** has been rewritten with more additions in the simplest possible narratives to make the grasp of the subject simpler for the students of media as well as the professionals in cinema and television.

Author

Act 1:

The Back ground:

The moment a producer decides to produce a film and he lines up all the resources at his command to go ahead, the first and foremost requirement is that of a *story and a screenplay writer.* No film can be completed without the active and creative support of a story writer, a screenplay writer and a dialogue writer. The story can be an author's original work or adapted from a published work of other writers, a novelist, a playwright or can be inspired from an earlier film, a drama or a new story can be conceived by a writer based on an *idea* however it requires a special skill to develop a story and its visual presentation on the screen. It has to come out of the original imagination and the visualization. The written form of presenting a story, novel, drama or an idea as it is seen on the screen is called *'Screen play'*. Therefore a *screenplay writer* is one of the most important persons who shape a story with his imagination and visualizing powers to prepare a blue print of the proposed film.

A *screenplay writer* is the first man who gives life to a character/s and creates interesting situations with his sheer imagination and grit. He feels the emotions and sentiments of the characters he creates, he sees the action and the events taking place in different situations he visualizes, he creates twists and turns, struggle and turmoil during the span of the story holding the hands of the audience participating and identifying them with their characters. It is the screenplay writer who makes his audience cry and laugh in the scenes he conceives. The writer is just not a creative person to achieve it but he also knows technical nitty-gritty of film making to manipulate technical support in the form of special cinematography, use of sounds including silence and dialogues and film editing. It distinguishes him from other writers who only play with words such as a Novelist who with his vocabulary skillfully developed and crafted sketches a verbiage by the effective use of appropriate '**words**' to provide a visual depiction of a scene. When a reader reads a novel, he is lost in the verbatim visuals, emotional expressions and interpretation caricatured in his mind. Author's success in his endeavor is in proportion of the reader's involvement in the story therefore it is not a mean task for a writer to create an engrossing and entertaining literary work.

Unfortunately a film writer is never accorded a place of dignity that he deserves. There is a common perception about him that he only integrates visuals and the words when he writes a screenplay on a predefined story, the characters and the situations, making any tom dick harry in the production think that anybody has the merit to give suggestions in the script conceived by a writer after lot of hard work and loss of mid night sleep. To an extent an Image of a poor looking man clad in loose tunic and trouser, long hair, unshaven beard, a bag hanging on his shoulders and slippers on his feet tagged with him since time immemorial, is also responsible for his pathetic conditions. The writers therefore have never been paid their dues and they always live life of a pauper. They always survive on the pleasure of their masters.

If we have a look at the historical perspective of a **writer** ,it is observed that he has been prevalent in every period and times. He was writing poetry and plays to sing praises of kings and emperors. He wrote to entertain rulers and the ruled, sometimes he wrote on social and economical issues to invite king's attention, he also wrote folklores and stories, he created literature for children's education and entertainment. In all these writings, he generally played with *'words'* which did not involve any technical skills. His concentration was on the creation of characters, actors and their dramatic performance however the actors or performers were given credit for the success of an enactment. Thus the writer is lost somewhere in the background, but in no way it undermines his contribution in its successful creation and presentation.

The Silent Cinema

Film is a transformation of an *illusion* to the *creative realism* through moving images recorded on the raw stock of picture negative and sound tapes or on a digital device during the shooting. This transformation takes place by creation of proper images, proper timing and proper placement of shots in chronological order of the script to provide an illusion of a real and continuous action.

Lumiere Brothers:

The advent of **Silent cinema** in the late nineteenth century was in fact with the capturing of real activities or events in a *single* *shot* pioneered by *Lumiere brothers* without a preconceived idea, a story line or a rehearsal by the performers. The purpose of these films was to entertain the captive audience by projecting the reality on celluloid film through moving pictures. The movies were a step forward of the earlier still photography. These single shot films by the Lumiere brothers included, *'A train leaving the station', 'Baby at the lunch table', 'A boat leaving the harbor'* and many more. The entire action was generally covered without a cut. Where there were more than one cut in the action, each shot was cut and pasted together in such a way that entire action looked a single continuous action but these multiple cuts were absolutely not planned and preconceived. The purpose of the multiple cuts with captions in between was to present the movement in the most realistic manners maintaining the continuity of actions.

After experimenting with the **'presentation of reality'** the *Lumiere brothers* moved one more step ahead to **'create an action'.** He preplanned the shoot in the film **'Watering the garden'**. A gardener is shown watering the plants with a rubber pipe. A cute baby enters and puts his foot on the hosepipe blocking the flow. The gardener is surprised at the sudden stoppage of the water. When he looks at baby, he releases the pipe and water flows out gushingly to wet him. Seeing he wet, the child starts laughing.' This was the first experiment in the history of silent cinema by the Lumiere brothers to make a film with the sole purpose to entertain people with a preconceived story and pre planed action.

Following the footsteps of Lumiere brothers *George Melies* did another experiment by creating special visual effects or trick photography   in the camera itself while shooting a film. Thus the practice of taking a scene in a single shot was at halt. This enhanced the possibilities of better story telling including special effects to make a film more interesting and entertaining. While the single shot series of films by Lumieres did not exceed the length of more than 50 ft each, the film *'Cinderella'* (1899) made by *George Melies* was much longer in length of 410 ft.. The *'Cinderella'* was shot in 20 parts, each part of the film was similar to the *'one- shot films'* of Lumiere however every part of *'Cinderella'* series was inter connected with other to take the story forward unlike the films of Lumiere brothers which were complete in a single shot. Revolving around a single character of *Cinderella,* the film had a definite story line with each part having a different title such as, *'Cinderella in her kitchen', 'The ferry, mice and Leaches',' The triumph of Cinderella' etc.* 'Cinderella' was the beginning of fiction films based on a preconceived story with characters and preplanned shooting style engaging actors to play different characters in a film. In the subsequent years more experimentation was carried out for a better and effective story telling.

In another landmark experiment *Melies* used his camera as an audience. The way people sitting in the rear watch an action played on the stage in a theatrical production, he fixed his camera among them to cover an action on a fixed background. In *'Cinderella'* and other productions of *George Melies*, though the continuity of story content was maintained, it was missing in context of the background, actions, continuity from one shot to another and the timing etc. captions were used in between the shots to carry forward the story idea. Influenced by the theatre, these films were close to one **'act'** of a stage play therefore it was clear that *Melies'* style was highly influenced by the theatre.

Edwin S. Porter, the first cameraman of *Edison* virtually revolutionized the style, presentation and technique of film making in 1902 by his film' ***The life of an American fireman'***. *Porter* was mesmerized by the actions and dare devilry of 'Fire fighters'. He shot an entire operation undertaken by the fire station. While the coverage was very effective, it lacked elements of interest and entertainment. He needed a story to make the film interesting therefore he introduced characters of a mother and a child who were trapped in the fire. A rescue operation to save them was shot accordingly.

The operation was divided in number of unrelated shots which individually did not convey anything but when joined together chronologically, they produced a different meaning taking the story of the mother and her child forward who were trapped in fire and recued. *'The life of an American fireman'* was a remarkable mix of reality coverage and dramatic enactments which kept its audience spellbound till the trapped family were rescued for their utter relief.

'The life of an American fireman'-

Defying his predecessors of shooting an entire scene in a single shot without a cut, *Porter* conceived a dramatic sequence having multiple shots as under, covering the scene from different perspectives and backgrounds maintaining the continuity of thoughts, action of fire fighting and rescue operation to give human touch with an emotional appeal by introducing the characters of a mother and a child who were trapped in the fire in a building. This made the film more gripping and interesting.

- The crew of fire brigade moves in to the place where fire is broke out.
- A building is in flames.
- In the background, the fire van enters in speed and stops.
- Orders are given to fix the engine. Water pipes are taken out of the van.
- Stairs are fixed on the windows of the building.
- Water is gushed with speed through hose pipes on the fire spots.

  (The scene is Dissolved to)
- In the interior of the building a mother with her baby are entrapped in the fire and smoke.
- They run around to save themselves but fail.
- They feel suffocated amidst the fire and smoke.
- The lady shouts from the window to appeal the surging crowd to save them.
- She is again entrapped in the smoke and a burning log falls on the bed in the room.
- A fire man (The Hero) breaks open the door with the help of a spade to enter the room.
- He tears the drapers and opens the windows of the room. He orders his other colleagues to put up a stair on the window.
- Immediately a stair comes up to the window.
- The hero lifts the lady on his shoulder like a gunny bag and climbs down with her on the stair.

  (The scene is dissolved to).
- Exterior of the building is seen burning.
- Lady in her night suit regains her consciousness and requests the hero to save her child.

- Hero calls his men to follow him and returns back with them to bring the child safely.
- He enters into the room through the window. Tension is built up for some time giving an impression that the hero himself is trapped in the fire and smoke and it was difficult for him to come back alive. After some time he is seen holding the child in his arms.
- He comes down and hands over the child to his mother ending the breathtaking climax to a happy end.

The story is conceived very intelligently in three parts to approach the *climax.* First part is the **establishment of a problem** that is the eruption of fire in a residential building. The flames increase with the flow of the wind. Another part consists of *a mother* and *a child* who is **entrapped in the fire** and smoke. They struggle to save themselves. Third part is the entry of the *Hero* who risks his own life and daringly gets in to the fire scene to **rescue** the lady and her child thus bringing relief to them and the onlookers. The continuity in action has been maintained by joining shots in chronological order to give a feeling of a continuous fire fighting and rescue operation. The film ends with the **resolution of the problem** when the lady and her child are saved.

If we take a close look at the difference in the style of film making of both these pioneer film makers, *George Melies* and *Edwin S. porter*, we can easily point out that if *George Melies* would have made the film *'The life of an American Fireman'*, he would have separated these parts with a Title caption to proceed with the story but *Porter* has treated every shot as a **'unit'** of a continuous action and joined them to carry forward the story without a jerk or a visual distraction. He had reversed the concept of telling one point at a time in a single shot. This has given greater advantage of creative freedom to a director. The continuity of events or action in the scene presented an *illusion of reality* to the audience for a better emotional connect and grasp. In *'The life of an American fireman'*, *Porter* had beautifully combined the reality and theatrical enactments without disrupting the continuity of a story line and action. This was the beginning of **'Fiction film'** making of today. It is another point that modern film makers concoct the reality the way they interpret it and want their audience to see it the same way.

Another advantage of assembling number of shots to a definite story line is that director can establish the event by squeezing the duration of the whole action which is also accepted by the viewers. *'In the life of an American fireman'* the entire action of fire fighting and rescue operations was contracted to less than 10 minutes of the real time of many hours however the audience was given the psychological feeling of the event in real time. In this film Porter has proved the following points very effectively-

1. No single shot can be a 'complete' action.

2. A shot is only a small 'unit' of the entire scene.
    The way bricks are properly fixed   together one by one with another to erect a wall, proper placement of shots when joined together creates a scene or a film. It is the basic principle of 'Editing'.

This basic principle of film editing was followed more precisely and systematically by *Porter* in his next film,' **The Great train** *robbery'* in the year 1903. Known for his innovative approach, the *'one shot transition'* was another innovation carried out by Porter in the film. In *'one shot transition'* technique an action was divided into many shots and in editing the action was completed by joining shots in the chronological order in the similar manner as we climb up a ladder step by step. The *'one shot transition'* was never used earlier by anybody.

The Great Train robbery-

Scene 9- Panoramic view of a valley. A group of robbers is running on the horses.

Scene 10- In the telegraph room of a railway station, the operator with his hands and legs tied by ropes tries hard to reach to the telegraph table but falls down unconscious. His little daughter brings food for him. She cuts his ropes and throws water on his face to bring him to consciousness. He becomes conscious. Fresh with the memories of the robbery, he comes out of the room to give alarm.

Scene 11- People are dancing in a hall. The door opens and the telegraph operator enters in semi conscious state. The dance stops and few people come out with their rifle.

'The great train robbery' was technically one step ahead of *'The life of an American fireman'* due to 'different actions' occurring at the same time in two different locations showed simultaneously. This is called *'Parallel action'.* *'The great train robbery'* was a very simplistic narration with effective use of **continuity of action'** 'and *'parallel action'* to convey a story however his presentation had its inherent limitations as the events were never preplanned, picked up haphazardly and

were shot in theatre style keeping the camera at a fixed distance. This restricted the observation and control of the director over the actions. It was on the actors to convey the meaning to the audience through their actions, mannerism and expressions. This technique had direct influence of the theatre in its execution. The shots in the chronological order were juxtaposed in the similar manner as we climb up the ladder step by step.

D.W.Griffith:

Almost after twelve years **D.W.Griffith** had liberally used this technique of *parallel actions* in his films. He not only accepted and executed the technique developed by Porter but also improved it. His creative experiments became mile stones in the history of cinema. To understand *Griffith,* let's have a look on the scenes and shot composition from the reel no.6 of his film, *'The Birth of a Nation'-*

Film-The Birth of a Nation: Assassination of Lincoln.

Benjamin Cameron comes out of Stoneman House with his friend Essle Stoneman. They move to a theatre to see a special performance which was also attended by President Lincoln. The performance in the theatre has started.

Scene 1:

Title- Arrival of the President Lincoln (Caption) Location- Auditorium

1. Full Shot. Interior, staircase,

The security guards of President Lincoln climb the stairs of the auditorium one after another and reach to the president's enclosure. After some time president arrives.

2. Mid shot, Interior, President's box.

President's box is seen from inside. His security men guard the box.

3. Full Shot, President's box, Exterior,

President removes his hat and gives to his assistant.

4. Interior, President's box as in shot 2.

Lincoln enters in to his box.

5. Mid shot, Interior, Theatre,

Essley and Ben are sitting in the theatre. They turn to see the president and get up to clap for him.

6.F.S. Stage in the long shot. President's box is on the right.

The audience stands up and turns to clap and welcome the president.

7.Interior, President's box as in shot 2.

Lincoln and his wife bow to thank people.

8.Long shot of the stage as in shot 6.

9.President's box. As in shot 7.

Mr. and Mrs. Lincoln take their seats after thanking the audience.

10.Full shot. Exterior, President's box,

President's security guards come out of the box and take their place. One of them scratches his knee.

11.Full shot. View of the stage from rear.

The performance on stage continues.

12.President's box, as in shot 9.

Lincoln holds the hands of his wife while seeing the performance.

13.F.S. View from the rear. As in shot 11.

Audience stops clapping.

14.Close shot of the stage.

Actors are performing.

15.F.S.Security guards as in shot 10.

A guard feels uncomfortable.

16.C.S.of the stage as in shot 14.

Performance is continued on the stage.

17.F.S.guards as in shot 15.

The guard in shot 15 shifts his chair behind the door.

18.Interior President's box as in shot 6.

Camera is near the box. The guard returns to his place.

19.Close shot of the box nearer than shot 18.

The guard sits in his place.

Scene 2 ,

Act-3. Assassination. Time -10.30. p.m.,

20. F.S of the hall, Stage view from the rear.

Lincolns' box is seen through a mask.

21.M.S. Essley and Ben in the hall.

Essley shows something to Ben towards Lincoln's box.

22. Face of John Booth through the mask.

23. M.S Essley and Ben as in shot 21.

Essley enjoys the performance.

24. M.S. Booth in mask as in shot 22,

Masked face of John Booth .

25. C.S. Lincoln's Box.

Lincoln watches the program.

26. M.S. Booth in mask as in shot 22.

Face of john Booth.

27. C.S. Stage.

Actors are performing.

28. C.S. Lincoln's box as in shot 25.

Lincoln smiles while watching the act. Feeling chilled he pulls up his coat and wears it.

29. M.S. Booth as in shot 22.

Booth looks up to get up.

30. C.S. Lincoln's box. Interior,

Lincoln watches the program.

31. F.S. Rear view of the stage as in shot 20.

Full shot. Mask is removed to show full view of the hall.

32. C.S Security guards behind the circular mask as in shot 19.

33. F.S.Booth

Booth exits from the door to come near to Lincoln. He peeps through the hole., takes out his pistol and prepares for the next action.

34.C.S. of the pistol.

35. Shot 33 continues.

Booth comes near the door and opens it with some difficulty and enters in to Lincoln's box.

36. C.S. Lincoln's box as in shot 25.

Booth stands behind Lincoln.

37. Stage as in shot 14.

Actors perform.

38. Lincoln's Box as in shot 36.

Booth fires at Lincoln from the back. Lincoln falls down unconscious. Booth escapes from the side steps and jumps out.

39. L.S. Booth reaches to the stage.

Booth screams on the stage.

The story of *'The Birth of a nation'* revolves around President Lincoln, carelessness of his Guards and his assassin John Booth. This simple story has been dramatized and presented effectively which not only entertain people but keeps them on their toes waiting for the next thrill. Porter might have finished this film in few shots but Griffith has very intelligently divided the entire story into four parts for which appropriate characters were conceived, prominent of them were the President Lincoln and His wife, President's Guards, assassin John Booth, Essley Stoneman and Ben Cameron. The group of performers is created for ambience and some dramatic effects in the auditorium. It seems that the group of performers is distracting the attention from the main event but in reality it is not so as the performance on the stage enhances the excitement and builds up tension that keeps audience glued to their seats so the performance too become a part of the dramatization. This makes the presentation more interesting. While doing this, Griffith has taken due care of principle of continuity and he has never broken it. He has also used parallel actions to show simultaneous happenings in different locations but at the same time. Parallel actions are imbibed so well that they assimilate with the theme very effectively without disturbing the flow of main story. Griffith has also experimented with the technique of **intercutting** which means dividing a shot in many pieces and using them at different places.

The difference in the working style of both *Porter* and *Griffith* is that Porter has divided his action into many shots because it was not possible for him to cover the entire action or incident in one single shot due to its duration and magnanimity but Griffith has deliberately conceived a story and characters in many parts to build up the excitement and dramatized the presentation in which ambience played an important role. The ambience helped the audience to be an integral participant in the story and happenings around. This is a great accomplishment of Griffith which separates him and Porter. However Porter's contribution and innovation to deal with a situation that forced him to divide his action in many shots cannot be undermined. Porter's technique was adopted and improved upon by Griffith that took him one more step forward to advance his cinematic creativity. With number of shots at his disposal for Editing, Griffith acquired extra liberty to be more innovative and experimental. While accepting Porter's traditions Griffith has added new ones in his urge for extraordinary experimentation in cinematic productions.

In the film *'The Birth of a Nation'* the director has worked successfully on many deferent aspects to obtain some cumulative effect. Griffith has divided the whole action in many components to recreate a scene. With this he has been able to touch the depth of storytelling or narration that had long lasting emotional effect on the audience. The detailed description and interpretation of the scene enhances the realism and brings the audience close to their personal experiences which is difficult to achieve in one single shot. Another advantage of having multiple shots is that the Director is able to conveniently manipulate audience's reaction to the ongoing events by associating characters actions and reactions with the main events of the story. The viewer thus starts associating himself with the characters on the screen and becomes himself a participant in the situation. Lets analyze *'the birth of a Nation'* to understand this factor appropriately.

'The Birth of a Nation' – an analysis:

Scene: The assassination of Lincoln.

- First fourteen shots in the film show the President arriving to the theatre and his welcome by the people present there. A caption here is an indication of some forthcoming danger.
- Next five shots are similar to porter's single shot action that show various actions of the guard, Like scratching his knee, feeling of boredom etc. in the shot no 15 the Guard is feeling uncomfortable, instead of 'what will he do or not do' scene shifts to the performance on the stage which the Guard wants to watch but cannot due to his posting so he moves to the door of the theatre in shot no17, 18, 19 but returns back to his place. This does not in any way distracts the mood and attention from the main event and continuity is maintained properly. In shot 17 and 18 the guards goes up to the door to see the action

on the stage but fails to see it and returns back in shot 18 and 19 . Another caption in this place reflects ignorance of the audience about impending danger.

- In shot nos.20-30 director heightens the suspense by showing mysterious activities of John Booth. An attempt has been made to prolong the suspense by interrupting Booth's mysterious activities with other happenings in the auditorium. Thereafter Booth is projected like an ordinary man so that there is no doubt about him. After some time Booth takes advantage of the Guard who once again leaves his place and Booth plans his further action as shown in shot no.33-36.

- Once again action in shot 36 is interrupted to show the actors' performance in shot no.37 thereafter continuation of shot no 36 is shown in shot no 38. Shot no 37 does not show anything new but enhances the dramatic effect of the scene. Suspense and horrification has been prolonged artificially keeping the President unaware of the danger therefore in Griffith's editing Drama is created in extended and simplistic form to avoid uneasiness and artificiality for the viewers.

- In shot no.21 Essley points at the Lincoln. It gives a hint for some time as if Essley has seen the assassin and some mishap are presumed. The audiences thus look at Essley with some hopes that he would take some action to prevent the mishap. In reality this shot of Essley has no meaning in the scene but it helps in increasing the suspense and drama. Before the assassin fires at the Lincoln, though the President is unaware of the future events, it seems that he could do something to avoid the unforeseen occurrence but it does not happen. His actions are considered to be his normal activities before he is murdered.

Griffith had realized that Porter's *single shot technique* in which camera was placed at a fixed distance to shoot like a stage performance, had its own limitations. In this style the viewers could only see the events from the perspective of a fixed distance. Actions performed from other variable distance were not visible so the actions and reactions of other performers at varied distances were not registered. To solve this issue Griffith had divided the entire scene in many fragments (*shots*) . While shooting each fragment he decided the actions and reactions of the performers to be covered by placing the camera at different distances for dramatic and horripilate requirements of the scene. He placed the camera close to actors to cover their minute reactions(Close shots). Like wise to establish a location and the ambience, he placed the camera at long distance (Long shots) for a wider view. Thus '**Long shots' (L.S.)** and '**Close shots' (C.S.)** were discovered during the shooting. In this technique the freedom and convenience to place the camera anywhere in between was also acquired. The use of Long shots, even unrelated to the plot helped creating better dramatics improving the technical quality of the scene.

Another important innovation by Griffith was the use of **'*Flash back'*** which became an important vehicle to convey actors' emotional state, memories of the past and previous events, his ideas and thoughts to the audience. Griffith experimented with this technique freely in his next film '***Intolerance'.*** He mixed '*flash back*' shots with the present one very simply to relate it with the past. In such combinations, *narrative continuity* of the story is more important than the *physical continuity.*

The greatest advantage of fragmenting a scene in many shots is that neither the director is dependent on shooting the entire scene or action in continuity nor he has to wait for the entire performance to take place at a time as the actions could be decided as per the requirement irrespective of the magnanimity and the duration of the scenes like war scene ,a gathering a celebration or a protest and procession etc. Everything could be shot in fragments with short enactments/actions as required however it made a bit difficult for performers to act in close shots; they were so far used to act for an audience sitting at a distance where they could hardly see their minute facial expressions. While Close shots were difficult for the actors, their effect on the audience was immense. In Porter's single shot technique actors had to indulge in overacting or loud acting to make an impact on viewers sitting at a distance. With the innovation of Griffith's techniques while the job of actors became more difficult, the responsibility to create dramatic effects had fallen on the the director. *'In the Birth of a Nation'* the suspense regarding Lincoln's assassination became more effective with the repeated use of shot no.37 than with the performance of actors. Therefore it is the director who has to decide how and where a shot has to be used to make the scene more effective and thrilling. The impact of a shot is not dependent on the actors' performance as it is on the talent, merit and creative acumen of the director. Similarly how and where the camera is to be placed, at what angle and composition shot has to be taken and how actors move during their act are better predefined by the director.

The pertinent question that arises with the use of multiple shots is that how long a shot should remain on screen and who decides it? Normally it is a joint decision of the director and the editor. In this context I would like to add a thumb rule that if the scene has to be fast paced, the length of the shots will be shorter and opposite to this if it is a slow moving scene, the shots will be lengthy. The duration of a visual on the screen is directly proportionate to the length of the shot as the universal speed with which a film stripe runs on the projector is 24 frames/sec. Generally action oriented scenes have faster rate of editing /cutting of the shots **(shorter shots /less duration)** than the dialogue scenes **(lengthy shots/longer duration).** The rhythm of the entire film is determined by the director based on the content and requirements of the scenes as there s no formula for determining the pace of a scene.

Griffith very successfully adopted the style of a *story teller* in his films. The way a story teller engages dramatic elements to sustain the interest of the audience from beginning to end including mannerism of actors, their actions and reactions, ambience etc and approaches to the climax, Griffith too employed the use of Long shots, Mid shots and close shots to provide variety of visual actions and emotions to the viewers to engage them till the end. That's where *Griffith* has surpassed *Porter* to be called '***The father of Editing'***.

It was not that in other parts of the world there was no experimentation in film production. Russian film maker **Eisenstein** had quoted about Griffith saying, *'Griffith has used literary style in his editing technique and translated the conventions of storytelling of a novelist in his films. Cross* *cuttings, close shots, flash back and dissolve too have parallels in the literature which were discovered by Griffith'. Griffith* had impressed many Russian film makers of the time but they also pointed out certain flaws in his technique such as his use of Close shots only for *'Parallel actions'*. Russians have used various shots to make a *'**Montage'**'* which had a different cumulative meaning and effect than the meaning and effect of individual shots.

According to this experiment *'**when more than one shots are joined together they have different meaning and effect than that of the original one.***'* Its parallel can be found in *'**Figure of speech'**'* in the literature where every word or phrase when combined with others gives a different meaning. A figure of speech is a word or phrase that has a meaning something different than its literal meaning. It can be *a **metaphor*** or *simile* that is designed to further explain a concept or a different way of pronouncing a word or phrase such as with alliteration to give further meaning to a different sound.

This similarity is evident in the *'Montage'* where unrelated shots mean differently when joined together. There was no *'Montage'* in Griffith's technique. His close shots, ambience, traits of actors/characters etc were used as an alternative to the dialogues of the main actors. In chase sequences, close shots of chaser and chased were alternately used to speed up the thrill and pace of the scene and not for increasing the importance or visual effects by *'Juxtapositions'* of the shots differently. Since the films made by Griffith were in their incessant years, his limited use of the shots should not be underrated but it should be appreciated as another step in the growth of cinematic explanation. Subsequent film makers after

Griffith not only used shots as a tool for story telling but also experimented for developing new editing techniques and deriving newer interpretations, intellectual meanings and effects.

According to *Eisenstein, 'film making in Russia was limited to the advertisement films to promote products and political ideology.'* Film production was not an organized industry at that time which restricted the knowledge, vision and imagination of film makers in Russia. Griffith's techniques and inventions have provided them an opportunity to think and explore the possibilities of developing cinema in their country. They picked up the basic theory of film editing from Griffith and worked to develop newer techniques and principles.' Neo film makers used film as medium to propagate their ideas among them *'Pudovkin'* and *'Kuleshov'* marked their presence in golden letters in the history of cinema.

Pudovkin:

Pudovkin worked to rationalize the basic principles of film making propounded by *Griffith*. While *Griffith* believed in resolution of the problems as per his needs, *Pudovkin* had pre-empted and assessed the issues to develop a new working system which is very important to the contemporary film makers even today. *Pudovkin* had formulated the guiding principles and system of editing for the generations of film makers.

To understand Pudovkin's principles of Editing, we have to analyze the role of a director. Apparently a scene shot in fragments (shots) by the director are not more than unorganized and incomplete pieces of celluloid which have no meaning as they don't convey anything individually. These shots are taken to cover different actions from different viewpoints and perspectives which are not conveyed by any single shot. It is like organizing *words* to make a *sentence* which has a meaning than that of individual words used in it. They either have no meaning or convey different meanings in different sentences. In the same manners each shot is only a fragment of an action and not the whole action. Therefore the exposed raw material brought by the director in fragmented form does not present a complete action, its timing and locations. These shots have to be organized systematically as per the editorial principles and practices to create a meaningful scene; it depends on the imagination, merits and creativity of the editor and the director of editing. While giving these shots a 'film form' unwanted actions and reactions, various intervals and gaps are removed. The editor has a liberty to decide about the timing of a shot to remain on the screen. This is called *'constructive Editing'* as per Pudovkin's principles of editing. The creative or constructive editing can be understood by the following example .Many times we are awed to see a character jumping from the height of a tower or so but the director pictures this action as under…

First of all in shot 1, the actor jumps from the height on a net spread down below. This net is not seen on the screen. In the second shot, the actor jumps from a lesser height to the ground. Both the shots are joined together in such a way that the action from top to the ground is seen continuous one. Therefore it is not really a dangerous action of jumping from a height to the ground as it is made out to be but is an outcome of editorial juxtaposition to create an emotional impact. Special attention is given to maintain the continuity of action by deleting unwanted intervals and gaps, waiting or getting up of the character etc. It is not a photographic trick or special effect but a presentation of an action by using editorial practices.

Pudovkin has converted Griffith's editing practices in to principles of editing. Griffith's use of Close shots to create dramatic effect was completely different than Pudovkin's division of the scene in shots. This 'pre shooting shot division' is now followed by the director during the shoots. Thus the editorial process for a director starts with the beginning of screen play writing itself.

Scene -1:

'A horse cart of a farmer is moving slowly on countryside's muddy pathway of a village. The cart is stuck in the mud. The disgusted farmer pushes his tired horse to move ahead. At a distant corner of the cart a human shape appears out of the dust storm. She wraps her clothes around to protect herself from the wind and dust, the passerby stops near the horse cart and looks at it amazingly.

The farmer turns to asks him, 'Is Nakhabin far away from here?' (Caption)

The man guides him pointing to the direction. The cart starts moving again. The man looks at the cart for some time and moves on to his route.'

The screen play is generally written in the above format. Since there were no dialogues in cinema in those days, scenes were separated by inserting captions in between the scenes. Director's comments or views about the scene/theme were also captioned in proper places. In the above example it is observed that actions and reactions are minutely detailed like cart's trap in the mud, disgusted farmer, tired horse, emergence of a human shape at a distant corner, wrapping of her clothes around to protect her from dust and gusty wind, surprise of the passerby etc. These details are similar to that of a literary writer creating a visual presentation in his story or a novel with the sole objective of taking his readers to the illusion of actuality from where they could feel the impact of the scene. The writer and the director of a film too have the same objective when they write a screen play. This is the time when the editing pattern of the film is also outlined. The shot division of the above scene would be somewhat like this-

1. **Long shot**-A farmer on his sores cart going on a muddy path.
2. **Close shot**-The cart wheel sticks in the mud.
3. **Mid** shot-The cart moves slowly.
4. **Close shot**-Farmer is disgusted.
5. **Mid shot**-The farmer pushes his tired horse to move faster.
6. **Long shot**-The cart in the foreground. A human figure emerges at a distance.
7. **Mid shot**-he wraps his clothes around to protect from the gusty winds.
8. **Long shot**-A passer by stops near the cart.
9. **Close shot**- He looks at the cart with surprise.
10. **Close shot**-The farmer turns to him and asks:
11. **Caption- 'Is Nakhabin far away from here?'**
12. **Mid shot**- The man guides him to a direction.
13. **Long shot**- The cart starts moving again.

14. **Close shot**-*The man looks at the cart moving away for a while.*

15. **Long shot**- *He moves forward on his way.*

It is amply clear from the above shot division that minute details and facial expressions must be shown in C.S. or M.S.so that viewers can experience the same emotions which would not be possible if the entire scene is shot in Long shot. Though viewers will be able to see the event in Long shot but the appropriate expressions and their impact on them will be missed out. According to *Pudovkin, 'Every shot in a scene should have different effect and meaning unlike in a monotonous Long shot which is occasionally punctuated with close shots or mid shots to show the details. Such shots neither serve any creative , dramatic purpose or reason nor contribute in creative editing therefore they should be removed.'* These inferences of Pudovkin were based on some of his own experiences and some on the experiments of *Kuleshov* in the process of editing which he considered was more important in story telling than the visuals.

Kuleshov:

According to Kuleshov's theory, **'By proper juxtaposition a new meaning or interpretation of shots can be derived which is not conveyed by original shots"**. This can be easily understood by the following example-

Shot No. 1.   Smiling face of the Hero.

Shot No.2.   A revolver.

Shot No. 3.   Frightened   face of the Hero.

When we look at the above shots in the same order, we see that the Hero is frightened when he sees the revolver. This explains that the Hero is a weak hearted person and his frightened face reflects his cowardice.

Shot No. 1.   *Frightened face of the Hero.*

Shot No.2.   *A revolver.*

Shot No. 3.   *Smiling   face of the Hero.*

In the reverse order when we see his frightened face first and subsequently the revolver and his smiling face in the above order, A frightened Hero looks at the Revolver and smiles that gives impression of his daring nature who feels happy and empowered with a revolver. Just by reversing the order of the shot we have been able to change the character and his behavior completely. It conveys another meaning and effect of the scene to the viewers. Otherwise all these three shots individually have no meaning but when they are juxtaposed differently, they convey differently. Thus the director can create the required meaning and effect just by shuffling the order of the shots. This is called 'Creative Editing.'

In another experiment *Pudovkin* and *Kuleshov* juxtaposed three different close shots with a neutral shot of the Hero intercut in between.

First shot-   C.S.   A Bowl of soup is kept on a table.

Second shot- C.S.   A lady lay wrapped in a funeral cloth.

Third shot-   C.S.   A baby is playing with her toys.

When the audience was shown these three shots inter cut with Hero's neutral shots, their reaction was astounding.

First shot-	*Close shot of Hero*
Second shot-	*A lady laid wrapped in a funeral cloth.*
Third shot-	*Close shot of Hero*
Fourth shot-	*A Bowl of soup is kept on a table.*
Fifth shot-	*Close shot of Hero*
Sixth shot-	*A baby is playing with her toys.*
Seventh shot-	*Close shot of Hero*

When the Hero looks at the lady in funeral cloth, the pathetic reaction of the hero was heart touching. Seeing the lady dead, hero forgot to have the soup kept for him on the table. When he saw the baby playing with her toys, he felt happy. The viewers appreciated Hero's versatile performance in these three combinations without realizing that all these shots of the Hero were neutral and devoid of any expressions but part of the same shot (used four times). An intelligent juxtaposition and intercutting gave different interpretation and emotional context to the shots.

There has to be basic material for any creative work which is arranged systematically, according to *Kuleshov*,' for a Musician or composure **'sound'** is the base material which is composed in particular rhythm and pace. For a Painter' his **'colors'** are the basic material which he arranges on a canvas. Similarly for a film maker the **shots** of the exposed film are the basic materials which are joined creatively to produce an effective and interesting scene.' Kuleshov opined that Film art does not begin with the performance of an actor or with the completion of shooting as it is only a basic procedure to prepare the basic material. The film art begins when a director starts joining the shots and achieves the desired effect after many permutations and combination of shots.

Griffith and Pudovkin - a comparison:

The difference between the editing techniques of Pudovkin and Griffith was in the level of emotional impact of the scene. Griffith used to concentrate more on the behavior, movements and mannerism of actors while Pudovkin worked on the details in the shots to incorporate more variety and dramatic effect. It was predominantly achieved through creative juxtaposition of shots. His technique is still followed by many film makers today. Griffith played more on human conflicts and Pudovkin emphasized more on ambience of the story and the surrounding actions. Pudovkin worked on simple plots based on common events where he devoted more screen time to explain the pros and cons and justify their importance.

Film- Mother   Director: Pudovkin

'Mother' is another example of a good continuity and experiment in juxtaposition of unrelated shots to establish the happiness of a man who is about to be released from the prison. Pudovkin has presented the scene very effectively.

According to his own statement, *'In 'Mother', I have tried to impress my audience with the psychological state of my characters along with some experiments in editing. The son is sitting in jail when he is handed over a piece of paper in which it is written that he will be released from the custody next day. I had a problem to show his facial expressions of happiness when he gets this information. Normally, to show him smiling would have not been effective. Therefore First I had shown his trembling hands followed by a big close up of his lower half of the face to include a corner of his lips with a short smile. I had juxtaposed these shots with few unrelated shots of different ambience like shots of brooks, spring flowers, sunrays falling on water, birds playing in a village pond and a laughing child. In this way by juxtaposing few different shots, I could establish the pleasure on the face of the prisoner'.*

When the scene is analyzed, it is not seen to be effective apparently but the director wanted it this way. Showing just a smiling face of the actor would not have the impact director wanted to create. He took the help of those elements from the nature which expressed happiness therefore the director juxtaposed those pleasure symbols from the nature to create a *'Montage'* where physically every shot seemed directly disconnected but each of them had indirect ideological link which expressed a definite emotion. According to *Pudovkin,' if the details of an event in the scene are fragmented and joined creatively, they produce tremendous effect on the audience.'*

Sergie Eisenstein:

Sergei Eisenstein however had a different view. He believed that,' *linking of various shots depicting details of a scene is very normal. To achieve continuous interest and regular flow in the film, it is necessary to incorporate elements of shocks and surprises at regular intervals. With every cut audience must be provided an opportunity to experience 'conflict' and anticipate further possibilities of 'what next'.*

Every shot of a 'Montage' should indicate forthcoming shocks and surprises. Such juxtapositions in editing help achieve the thrill. Eisenstein imagines *'Intellectual Montage'* when he compares cinema with other art forms. The intellectual Montage can be understood by the following interpretation of shots:

Shot of Dripping water + eyes	=	*Sense of crying.*
Shot of an ear + close to door	=	*Sense of Hearing.*
A Dog + face	=	*Sense of Barking.*
A face + Child	=	*Sense of shrieking.*
A face + a Bird	=	*Sense of singing.*
A knife + a Heart	=	*Sense of sorrow.*

For Eisenstein such 'Intellectual Montage' is cinema in which each shot has a different meaning and emotion but their content is always 'Neutral'. When these shots are juxtaposed together in the intellectual context, a series of intellectual interpretations is created. Director should choose his shots conflicting with each other and proceed further discovering inherent meanings and emotions of the shots in the content to provide his audience an opportunity to feel shocks and surprises. These shocks and surprises can be created by the variety and contrast in the composition of shots, Distance from the camera, Back ground, Depth of field, cinematographic technology and gimmicks, special lighting arrangements etc. This can also be created by connecting some disconnected shots .The duration of the shock is not important , which can be short or longer as decided by the director.

In the *'Intellectual Montage'* of Eisenstein the problem is not that of the juxtaposition of shots but of how easily the viewers will be able to grasp its inherent meaning and emotions. It is possible that they may not understand it when they watch it first time or they may have to tax their mind to understand by watching it many times for which they may not have the time and patience. In such a situation director may not be able to properly convey what he wants to say. But whatever it may be, by his concept of 'Intellectual Montage' Eisenstein had definitely created a new 'Genre' of film making which can be called' **Intellectual or Experimental Cinema'.**

It is correct to say that only one person is responsible for creative expressions or creative ideas like a painter for his painting, an author for his story, novel or poetry, a musician for his compositions but it is not so in cinema . In the early phase when films were silent and more experimental, films of Lumiere Brothers might have lacked creativity in expressions as films presented live events that had no preconceived ideas and exceptional planning. The moving images of 'Arrival of a Train', 'workers leaving the factory', 'A demolition', etc on screen attracted people from all walks of life to a new medium and experience. There were no writers, Recordist or an editor for such films. The director many times himself wielded the camera in the absence of a cameraman. In fact these films were made solely by one man's imagination and efforts. In the year 1903 Edwin S Porter made 'The great train Robbery' with a preconceived action sequence and laid the ground for films on preconceived story line with a well thought of execution plan. He divided the scene in many fragments (shots) for shooting and subsequently joining them in chronological order introducing a new element in cinema called *'Film Editing.'*

Porter analyzed the *'space'* and *'depth'* in the moving images to establish a relationship with other images/shots. This resulted in **'visual continuity'** when shots were joined together in chronological order keeping the consistency of Time, Place and the desired emotional effect . Porter is credited for introducing an effective **'Narrative form'** of a storyline which is still accepted by film makers the world over.

XXXXX

'Screenplay writing, direction and editing are three basic milestones in the process of a film production.'

Act 2:
Screenplay Writer: An Introduction

When *Lumiere brothers* discovered *moving images* and made their first silent film *'Arrival of a train'*, there was no place for a writer as the films during this era were the coverage of reality as they took place. *'The great train robbery'*, *'Workers coming out of factory'*, *'Fire operation' etc.* were such films shot by Lumiere in *'single shots'* . Neither was there a need of writers nor the technology was as developed as it is today. Gradually with more film makers experimenting with cinema technology in other parts of the world, films started to leap in due course. Reality coverage moved to shooting of live stage performances and plays. The events and incidents were conceived to entertain people. It was this time when the need to engage a writer was felt by film makers. Though cinema was a visual medium, it was not necessary for a writer to have knowledge of film technology so once again he remained an underrated and under paid person. If the film got success, he got some raise in his remuneration otherwise he vanished in to oblivion however film directors realized a fact that a film could not be made without proper planning   so it was necessary to have a properly conceived, developed and planned screen play before   shooting. In the absence of a predefined script, director could be rendered helpless. Neither he could pass proper instructions on the set nor a camera could be taken out of it's box, neither an actor would know what to perform nor an editor would be able to edit the film and so on. It's a pertinent question then, if a writer is so important in making a film why he is so incognito? The answer to this lies in the attitude of those who think a writer is a useless person who is there only to write and that is the best he could do and nothing else. When we talk of the attitude towards a writer, it is not restricted to cinema but it is found in other fields of writing as well. An author is rarely paid his royalty by a publisher who thinks that by publishing a writer's work, he is being obliged. More so many publishers demand them to contribute *'printing cost'* to publish their work and make up their loss citing the reason of people having lost touch with books. Many times a writer succumbs to their demand if he has to find a foothold to stand in the world of writing. This practice has been given a fancy name of *'Vanity publishing'* by unscrupulous publishers who thrive at the cost of an author. So until there is an attitudinal shift towards them, they will continue to languish in the dark.

With more than three decades of my experience in writing short stories, screen plays, production, direction and editing for fiction, shorts and animation films, I define screenplay writer as:

'The Screenplay writer is a person who takes the first step from an idea to develop a detailed story confirming cinematic parameters, visualizes scenes imbibing his philosophy, experiences , ideology and situations, that takes his audience to an emotional voyage along with the characters they identify

and live with in an interesting presentation that not only entertains but also gives a massage to the society as a whole at the end.' In all these facets the writer displays his originality of thoughts, ideas, imagination and visualization which is expressed with the effective use of sounds and images that creates a good cinema.'

Cinema: an exotic journey

Film is a unique combination of multiple art forms such as writing, music and dance, make up and painting, animation, architecture and construction, interior decoration, fashion and costume designing, acting and other performing and creative art forms integrated with exotic locations, special sounds and visual effects etc. The writer takes people to an exotic visual journey imaginatively planned with the use of *'speed'* and *'sounds'* giving a meaning to scenes, reducing or increasing the time span of story with effective time management that enhances the emotional and sentimental value of scenes, situations and characters. It is possible only in cinema where there is an unbridled scope of imagination and creativity beyond the limits of an individual thinking. While people watch a film in their present, they can be interestingly taken back and forth by their onscreen characters that sail with them with the flow of the narration. Like other forms of writing where words dominate the imagination and interpretation of the readers, cinema gives them a wholesome visual and realistic experience of living with the characters. This takes cinema to another pedestal where other written forms including a novel, a drama, short story or poetry fail to compete.

The film writing should not be linked with technology that only complements the writer to convert his imagination in to a film form. Technology is used to confirm the requirements of the director to transcend the imaginative visual images written in the screen play to a cinematic medium that is projected on a large cinema screen.

Content:

It includes narrative of the story the way it is unpeeled in layers, development of characters and performers, theme, locations, the target group, the message given by the characters that can be identified by the audience with their own life etc. These are few of many factors that are included in the content when the writer writes screenplay for a film or television. An effective story teller combines the methods of yester years and the contemporary dramatized style of story narration by appropriating cinema technology in its content. It proves to be more effective and successful.

Observation, Experiences and creativity:

Creativity is an outcome of the experiences of a creator. These are the experiences that are gained from the activities and the events taking place around us, from others experiences and from the emotional fluctuation in our life. The experiences of a writer are like bank deposits that provide him inspiring content and emotions for writing whenever needed.   Experiences deposited in the memory of a writer inspire him with different contents, views and plots for the stories. These experiences are a raw material for him. They hide an artiste's restlessness, urge to express, sensitivity, emotions and turmoil. The way diseases, their treatment, research etc are the raw material for doctor or laws of the land, constitution, different judgments given in different type of cases are the raw material for a lawyer; the experiences of a writer gained during his life time from his personal life, from others or from his constant observation around are the raw material for him therefore a he must seriously analyze everything he observes and gains in his life. Such analysis should be conducted on the basis of their emotional and sentimental value. One derives experiences mainly from three sources:

1. **Own experiences:** They are based on real events, situations, their outcome, pain and pleasure, causes and effects that an individual experiences physically, mentally, emotionally and spiritually. During such experiences the person is directly involved with the events. They are the *first hand experiences* of a person that are more serious, emotionally intense and have direct and deep lingering impact therefore their expression too is more realistic and effective.

2. **Second hand experiences:** They too are based on real happenings and events but there is *no direct association* and involvement of a person but he witnesses them *directly* as an *'other person'* with knowledge of details, causes, actions and reactions of people associated with the events, their agony and happiness etc. Since they are not first hand experiences but of the second person, they are called *'second hand experiences'*. They also leave a lasting effect on an individual but with less intensity, for example an injured person feels more pain than those who have just witnessed him getting injured or those who take care of him later.

3. **Third person experiences:** They are not real experiences but created, acquired, felt and gathered one while seeing a play, film or a television show, by reading a news paper , a magazine, a novel or any other literary work or by hearing descriptions, hearsay, rumors, stories, folk tales etc.. Such experiences though may have some information value, are superficial in knowledge and have little emotional effect as they are aquired from the experiences of a *third person*. There is no direct or indirect association of the individual in such cases therefore writer must preferably acquire first hand or second hand experiences. Third person experiences are important to acquire knowledge about them in the absence of the first two.

A writer must continue to gain fresh knowledge and experiences for an effective communication. More the experiences better will be the quality of his writing. A writer rich with experiences, practice and knowledge has better imagination and communication as they come handy while developing a story. We observe, see, hear and experience many things from the sun rise to its setting every day but remember only few of them that we are associated directly or indirectly that leave an impact on our mind, rest are lost in the depth. Forgotten are normally those activities that are common, regular and routine in the chronology of our daily schedule. It is neither advisable nor is practical and possible to remember all of them as a story is not created by routine and common activities but is inspired by special events with a *cause and effect* therefore a writer must concentrate more on such special activities. It does not mean that one should completely ignore these common activities as they too are important to develop a scene. They provide life to the characters. Every scene in the screen play cannot be special or every event cannot be important. It is to remember that the characters of a film, play or a television shows are replica of real life people and they too live the way we live except when a story is based on pure imagination, a fantasy or on alien characters. Since the characters of a screenplay are driven from realistic situations, the writer must find a plot that is based on real life so the he must keep on enriching his treasure of knowledge about Events, characters, emotions and sentiments, pains and pleasure by developing a habit to observe everything around. No observation is waste for a creative person in general and for a writer in particular.

Writing for Cinema:

Writing for screen is a process that requires a continuous research, creativity, knowledge of cinematic and dramatic elements, technology. A Screenplay is a combination of creative expressions and cinematic techniques that is capable to invite attention and the interest of the audience during its entire period of play. The screenplay is only an expression of the story in cinematic form. The writer who is well verse with cinematic requirements cannot avoid their inclusion in his narration. In fact the knowledge of cinema inspires him to conceive effective visuals and the sounds in the blue print of the film. A common writer creates his scenes in **'words'** while a screen writer thinks in terms of **'visuals'** and **'sound'** to give life to his characters in different situations that are relevant to various socio-economic conditions and thereafter descends them on paper. This screenplay is given life on celluloid in the form of *moving images* by the director with the involvement of film technology.

What a film writer needs is the *original vision* which means originality of thoughts, originality of concept, originality to create convincing situations and the characters and the original presentation to convey through a pleasant cinematic experience. He should be able to place himself in the situations of his characters and experience their emotions. Sometimes it may so happens that scenes are devoid of successful translation of his vision on the screen due to many factors like inability of the actors to perform as expected, cinematographic and lighting restrictions, variations between the writer's imagination and director's execution however they all work hard to realize the original vision of the film to the best possible extent or better than what has been conceived in the script. To avoid this uncomfortable situation there is always a need for a better understanding and coordination between director and the writer. This also avoids occasional conflicts between them.

It may be inappropriate to say that the talent of writing is a gift of God which everyone may not possess; it is also not be correct to say that anybody can be a writer, but everybody has something to say. He has to develop the skills to effectively communicate what he has in his mind. A writer should be a keen observer of different social norms and traditions, economic status, their behavior and mannerism, living style, knowledge of different religions and their rituals, philosophical and ideological differences, history and culture of the country or the society, literature and various art forms, technical knowhow of cinema and television production etc. It is said that it is never late to learn new things in life so a writer can start acquiring such knowledge anytime he wishes if he has the passion. Learning and observation is an unending process for a creative person particularly for a writer and the director.

Generally a story is developed from an *idea* that is extended to a series of scenes involving different characters, situations, struggle and accomplishments in characters' life. The script consists of conflict and opposition, changes and resolution of the issues with a predefined beginning, middle and the end that is also called a *climax*. The ups and downs in the life of characters, different moods, heart touching performance of actors, emotions and sentiments generated in different acts of the story, timing, pace and speed etc are essential ingredients of a screenplay. The entire body of the screenplay should be such that audience has no time to stray elsewhere in their thoughts, attention and concentration from the events on screen. Effective use of lights, sound, Location, composition of shots, color scheme, set design and setting, music and actors' performance contribute in effective visualization of scenes. Screenplay should bring its characters to life by giving details of their actions and behavior, effective dialogues and variations in their mood and emotions. The challenge for a film writer is to make people glued to their screen without losing interest from the beginning to the end. Loss of interest of few minutes in the entire film too may cost it's box office collection. Most of the factors including technical parameters ,technical functions and team involvement, for film and television are similar so when writing screenplay for either film or television the writer should follow the same process as that of a film.

Writing for Television:

Basics of the screenplay writing for film and television don't differ much in style and patterns except some differences in the presentation due to their inherent qualities. The film writing requires a continuous narration of the story that should end within the stipulated screen time of a show that is generally between 100 minutes to 180 minutes while a television show lasts for 30 to 60 minutes of telecast time. A television serial is divided in many episodes which may continue for weeks, months or the years, if their *'Television rating parameter' (TRP)* is within acceptable limits. So the writer for a television show has to write every episode in such a way that people retain their curiosity for the next episode which would be telecast on a fixed slot.

Cinematic genres:

'Cinema is a strong medium of artistic expressions'. As is generally believed, ***'A moving image is thousand times more effective than a million written words.'*** Therefore cinema becomes an effective tool to communicate about many of the social issues. It has been successfully used to meet such social obligations. Cinema cannot be restricted to merely a means to entertain people but can be effectively utilized to inform and educate them. Like any art form, Cinema is also influenced by what happens in the society, in the country and in the world where people have different opinions on a particular issue. Cinema thus becomes a form of *'interaction'* between the interested groups, individuals and intelligentsia. Earlier when it did not gain importance there were many creative art forms to communicate such as literature, theatre, painting, music, songs and dances etc. Cinema extended an opportunity to all these art forms to integrate and interact with people in the most creative, interesting and entertaining manners. This gave rise to many *cinematic genres* each with a different purpose. Fiction films the most common genre, has always remained most popular, other genres too cropped up to fulfill variety of social objectives like Information, education, advertisement and promotion etc. Few enthusiastic film makers started experimenting with cinematic grammar and made experimental films like an artist would make an abstract painting. The concept of canvas painting has been extended to make Animation or cartoon films with a series of drawings giving an illusion of movement.

Fiction film:

The urge to be entertained has always been there in the back of human mind since the time immemorial. They devised various forms of entertainment and creative expressions from music to dance, drama, sporting activities, celebration of different occasion and events in life, writing, painting, sculpting, photography and many more. Cinema, the moving images, was an extension of still photography. The silent cinema of Lumiere brothers and others which brought a revolution in cinematic expression in decades to come, was a major discovery in the field of entertainment. While cinema in its initial phase was based on reality, it did not take many years to adapt itself to the ancient form of entertainment like drama, music, songs and dances, mythological and social content. In its raw form the silent cinema started live filming of popular stage plays with the captions in between the acts to communicate and move the story forward.

The evolution of cinema is also the evolution of *'planned cinema'* where a story is selected, screenplay written and shooting is done as planned. The technological revolution too played a very significant role to enhance *on screen experience* from increasing the size of cinema screen to the stereophonic or Dolby sound recording systems. Celluloid projection gave way to digital projection with flawless visual quality. Single screen cinema halls transformed to small and cozy mini theatres with maximum comforts for the audience.

The story telling in fiction films too changed drastically from melodramatic clichés to normal life experiences. Fiction films evolved two distinct patterns, one to cater to general entertainment and other for stirring the intellect of a target audience. They were later defined and identified as **'Commercial cinema'** and **'Art/Parallel cinema'**. They both have their distinct audience, style of production and presentation. While commercial films are meant to earn money, the Art films take up issues related to the society and the humanity at large. Gradually the lines between a commercial and an art film blurred with the changing tastes and intellectual levels of audiences.

Non- fiction Film:

The beginning of twentieth century saw a new medium of moving Images that later came to be known as 'Cinema'. It generated equal interest and excitement from film makers to film goers. It was an extension of still photography. It captured *live actions* with a camera running in the speed of 16 frames/ second. Every frame captured a friction of an action that looked 'live' when projected on a film screen in the same speed. The pioneers Lumiere brothers produced their first cinema in the year 1895 by capturing *'Arrival of a train'*, *'Workers coming out of a factory'* and many more. Thereafter other film makers like DW Griffith, Eisenstein, Edwin s Porter came in to the scene and experimented with new methodology and technology to further the impact of cinema. This discovery also generated lot of interest among people to know more about people, Places, countries and events etc. If we ponder in the history of cinema we come to know that the films made during the initial years were all *nonfiction* or *actuality films.* Such films were mainly based on the live coverage of real events like coronation ceremonies, Places of interest, News events, Views and opinions etc. These films were a *visual documentation* of reality that's why they were named as **Documentary films**. In the coming years, the documentary became an important means to preserve the history of a country or a civilization in the celluloid format. Film archives in most of the countries, still preserve the visual history to keep further generations abreast of the past glory and achievements, the struggle and turmoil of their country.

During the course of time Nonfiction films have developed many other forms to cater to different purpose. News reels, Biographies, scientific research and innovations, Research and development, Promotion and publicity, Information, education and training films etc became order of the day for film makers to choose a film form of their choice. In a way all these films are an offshoot of Documentary films except few differences in their treatments. Some activist film makers make documentary films to highlight the issues plaguing the society and to protest against certain policies perused by the government. Like any other medium, cinema also has its grey areas when some anti social groups start making provocative films to create unrest and divide in the society on the lines of region and religion, bigotry, cast and creeds or to thrust and propagate their individual opinions. The nonfiction also gives ample leg room to film makers to experiment with different ideas and vision.

Non fiction film making in general and documentary films in particular are considered to be tougher than making fiction films. It is because documentary films are not based on a predefined story or screenplay. The concept is generated from an *idea* that keeps on developing and changing with the research, information received from various resources in different times and constantly changing perception of film maker during the thought process. In fact there cannot be a final screen play for a documentary film. Many times what is written in the script is not possible to shoot on location and the same cannot be recreated as documentary films are based on *'actuality'*. It is believed that all the technical departments in the production of a fiction film must be excellent but in documentary films it is the Director who should be excellent as other technical qualities here are not as important as the *presentation of an idea.* In a fiction film the director is the captain of the ship while in a documentary Director's imagination is the key. A documentary film maker recreates the scenes within the limits of *'reality'* but staging the same has the potential to kill it.

Advertisement films:

With the growth of consumerism, competition and industrialization a need was felt to reach out to people with the information about products and the services at their disposal. The manufacturers of goods and service providers realizing the effectiveness of moving images, embarked aggressively to the production of advertisement films that are released simultaneously along with the feature films in cinema halls and the television. Gradually advertising has become an industry in itself. Corporate houses earmark a fixed budget for their annual advertizing activities. Then came directors with specialization in marketing who know the pulse of their consumers and try all tricks of the trade to induce and confuse them. These advertisement films hit the psyche of gullible people to make a purchase decision. The success of an advertisement film is measured through how many people are influenced by it? This is reflected in the account books of the company.

Serials and Sequels:

In the adolescent age of the cinema when the technology was not so developed, the events or a story could not be filmed at stretch and were exhibited to the audience in a closed hall on weekly basis in bits and pieces. . In such a situation the story was divided in many parts and every part was released separately week after weeks in a series. Every episode was an extension of the last one and in such manners the story progressed. The current format of television serials can be credited to be inspired by the series of scenes filmed and released in early years. A story is serialized and every episode takes the story further. Fictions or nonfiction television programs which run more than the required duration/length of the telecast time or single release slots, can be made in to a 'series'.

The trend of making *'sequels'* which has long been very popular in the west has taken its roots in Indian cinema too where feature films made in number of sequels or prequels are released separately. The programs which can be telecast within the fixed time slots and are complete in its specific content in a single episode can be telecast any time however a series has to have a fixed and regular time slot otherwise its *'different telecast time'* will lose its continuity, purpose and interest of the audience who dedicatedly are glued to their television at a regular and convenient schedule.

Animation Films:

Unlike the films shot in 24-25 frames /second which is the running speed of the camera (The standard speed for film camera is 24 frames while for digital it is 25 frames/second), the animation camera runs on *'single frame exposure'* at a time shooting a series of still drawings or caricatures which have inherent continuity of movements in their characters/objects.

One might have noticed in a film stripe which has number of still photo frames and every frame or a photo has a friction of a whole action. When the same is projected in normal speed we experience an illusion of a continuous action. In live shooting all the actions are recorded in normal speed of 24 frames /second while in Animation or cartoon films a friction of every action is shot in single frame. When an animated film is projected in normal speed, we see a continuous action created in continuity of each drawing or a caricature one after another in chronological order.

Creating animation is very complicated and time consuming process as an artist has to draw hundreds of drawings manually which means he has to create 24 designs for a second of film time therefore preparing thousands of designs for few minutes of animation is not a mean task. Dozens of artistes are engaged for making these sketches, caricatures or designs. It takes months or years to make a full length animation film. These designs are prepared on transparent cell papers. Every character is drawn in separate sheets and every design must have some movement of the character. There are separate designs for the background which also requires having some actions/ movement such as movement of the tree leafs in the forest or the birds flying.

Now of course with digital technology, animation is created faster in computers. In fact, it has taken multiple leaps and revolutionized animation technology which did not remain confined to just drawings and caricatures but has expanded to create special effects.

Now, special effects created by digital technology have become an independent genre in filmmaking that gave way to produce fiction and nonfiction films predominantly with special effects. The computer animation has eased out the labor of artistes but process has more or less remained the same. The designs can be prepared and action of the characters can be created in computers faster than the manual ones. The special effects and computer animation has become an inseparable ingredient of any film or television production and also revolutionized the *'action'* in cinema.

XXXXX

'Motion picture is a grand art that uses elements from all other art forms. So if you consider literature, photography, music as arts, then you would have to consider filmmaking an art as well because they are all integrated.'

Act 3:

The First step:

Writing is not only an art but also an experience that comes by practice. A writer hones his skill by writing as much as and whatever, whenever and wherever he can. There is no restriction of time and content for him to write. The regular writing habit not only embellishes his language, style and thoughts but also opens up the flight of his imagination like a kite in the sky. There is a very popular incident of **Swami Vivekananda,** the great Indian philosopher, who was to address a gathering in 1893 in Chicago, USA.

Swami Vivekananda... the famous disciple of Sri Ramakrishna Paramhansa who had reached higher realms of spirituality, always spoke extempore so much so that he never had to refer a single book in his lifetime. All his speeches were always extempore... no matter what.

Once it so happened... he was invited for a talk and the organizers wanted to make a fool of him. At the venue of speech, Swami Vivekananda found a white cloth tied between two trees and in the center of the white cloth was a dot... a black spot. Swami Vivekananda understood it all and started his speech on **'Zero'.** People gathered in the gathering were awed by his phenomenal spiritual powers. None had told him what he was supposed to speak about path yet. Swami

Vivekananda spoke on *zero... the tiny black spot*. Swami Vivekananda expressed that the whole cosmos grew from a tiny spot... the size of half thumb. And the lecture that was delivered by Swami Vivekananda made the organizers flabbergasted. They simply could not believe their ears. It was not his topic of speech but he spoke unbridled for over three hours and audience was spellbound by his oratory. This could be possible because of his wide knowledge on various subjects and his command on the language. The same is true with a writer who has to acquire wide knowledge on various subjects that include traditions and cultures, festivals and festivities, social and political order of different societies and nations. It is achieved by extensive observation, reading of literature and works of writers of all hues, regions and languages.

If you feel that you have spark to be a writer, pick up a pen and diary and start writing whatever you have seen, heard, experienced and informed about things of your interest and appeal. You can express your innermost feelings and sentiments that you have suppressed for long time in the depth of your heart, it is the time you can express them in your most confidential diary that will not only relieve you of your emotional baggage you have carried so far but also mirror your own imagination and create a writing style of your own. In due course, this diary becomes your most admirable companion. You must make it a habit to write something every day. You must keep your diary handy so that whatever comes to your mind any time of the day and night, you may jot it down before you forget. Within few days, writing becomes your regular habit. Words will be restless if they are not unleashed from the shackles of your thoughts. Your mind will always want to search for an *'Idea'* that you could express and store in your memories for future reference. This practice will not only inspire you to write something whenever you feel like but also increase your *'observation'* of things happening around you. You will start observing minutest details of everything, every situation, every character in your family, in your surrounding and in the society in general. Observation educates you about their habits, their personality, their behavior and their socioeconomic status, their living. This will help you to think about different characters and situations you will be creating for your story . Initially all this happens **'consciously'** but later when observation becomes part of your behavior. You continue to observe things **'subconsciously'** and preserve it in your memory for longer duration. It is like driving a car , you are conscious of every move when you first put your feet on the start and break peddles, your hands tremble to steer the wheel but later after a regular practice you drive it effortlessly. How soon you assimilate *observations* in your thoughts depend on how much serious you are to be a writer? If you are serious enough to meet your objective, the road ahead will be smooth otherwise you may face some road blocks on your way.

The creative process:

A *creative activity* is a comprehensive process that starts from the moment one gets attracted to a subject subconsciously, discover and analyze earlier experiences consciously and relate them to the subject of attraction till he is convinced of the final effect of the outcome. The entire process passes through many conscious and subconscious stages of creator's mind before the best solution is found.

Stage 1. The attraction-

A creative process of an artistic form is the result of a

conscious state of mind that is attracted to an interesting object, event, person and experience. Whenever something attracts him, he tries to know, feel and experience more about it. In this process the emotions stored in his memory bank inspire him to express his opinion, feelings, sentiments and emotions about this subject. It is the phase when a writer is completely ignorant about the outcome of his *attraction* as there is nothing concrete in his mind. Sometimes it may happen due to lack of self confidence, effective expression or the knowledge of language that includes proper vocabulary therefore it is necessary for a writer to have sufficient knowledge and the confidence on his merit and imagination. This inspires him to explore relevant experiences, subjects, characters, events and threads that lead him to link a story with his subject.

In reality, it is a difficult task to dig out relevant material from the warehouse of the mind. There is a dilemma about the relevance of certain facts, feelings and information about the attraction. In this indecisiveness something important may be pushed back but it always keeps on knocking at the doors of the consciousness. It can happen during awaken stage, during the sleep or dreams. In this stage of indecision, writing may not make a possible ascent but there is nothing to be worried and disappointed. It is common when the concept is misty and vague.

Stage 2. Discovery of relevant material from scattered storage of information and experiences- As the mist clears gradually, the relevant information and experiences about the 'attraction' too start surfacing on the consciousness to link it with main event. There comes a feeling of comfort that makes it easier for him to create a story and characters. He is able to suddenly find answers to many of his questions and resolution of many problems. It can happen at any time of thinking process from morning to noon, evening, or during conscious or subconscious stages.

Stage 3. Short listing of relevant experiences in subconscious mind-

After the discovery and analysis of relevant experiences, it is important to know about the solutions to the main issue. It is considered a very important phase in writing to find the most effective solution that also includes elements of cinema, the stage and different personalities of characters during the imagination and conception of the story. Once the best solution is found rest are discarded and concentrated on the main one.

Stage 4. Analysis of *'Experiences'* by conscious mind-

If the writer still feels that what he got is not the best and wants to continue with further research and exploration then he has to revert back and repeat the entire process till he is satisfied with the best solution.

Stage 5. Analysis of *'Relationship'* by conscious mind.

When the writer is sure of finding the best and most effective material, he creates an imaginative sketch of the story. It is in this stage that writer visualizes his scenes that he can see, hear, feel and talk to his characters. At this stage the dramatic and cinematic elements are integrated to create scenes according to cinematic requirements.

Stage 6. The Writing process -

Once writer has clearly visualized and conceptualized the **story**, in the next move he has to translate and transcend his visualization in *words* on paper. The similar process is followed to create **scenes** in a chronological order till the story comes to an end.

The creative process is the management of scattered thoughts and different experiences stored in subconscious mind. After understanding this process it is imperative for a writer to continue storing different situations, events and characters in his subconscious memory and continue to repeat this creative process. There is a constant churning of creative ideas and experiences in this process. The writer subconsciously continues to enrich himself with new ideas, experiences, sentiments and sensitivities, different situations and characters in order to discover new plots, new answers to various questions and new solutions to different issues. He has complete command on his creative surface. He lays his hands whenever he wants during this process. He should never be in search of instant solutions or quick answers as they may be stumbling blocks in the development of his ideas. He should analyze all his options on the basis of *cause, action and relationship* before zeroing on the best solutions to avoid indecisiveness, ambiguity and uncertainty. Thereafter he should pick up the right words for transcending his imaginative ideas and images on paper.

The Creative process is defined as complete assimilation and unification of actions, reactions, emotions, feelings and expressions. The material stored in subconscious is ready to be explored and expressed by a conscious mind. The process may be different for every creative person however the end result must be the best and most effective in all cases. Creativity flourishes in the domain of a writer who picks up only those subjects that attract him. He has his discretion to choose its timing, place, centrality, main idea, experiences and feelings, sensibilities and expressions etc in the plot

The writing of a screenplay begins with a *story* or an **idea of a story**. No screenplay for a fiction film can be written without it. The moment a decision to make a film or a television serial is taken the search for an interesting and entertaining story that appeals maximum people starts. The search of a story is normally undertaken by the studio, the producer or the director based on their individual liking and the field of interest, the budget and its probability of a commercial success. It is possible that a screenplay writer himself is a story writer or a story writer may like to write the screenplay himself. The difference is only of **'originality'** between the two. When the person other than the author of the story writes a screenplay, it is not his original concept but borrowed one. In this situation the script writer has to work closely with the story writer to understand his concept along with the producer, director, cameraman and actors as a **'team'** to incorporate their suggestions and opinions. This happens during the course of the development of the story and the screenplay. When the writer of an original story is engaged to write screenplay, he must cease to think himself as its *'author'* because the story is a piece of a literary work based on **verbal expressions** while as screen play writer he should think in terms of a **visual presentation** that he can achieve only by a complete metamorphosis of his original concept except picking up the main outline of the story. It may be hard for him to temper his own work to integrate it with cinematic language but it is a bitter pill he has to swallow however many of the authors are not able to accept it that creates conflict between them and the director.

The origin of an *'idea'* can be from any of the sources such as -

1. Recall of the writer's *own experiences and observation,*

2. Inspiration from the *second hand experiences* of other people you know and

3. *Borrow* from the expressions, experiences and communication material created by *others not known personally* such as literary writers' work, biographies ,reports and speeches, features published in news papers and magazines, real life events and experiences of third party, folk tales, inspirations from the films ,drama or television programs made by other directors or any other sources. This idea has to be scrutinized by the writer or the director to ensure if the same fulfills the criteria for making a film or a television show in terms of cinematic elements, entertainment value, visualization , scope to develop interesting characters and situations that can entertain and involve audiences when they watch the film or a TV show with apt attention.

The Plot

A Plot is generally perceived as a raw, desolate and uneven piece of land where any type of structure can be erected with proper concept, clarity of purpose and planning as required and imagined by the developer. Similarly in cinema a *plot* means a vague concept that needs to be developed to a story with proper vision and imagination of the Producer, writer and the director. *Plot* refers to the series of questions hidden within its meaning which affect its characters through the principle of cause and effect. The causal events of a *plot* can be thought of in a series of sentences linked by "***and so.***"

The 'Plot' in a sentence:

1. ***Naina was mesmerized by the charm of Manu's personality when she met him after many years.***

Story Idea: Naina and Manu were infatuated since their childhood. She left the city along with her family when her father was transferred to another country. Thereafter she did not see him for long time however they could never forget each other. When she returned back, she was still mesmerized by the charm of his personality after many years. What happens next, whether Naina and Manu could reunite? Were both of them married in their respective life? Will they unite again? How far this reunion will take them or will they meet the same fate and separated again?

2. ***Anupriya lost interest in her life when she realized her mistake for not being aware of the fact that Sudeep saved her life when she attempted suicide and wanted to accept him for life but it was too late.***

Story Idea: Anupriya is not happy in her married life. She meets Sudeep by chance in a party. They become friends. Sudeep is disturbed when she turns down his proposal to marry her accusing him to take advantage of their friendship. Frustrated by her husband's behavior towards her, Anupriya attempts to commit suicide by jumping from a river bridge.

She is saved by Sudeep in her unconscious state. They fall in love but don't express their feelings. Will they ever commit to each other, will she come out of her married life, will he go out of the way to patch up their marriage or help her to take a final call , will his family accept Anupriya for Sudeep or will she fall from fire to frying pan?

3. ***The strict discipline of Col. Vishwajeet forced his only son Srijan to run away from the house and take revenge with his father.***

Story Idea: Col. Vishwajeet is a strict disciplinarian in his office as well in his home. His wife Parineeta and only son, eight year old Srijan is always scared of him. He strives for his fatherly affection. Once beaten blue by him for securing low marks in his class-test, Srijan decides to leave the house and his mother in tears. He vows to take revenge with his father. Srijan is brought up by a businessman. After few years too, he could not excuse his father for the humiliation and torture inflicted on him. What is there in his mind, how is he going to take revenge, will his mother support him . Will col. realize his mistakes ?

4. ***Ram Chandra is not happy when he gets a job in reserved quota as it undermines his own self respect and merits.***

Story Idea: Ramchandra's family is happy when he gets a job as a govt. officer but he is not as he feels that his merit is undermined due to *reservation*. He has worked too hard for this selection. He faces ridicules from his colleagues and staff. He feels out cast in the office. Will he be able to function and control his staff, how will his staff treat him on duty, will Ramchandra pull on with this humiliation or will he quit, what will be his next move ?

5. *Dayal at the sunset of his life, is still waiting for the return of Laxmi, the women he loved and lost forever.*

Story Idea: Dayal keeps on gazing at the last *token* of memories of Laxmi who left him few decades back. Few are of the opinion that she might not be alive but Dayal never believes them. He has an intuition that before he closes his eyes he will be able to see her again. Will his wish be fulfilled, will Laxmi return back to him, is she really alive, why she left him if she too loved him, what is the significance of the *token* he has preserved for so long?

These are few of many *story ideas* one can discover within a '**single sentence'** with many questions hidden in its depth. The answers to these questions may leads to a **story**. It depends on the fertility of imagination of a writer as what he looks for in a sentence. He can discover many more questions and interpretations out of these sentences. A *plot* can be construed as a single line concept of a story which needs to be developed. The content, characterization, dialogues, emotions, pace and rhythm, presentation and the production are few of many factors that directly or indirectly influence a story. It is not necessary that all these factors should necessarily be present in an average or in fixed ratio in the content. Many times the economic compulsions of a production house too decide about their ratio. In some stories emotional quotient may be dominating while in others it could be action. They all influence the basic factors of a story. Some stories may have simple characters while in others they may be difficult to deal with and understand easily. The beginning of a film could be a mix of the present or past events which are relevant to the social context, period, place of incidents and beauty of the locations etc.

The Theme.

There are many and different school of thoughts that define a *'Theme.'* There may be different routes and process to develop it but the existence of an *'Idea'* is very essential for a theme . Without a definite idea no theme can be developed in to a story. The *theme* is an objective that is ultimately to be achieved at the end. In fact the writer should not tread to write without an idea. Few believe that a writer never has a definite idea about a theme, it could be true as no plot or a theme has a predefined form . No writer knows what may inspire him the next moment. He generally does not start writing until something makes him crazy and restless and he is itching to explode. In the process of expressing an *idea,* a *'theme'* begins to take shape on its own. It is similar to that of a painter who has absolutely no idea about his final outcome till he picks up his pencil and brush, he has no definite plan to proceed about it. He just starts sketching and splashing his colors with a vague idea of what he wants to paint. Similarly a writer starts pouring his experiences around a vague idea that he has in his mind therefore writing is also as creative an expression as that of a painter . The difference is only in the medium. While a painter uses colors , a writer uses his words as a medium of expression. So there cannot be a precise definition of a *theme.*

'A 'Theme' is a creative expression of social and cultural

values, objective and the message to the audience. This separates a theme with a plot. The plot is an event or incident or an idea around which a theme is developed that connects all the relevant issues in to a single thread.'

A plot and the theme complement and supplement each other. They walk together in the journey of the development of screenplay. **If 'plot' is a beginning then the 'theme' is an ultimate (objective)** so the writer should never forget the plot around which he is forging a story to meet the objective. Without a plot no theme can become a story and without a theme all the incidents and the events are merely a chronological collection which lacks a purpose, emotions and sentiments like a crowd where no individual has an identity , purpose or significance. The audiences are devoid of their participation and involvement and they fail to connect with the characters. A screenplay is the reflection of our own life where we are carried away by our emotions, sensitivity, honesty, change and the growth.

Story telling:

Since the time immemorial *'story telling'* has not merely been a means of entertainment but stories were also the carrier of cultural traditions and social values to the next generations. Stories narrated by grandpas and grannies provided education and a small dose of entertainment to the children. Due to various changes and the development in the society, the story telling has also gone through many changes in the methodology, style and the medium but the fundamentals of storytelling remained the same. We still express things through stories that we feel passionate about and are of the opinion that they must be shared and conveyed to those who are affected or those who can make an impact on others. In contemporary writing, stories are inspired from problems and issues being faced by people around, social and economical discrimination, individual sufferings, struggles and their journey to fight with them either to fail or be a winner. As it was prevalent in ancient times there still is a formula to tell a story that will continue to be followed in future-

1. **Once upon a time....**   *(Time)*
2. **In a city....**   *(Location)*
3. **There was...**   *(person or people)*
4. **Because of/ due to....**   *(Initial action and reaction)*
5. **After all his efforts....**   *(Struggle)*
6. **Winner or failure in the end...** *(Change in situations)*
7. **It means that...**   *(Theme/objective/message)*

Most of the stories begin with time, person or people to explain the situations and the characters including main protagonist, antagonist and others', their actions and the reaction which bring change in the situations and in the behavior of different characters leading to the culmination that meets an objective. The victory or a defeat conveys a message that writer feels passionate to communicate. This message is the *theme* of the story.

It is a story-

Every story has the following ingredients:

1. A Problem:

- There is always a problem,
- There is a resolution or the decision to solve the problem,
- A main character plays a vital role in the resolution,
- There is a new beginning of life after the problem is solved.

2. Struggle:

- continuous struggle and efforts to face it,
- cropping up another issue/problem after one is resolved,
- complicating the situations with new developments,
- defeating the opponents with newer efforts,
- trying to get rid of the past mentality/attitude,

3. Culmination:

- Failure to meet the objective/purpose,
- Non acceptance of the dangers or acknowledgement of warnings,
- Success at the end,
- Bravery or a bold act of a person or the character,
- Success of a man and the birth of a new person.

4. Theme:

There is always a **theme** of a story that conveys something to be accepted or not accepted such as:

- Refusal to what is non attainable,
- Leave it to destiny whatever is not possessed,

- God is one. There is always something good and bad in the world,
- One should acknowledge the power within and not search it outside,
- Self respect is restored with out disrespecting others.

It is not a story-

One should remember that everything which is told may not be a story; it needs to have ingredients of a story as discussed earlier. Following may not be considered suitable for a story:

- The news, reviews and editorials published in a news paper even though the writer is convinced of its credibility and expects that it will be accepted by everyone but there is an absence of struggle therefore even though people may be convinced of the facts, they don't get involved. It is not necessary that a reader must accept 'the end' as written in the write up or an editorial as it is considered to be personal opinion of the writer.
- A joke, a taunt or something expressed in sarcasm is not a story though it may express an opinion in one line. Readers may or may not agree with it. It lacks struggle and emotions that drift away readers from the issue.
- A speech, a pamphlet or an appeal doesn't make a story even though the speaker or the propagator may have put his views strongly with conviction but ultimately it remains his personal view point. It is devoid of other ingredients of a story which don't make it an effective piece of writing. It lacks struggle

and an effort to overcome the problem. Since it is only a personal expression, it fails to interact with readers.

- Radio and Television talks and News too don't make a story as they present an event or an incident as it happens. People may be curious to know more about the issue, its background, people involved, their intentions and objective but it does not lead to a resolution. There is no end of the issues raised in a news item or a talk show. They also don't present a goal. Such issues or event may provide elements of curiosity, conflict, cause of struggle, possibility of people's participation and involvement and a theme but until all these elements are organized and integrated interestingly, they do not make a story.

- A specific incident of an individual's life which creates a purpose, struggle, conflict and confrontation,, cooperation, meeting of an objective by constant efforts, victory or failures etc may be a catalyst for a story but till these ingredients are systematically integrated, they don't create a story.

By this analysis you must have understood how these elements and ingredients are essential factors to write a story that invite people to participate and involve in every aspect and event caricatured in it. If they become an inseparable part of the story, it is sign of a writer's success.

The Situations:

The common viewer of a film or theatre normally ignores the present situations as they are not aware of their inadvertent impact the story would make on their mind. The present situations only affect a story or the growth of characters. In the absence of present situations the characters would be groping in zero space and the audience would be left confused. The present situations only make a character sensitive and full of feelings. They take their audience to a journey to their past and the future so the *'present'* itself becomes the present of the characters and the viewers. These situations play a covert role in the plot and weave new characters, events, stress and curiosity, twists and complications to take the story forward. These situations generate audience's acceptability of the characters and their authenticity. In these situations audience look for the period of the story, cultures and the traditions, life styles and the behavior of people and the characters, therefore the knowledge of periodic situations and circumstances, place of events, social fabric and their cultural traditions, general Intelligence, Law and order and political back grounds, Religion and beliefs of the people etc. is essential.

Many decades ago in the year 1919 an English author *'Wycliffe A. Hill'* discovered elementary aphorisms of a story. He believed that there were only *36 maxims* to create a plot. All the stories are generally based on these formulae and have their variations.

A. Happy Situations:

1. Rescue
2. Lost loved ones recovered
3. A miracle of God

B. Pathetic situations:

4. Entreaty
5. Love's obstacles
6. Rivalry between unequal
7. Rivalry between kinsmen
8. A mystery

C. Inspiring situations:

9. Loving an enemy
10. Sacrifice of oneself for an ideal.
11. Sacrifice of oneself for Kindred

D. Disastrous situations precipitated without criminal intent:

12. Possessed of an ambition
13. Fatal indiscretion
14. Pursuit
15. Rebellion
16. Enmity between kinsmen
17. Effort to obtain
18. Daring effort
19. Vengeance
20. Kindred avenged against kindred
21. Mistaken jealousy
22. Involuntary criminal love

E. Disastrous situations precipitating with criminal intent:

23. Struggle against God
24. Abduction
25. To sacrifice all for a passion
26. Adultery
27. Adultery with murder
28. Criminal love

G. Tragic situations over which the victim has no control:

29.Loved ones lost

30. Falling a prey

31. Disaster
32. An innocent suspected
33. Obligation to sacrifice loved ones
34. To learn of the dishonor of the loved ones
35. Mental derangement
36. To kill a kinsmen or a friend
37. Remorse

The period and the Span:

The suggestions of *'Period'* *is the time (Present, past or future)* when the events take place, facilitate the audience to travel to the particular 'period' immediately and they become part of that era.

The *'span of the story'* is the cumulative duration of the events occurring in the entire plot. The span may vary from days to months and the years. In this span every event has its own period and the season of occurrence which gives it a definite identity and purpose.

A film or a part of it can be designed in any **season** such as rainy, winter or the spring if the story has specific relevance and requirements. Similarly the story may also emphasize a particular festival, occasion or the boundary.

The Dramatic *duration* of an Act is the *'Time'* taken by an event or the scene of the story or the drama to travel to the next act'. This helps to complete the entire chain of events in the story with in a limited time frame. This timing can vary from one scene to another if required. While writing the screen play every scene may be allotted some days or weeks of *dramatic duration* to maintain continuity of events.

Physical environment and the Locale:

As it suggests **it is the environment, atmosphere and the ambience where the event or the action takes place**. The physical environment of the place is detailed minutely In the narration to increase the impact therefore the director must acquire a thorough knowledge of the place, its history, environment and culture, society and the traditions.

The 'Locale' means the country, the area, the district or the village where the story unfolds. The geographical locale can sometimes be informed through dialogues however the emotional relationship and the impact of this in the narrative of the story must never be ignored and the writer should make full use of such provisions.

No event or action can take place without a specified *location*. This physical location should by all means be decided by the director while writing the screen play however unnecessary details at this stage are not required and may be avoided to give him more liberty to roam freely in his imagination and creativity to make necessary changes in the scene accordingly. The details which have the potential to enhance the effect of the scene may be included in the script.

Extending his list of common plots *Wycliffe* also listed *common locations* where generally a film is shot or the events take place. They are-

1.Aeroplane, 2.Ship, 3.Train, 4.Advertising agency, 5.erospace, 6.Dictator's headquarter, 7.House of dignified person, 8.Army post, 9.Artist's studio, 10.Stadium, 11.Foriegn township, 12.cotton fields, 13.Court, 14.Dance floor, 15.Shop/store, 16.Desert, 17.Shipyard, 18.Factory, 19. Farm fields, 20.Fishermen's colony, 21.Lake, 22.Advocate's chamber, 23.Light house, 24.Cattle shed, 25.Mansion, 26.Matro city, 27.Mining center, 28.Embassy. 29.Motel, 30.Police station, 31.Prison, 32.Publication house, 33.Racecourse, 34.Radio/television station, 35.Railway station, 36.Trench/Pit, 37.Bank, 38.Warfield, 39.Seaside/beach, 40.Grove, 41.Cave, 42.Broker's office, 42.Sharemarket, 43.Cabrette,Camp, 45.Forest, 46.Gamblers' den, 47.Criminals'den, 48.Playground, 49.Port, 50.Hospital, 51.Hotel, 52.Island, 53.Laboratory, 54.Film studio, 56.National Borders, 57.Newspaper house, 58.Night club, 59.Brothel, 60.Astronomical laboratory, 61.Execution home, 62.Culvert, 63.Pirates'den, 64.Gardens, 65.Rest house, 66.Rice /grain fields, 67.River, 68.Sailoon, 69.Ocean, 70.Small town, 71.Godown, 72.Stage, 73.Stock exchange, 74.Hot regions, 75.Underground activities, 76.Waterfronts, 77.Village, 78.Snowfields/places, 79.Zoo, 80.Office, 81.Hutments, 82.Chawls, 83.Dispensary, 84.Places of worship. 85.Streets, 86.Lanes/by lanes, 87.Bridges/flyovers, 88.Flowerbeds, 89.Hill stations.

Social context:

The plot of any story revolves around various social groups among us. They may be our family and its members with whom we have intimate connection or other groups who are directly or indirectly related to our lives at various levels. All these social groups differ in their back ground, ideology, behavior, socio economic situations that give them their distinct identity and influence personality of their people. In the stories that are conceived around a family, realistic situations can be portrayed around intimate relationships but in other social groups that are devoid of emotional intimacy, such portrayals may look concocted and clitche thus make no impact. Sometimes such characters are created deliberately for the sake of entertainment who do not look real. In other social groups friendship, professional relations or relations based on various socio economic status, romantic liaison is important. The members of such groups have different behavioral pattern which is reflected in the development of the characters.

1. The family:

Family comes first among all the social groupings. Everybody is connected with his mother, father, brothers, sisters and other relations. A family is the basic unit of a society which cannot be ignored. The family establishes an identity of characters that links them with the audience. Every person in a family has a different role to play which is the basic constituent in his growth. The writer must be conscious of the sensitivities of every relationship which has to reflect in each of the characters.

2. **Friendship:**

Next to the family comes friendship which is out of the family's periphery. Friendship differs with the situations and the immediate circumstances. It has many types but the common thread between them is *friendly connections.* Another dimension in friendship is that of *romantic relationship* which is normally established between the persons of opposite sex. The main difference between a friendship and romantic relationship is that of an *'attraction'.* It is not necessary to have an attraction and emotional link in friendship which is essential for a romantic liaison. This variation makes a difference in the development of various characters.

3. Professional:

People engaged in similar profession or institutions develop a functional relationship and expect special considerations. Everyone in such group follows set parameters and discipline as in Navy, Army, Police or any other profession. Their specific behavior and personality authenticates their profession.

4. Dignitaries:

People in this group represent a special category of high and mighty in their social, economical and the political status. They give orders to the people who are comparatively rank lower in education and professional strata. The difference between high and low can be easily noticed in their behavior and mannerism. People in subordination greet, salute or wish them humbly bending forward while those in higher peddles look them down with authority and arrogance. This discrimination between classes of people is the result of traditions and ethnic culture which is easily identified with their dressings, ornaments and jewelry, language etc. This class discrimination provides a definite identity to various characters in the film.

5. Social standards:

Every society or a social group consists of some definite traditions and behavior which is expected to be followed by everybody. This behavioral pattern is ingrained in their etiquettes. Most of the people display their personality which confirms to their social and economic standards. Any change in their behavior marks an aberration and is then protested by those who profess it. Traditionally such class differences were created by religious, political and cultural parameters. In modern times of scientific innovations and applications, these traditions are still followed by middle class in respect of equality and inculcate law and order in the society.

6. Economic system:

The economic system created by the state affects everyone irrespective of their social groupings. There are two classes of *1. The Ruler and 2. The ruled*. They have distinct identity in public and private domains. While a ruler displays his freedom of action and ideology, the ruled display signs of slavery and subordination.

7. Politics and the Law:

The laws of the land are governed and enacted based on the political and legal decisions of the state. They affect every one differently therefore the writer and the director should have fairly good knowledge of the politics and the laws of the nation.

8. Intellectuals and opinion makers:

The intellectuals and the opinion makers have always been a

great asset since the beginning of humanity. Their opinion provides a direction to the society by influencing the minds and beliefs of common men. This group includes religious preachers and priests, teachers, leaders, journalists, actors and other performers, celebrities and professionals etc. Their daily discourses and ideology influences day to day life of people. These intellectuals and opinion makers are the instrument in preserving the social and cultural heritance and traditions Therefore to develop such characters an extensive research is important and necessary to ensure how a character from this group will behave and how he can influence people in general.

9. Faith and beliefs:

Every society has its own religious factors, rituals, festivals and traditions which influence people since their birth. These faiths and beliefs not only influence their life styles but also their ideology though the intensity of influence may vary due to many social and economic factors. It is not necessary that everybody is influenced equally. It depends on the intellectual level of an individual which decides the amount of his faith and beliefs in religion and traditions. It is the reason that we see two types of people 1. *A theist* and *2.An atheist.* This attitude is evident in their characters and behavior. It is very common these days by a group to protest against depiction of certain faiths and beliefs in the excuse of *'hurting their sentiments'.* Sometimes these protests damage a film's collection but most of times they are used publicity.

The writer and the director must ensure that when they are developing a character from any of the above groups, they must study them thoroughly as their depiction is closely observed by the audience while they watch a film, a drama or a television serial. A wrong depiction not only nullifies their effect but also questions their authenticity and makes the characters hollow and laughable. This is one of the major factors of the failure of a film, drama or television show that concocts the situations and characters which are not natural. These things are not taught in any school but the writer and the director must learn themselves by minute observation around.

The writer must ensure while writing screen play or a drama that all his characters should have born before their entry in the script so that they have already taken a shape and there is no need to waste time to show them growing until and unless there is a need to show its subsequent growth. The past of a character shapes his present and future behavior and actions.

Selection of characters:

It is next important task for a director after he is aware of the main characters and the locations. According to **Wycliffe** there can be a protagonist, an antagonist and the female lead character. Thereafter few or more characters and locations as required in the script where most of the events of the story occur can be selected.

Common characters:

Wycliffe A. Hill during his research on the stories not only discovered common themes but also analyzed them to enlist **Common characters** used in these plots. These characters, consist of various socioeconomic groups drawn from different geographical backgrounds prepare the ground for an entertaining story line.

These characters include- 1.Actors/Actresses, 2,Advertiser, 3.Representative, 4.Protester/Agitator, 5.Anarchist, 6.Relegious preacher, 7.Performer, 8.Astrologer, 9.Astronomer, 10.Blackmarketeer,11.Blacksmith, 12.Blind, 13.Librarian, 14.Agent/Broker, 15.Pirates, 16. Builder, 17.Tyrant, 18.Thief, 19.Quality controller/inspector, 20.Hero/Brave, 21.Priest, 22,Driver, 23.Pharmasist, 24.Microanalyst, 25.clerk, 26.Joker, 27.cobbler, 28.Funnyman/comedian, 29.Body builder/Athlete, 30.Accountant, 31.Motor racer, 32.Pilot, 33.Player, 34.Dacoit, 35.Banker/cashier, 36.Fool, 37.Prince/Ruler, 38.Begger, 39.chef,,. 40. Cannibal, 41.Wealthy, 42.Captain/Boss, 43. Forest thief, 44.Cartoonist, 45.Treasurer,Animal thief, 46.Horse rider, 47.Cavemen, 48.Socialist, 49.Conducter, 50.Trustee,

51.Leader, 52.Magician, 53.Police constable, 54.Contracter, 55.Convict, 56.Police, 57..Fraudester, 58.Shephered, 59.Disable, 60. Truthful warrior, 61.Dancer, 62.Deaf, 63.Dentist, 64.Spy, 65.Devotee, 66.Diver, 67.Divorced, 68.Legger, 69.Naughty, 70.Forecaster, 71.Gambler, 72.Criminal, 73.Jewelthief, 74.General, 75.Swordman, 76.Governer, 77.Abductor, 78.Mortgaged, 79.Hunch backed, 80.Hunter, 81.Hypnotist, 82.Inventor, 83.Invester, 84.Jailer/Prison superintendent, 85.Jweller, 86.Psychic, 87.Marine, 88.Martyr, 89.Companion, 90.Mayer, 91.Doctor, 92.Businessman, 93.Minister, 94.Miser, 95.Crowd puller, 96.Alcoholic, 97.Drug manufacturer, 98.Editor, 99.Embezzeler, 100.Expatriate.

101. Engineer, 102.Accontant, 103.Firefighter, 104.Fisherman.

105. Fraudulent, 106.Guard, 107.Guide, 108.Gunmen, 109.Vagabond, 110.Mercyless, 111.Physician, 112.Saint, 113.Highway pirates, 114. Professional riders, 115, Judge, 116.King, 117.Warrior king, chief, 118.Labourer, 119.Advocate, 120. Life savior, 121. Creditor, 122.Model, 123.Nuisence talker, 124.Killer, 125.Musician, 126.Dumb, 127.Lame, 128.Womanizer, 129.Ideal person, 130.Author/Novelist,131.Nurse,132.Officer,134.Poet,135.Singer,136.Absconder,136.Areligious, 137.Child labor, 138.Dramatist, 139. Burglar, 140hunt –thief, 141.Chairman, 142.Herdsman, 143. Wrestler, 144. Rebellion, 145.Correspondent, 146.Mariner, 147.Wild, 148.Educationist, 149. Scientist, 150.Worshipper,

151.Scout, 152.Social worker, 152.Short and fat man, 153.Steal maker, 154.Textilemaker, 155.Stenographer, 156.Homeless, 157.Rowdy, 158.Swimmer, 159.swindler, 160.Union leader, 161.Grabber, 162.Devil, 163.Vampire, 163.Brutal, 164.Indecent, 165.Throttler, 166.Guardian, 167.Soldier, 168.Watch repairer, 169.Watchman, 170.Reciever, 171.Extravagent, 172.Professor, 173.Psychologist, 173.Boxer, 174.Marine cashier, 175.Horse Trainer, 176.Horse racing coach. 177. Bribe taker, 178.Annoncer/Anchor, 179.Servant, 180.Sheriff, 181.Bishop, 182.Captain of the ship, 183. Water queen, 184.Suspicious, 185.Slave, 186.Smuggler,, 187.Tailor, 188.Skin specialist, 189.Telegrapher, 190.Telephone operator, 191.Hunter, 192.Dictator, 193.Bruital, 194.Ampire, 195.Responsible, 196.Black magician, 197.Specialist, 198.Maid servant, 199.Homemaker, 200. Student.

201. Roughen, 202.Adulterater, 203.Lover boy and girl, 204.Informer, 205.Engine driver, 206.Ticketcoleector,

207.Shoppkeeper, 208.Filmmaker, 209.Publisher, 210.Traditionalist/religious, 211.Historical, 212.Imaginative, 213.African/Negro, 214.Mangole, 215.Englishman, 216.Assistant, 217.Delivery Nurse, 218.Person who assumes various characters, 219.Crafty, 220.Washerman, 221.Coolie, 222.Women carrying water on head, 223.Carpenter, 224.Farmer, 225.Landlord, 226.Atheist.

The first move:

The plot as we all understand in layman's language, is a piece of land which is uneven, undeveloped with lot of shrubs and unproductive grass, trees and plants etc. This plot needs to be worked upon from its leveling to prepare a concrete plan of Structure. Similarly in the plot of a story whether it originates from an idea, concept, a short story, a novel or any other work of writing, there comes a series of changes and modifications by the time the screenplay reaches to its culmination. Most of these changes are carried out to sustain interest and ease the grasp. The common thread to these modifications is the *continuity and integration* of various facets of the story which restricts the diversion of the main content. This forms the *'theme'* of the story.

Assessment of a story:

The first step towards the screenplay is to carry out an in depth analysis of the story to underline its salient feature and important events that may interest and impress people to associate with them. If there is a doubt that story may not be able to connect with them, the writer must immediately remove those points or discard it entirely as it is not advisable to move on with such a content. While carrying out this analysis writer must ensure the cause, the effect and the relevance of every event, action and reaction , character and the situation is relevant and realistic. While watching the film, audience 'mind' constantly keeps on analyzing them to remove unwanted material projected on the screen. Therefore it is important to include only those events and characters which are relevant and have some lasting impact on the audience.

The way a **written play** is the base of a '**Drama**' before it is staged; **Screenplay** is the basic requirement for a **film** before it is shot. The *screenplay* in fact, is a detailed written impression of the film that is envisaged to be seen on the screen. In simple words one can say *'a screenplay is a film on paper'* which contains a detailed visualization however it's outcome depends on its effective execution. It can easily be surmised that *written words* in a story or a Novel are complete expression for a writer; they are complete in screenplay only with the integration and incorporation of various genres of art forms and cinematic technology. An author of a novel or the story does not need any other tool, means or technology to complement his creativity other than the words. Words are the only bridge required between him and the reader but is not so in the production of a play or a film where words are only a means to take off the flight of imagination to write a drama or a screenplay.

The imagination poured in the screenplay can be realized only with the support of sensitive performances of actors, effective dialogue delivery, attractive set design and the setting, special lighting, soulful background music etc beside eye catching cinematography and flawless editing. In their absence the film is neither complete nor effective. Therefore it is confirmed that a screenplay is not complete in itself and it is just a **plinth** for planning structure of a dramatic enactment or a film production. There is always scope for improvements at various stages of a film production.

The Idea:

The take off point is an '**Idea**' that inspires a producer to decide about the production of a film or a television program. Once an idea is spruced up, the producer needs a writer to work out the story. The idea can be developed for any genre of films such as documentary, fiction, talk show etc but a script is always needed prior to the execution or its actual production. Screen play is written by the writer in consultation with the Producer and the Director. It is not advisable to jump in to production without a proper and planned script.

The *idea* that is picked up for a production is vague in the beginning. No one actually knows about what shape it would take and how much effective and appealing it would be after it takes a form, how the idea would be developed therefore writing for a film and television show becomes a very specialized job. The writer must have the knowledge of fiction writing, novels, drama and other art forms besides having functional technical knowledge of the medium. As you know by now that film and television are basically visual medium and express through moving images. The professionals engaged in this field require technical knowledge, creative pursuits and power to visualize scenes . *'In film and television writing, 'words' and 'action' are not written or spoken but* '*shown visually*' therefore the 'words' written in the screenplay don't have to reflect writer's expertise of language and literature but display a series of *moving image* . These moving images include emotions and sentiments of human life . A laughter, a cry, an anger, sympathy and romance etc have more impact when shown visually than in written words therefore to be précised, we will here discuss specifically about fiction film and television programs which start with an '**idea**'.

The idea can be picked up or inspired from original concepts, events and incidents in our life, personality, news reports, political situations, social issues, literary works, plays and films etc that can be conceptualized as a plot for the story.

Development of a story:

The development of a *Plot to a story* is undertaken in following steps such as-

1. **Establishment of the Problem:** In the first step the problem and the characters are introduced in which various dimensions and contradictions of the issues are brought to the notice of the audience. The objective of this introduction is to make people start thinking about the solution but it is not to make them aware of the issue or bring them on the same wavelength as that of the characters or to instigate them to chase for a solution. The resolution of the problem should be revealed in layers gradually and not at a time. The beginning and the built up should not take more than 1/6th of the total time.

2. The Complications: The cause, action and relationship are used logically to create complications, conflicts and the tension in the story otherwise the story will be a poor narrative without twists and turns that will not interest anyone. The chain of complications and conflicts followed by one another immediately after the resolution of a problem is necessary to build up interest and subsequent release of tensions till another complication appears. This provides relief to the audience after intense situations are resolved.

Complications can be long and short but they should have appropriate relevance and reasons. If there is proper coordination and linkage between them, the story will move forward without interruptions in its continuity and they will complement each other in the progression of the plot. If exclusion of any of them does not make a difference to the narration then such complications are not acceptable hence removed.

3. **Contradiction, confrontation and relief:** This should take about 2/3 of the total time of the film which includes different ups and downs, tensions, confrontation and opposition etc. It is like ECG graph where modulations go up and down then there are straight lines before modulations go up again. This forms a major portion of the film or television story where characters play their established roles and help built up the conflicts and release of tension. Special attention is to be paid to develop this part which is also called *'the middle'*. It requires a great deal of vision and creativity. While doing so *'Cause and effect'* should be used with logic and precision. A scene without a logic and reasonability destroys its dramatic effect. Similarly the unbelievable complications which cannot

be easily digested by people should be avoided as they don't not impress people and leave them confused.

Romance plays a very interesting role in screenplay or television drama. It has an inherent emotion of everybody's life. Their internal and mostly suppressed feelings are awakened when they see another couple romancing on the screen. It is not necessary that every romance has a similar angle. As we have seen in the list of 37 plots, there are only few of them which have romantic connotations however *'Romance'* should always be integrated in the plot as it has the potential to have people glued to the screen.

4.The final solution- This part of the story takes the audience to its logical conclusion which includes its climax. There is no formula to have a set resolution of a problem. It largely depends on the sensitivity of the story, type of audience, personal preference of the director and the writer who decide how to approach a resolution whether it should be tragic or a happy one.

While deciding so, the basic nature and the emotional factor of the story should not be ignored otherwise the impact of the climax will be diluted and the audience will leave the theatre unsatisfied. There is a general tendency of those who see films only for entertainment to appreciate a happy end of the film however director is not bound to accept it.

Setting the Goal:

Now any one of the 37 basic plots mentioned above can be chosen for a plot to develop a story. There are only three **objectives** of a protagonist to accomplish-

A. To acquire an authority, possession or ownership

B. To get rid of something,

C. Revenge

These three points can be explained and analyzed as under-

A. Authority or ownership: 1.Vehicle or an aircraft or a ship, 2.Means of luxury, 3.Family, 4.Children, 5.Kids,6.Clothes, 7.ornaments and jewelry, 8. Immovable Property, 9.Other's possessions, 10.Popularity, 11.Formula, 12.Wealth, 13.social status and Dignity, 14.Knoledge, 15.Inheritance, 16.Love, 17.Map, 18.Fortune, 19.Pet animals, 20.Authority and the post, 21, independent Identity.

B. Getting rid off: 1.Law breaker, 2.Critic, 3.Killer, 4.Insult, 5.tyrant, 6. Enemy, 7.Advocate, 8.Opponent, 9.Decoit, 10.Desreputer, 11.Rumour monger, 12.Dictator,

Road blocks:

To accomplish his objectives the protagonist generally faces the following road blocks or the hurdles-

1. Facing a person who is more experienced, powerful, knowledgeable, wealthy, influential, beautiful or balanced than him.

2. Poverty, filth, domestic, incompetent, foolish, sick, lazy, latecomers, weak, stranger, Misinformation, mistaken identity of a person, Place and Object, Identity marks, Bloodstains, Disable, ugly, criminal, Blind, Deaf, Dumb.

3. Suspicious, Convict, Infamous, Mental, Loss of memory,

Misunderstanding/misunderstood, Hate, Loathsome, Unwelcome.

4. Gutless, Power, Friend, Influence, Dignity, Freedom, Closeness, Defensiveness, crime, Investigation, Extradited.

5. Opposition from an enemy, competitor, tyrant, executer of a punishment, punishment, Voice of conscience, Ego, Pride, Conventions, Rituals.

6. Duty bound, Commitment, Traditions, Religion, Status, Vow, Rules and regulations, Legalities, Laws, to save a friend or close relatives. 7. Disabled by extra baggage, Lack of identity, Truthfulness, Honesty, Dead end to prove ones merits.

The hero has to face and overcome these hurdles to achieve his ambitions and hit the targets. They can be accomplished by Begging, sacrifice or confrontation to win the targets.

A. Begging-The protagonist begs the giver to hand over his desired object. In most of the cases his request is accepted. Following can be the reasons for prayers/request or begging-

1. A right opportunity, another opportunity, Mercy.

2. Selling oneself at a cost, Duty, Devotion, service, Misunderstandings, Innocence, Fair intentions.

3. To honor a commitment, Vow, , to prove innocence, to save/defend others.

4. Defensive actions against an opponent to save a friend or relative or love from harm.

5. Crime instigated by other, Misguidance about an identity,

Revenge for a friend, relative or love.

B. Sacrifice-In the eventuality of a sacrifice there is a compromise between two opposing groups where both of them sacrifice something for other with certain conditions. This can also be termed as 'Compromise on mutual consent. Once this compromise is reached both the groups/parties are bound to honor the commitment made in the compromise terms and conditions. Normally following materials are sacrificed in a compromise-

1. Life, Love, Dignity, Health, Relation, freedom for self or loved ones.

2. Trust, Pleasure, Status, Valuable possessions, Friendship, respect for self or loved ones.

3. Self respect, Duty, Honor, Dignity, Vows and commitments, Time, Soul, Post, Money or property, Defensive actions.

4. Right to revenge and wining.

5. Pleasures and materials, essentials of life, important information or mystery, Getting rid of unpleasant situations of a friend, relative or loved ones.

C. Hitting the target or revenge- In the efforts to win and achieve its objective both the parties try their best of muscle power and physical strength, mental and spiritual powers and convince each other to give up their obstinacy. These persuasive powers can be in the following forms-

1. Arguments, threat, physical conflict.

2. Right to conquer and hitting the targets.

3. Stop further progression, Capsize, Sudden attack or loss to enemy, misinformation, revenge, convince him to change his mind and attitude by physical strength or talks., Disarming of fighting weapons, Injuring or killing the enemy,

4. Physical and mental dismemberment of the opponent or forcing surrender.

It is not a child's play to write a story but a writer can follow the conventional methods of selection of characters, places, events and integrate them logically with the convincing cause of action related to reasons, actions and relations. One should remember that any story starts with an Idea which is developed with great efforts and application of knowledge, language and technical skills. The story develops gradually step by step to its culmination. There s a regular chain of events when an idea takes off to its expansion till its climax. There are few common climaxes or end for a story such as-

1. A sick, disabled or a lost person appears suddenly.
2. The victory of the antagonist converts to his defeat and destroys him or there is a sudden victory of the Hero who almost lost his battle.
3. The crime was just a misunderstanding.
4. The character is either identified wrongly or he appears to be in disguise.
5. Unexpected sacrifice by unexpected characters.
6. There is a windfall for the person who sacrificed everything.
1. Acceptance of guilt by the antagonist or his surrender in the end.

2. The person gets a life that lost all hopes to live.
3. Submission of a evidence by a small character that decides the guilt and the defeat or punishment of the antagonist.
4. Sudden Change or reversal of situations between the protagonist and the antagonist.
5. Sudden appearance of some evidences that proves the truthfulness of the character and removes misunderstandings.
6. A miracle that reverses the entire scenario of disappointment to a pleasant surprise.

According to Wycliffe there cannot be any plot formation beyond these contents. Imagination can create an entertaining and interesting story out of any of the above suggestions. There can be '**experimental plots'** which can defy the set formula of storytelling and the contents. It depends on the writers or director's innovative thinking and creative imagination.

Wycliffe never promises to make anyone a story writer but only guide him. Every writer has its own style which is embellished by practice during the course of time therefore it is suggested that all the writers read as much as they can to acquire knowledge and understand writing styles of different writers of different genres and work out his own unique style of story writing.

It is true that production of film and television program is technical and also an amalgamation of many other art forms where people connected with them contribute. They are exponents in their profession. These art forms include writing, painting, music and dance, designing, drama, construction and many others. Beside them there are many more functions that involve technology as well as individual creativity. No one person can actually take the credit of the production of a film or television program however the punch of its failure is felt more intensely by its Producer as he is the person who takes lead from the decision to produce it .

The extensive technical details about a scene are best avoided or reduced to minimum if their mention is indeed important, such as camera angles, special sound effects, specific expressions required in actors' performances may find a place in the scene to enhance the reading effect. *'Actions'* of the actors , camera angles and movements may be specified before shooting. It is not appropriate to decide the *'action'* as per the shots but shots should be divided as per the action required in the screenplay. It is also true that after a long experience only a director is able to form a clear visual concept but still he should make extra efforts to visualize the scenes beforehand along with the writer. It makes it easy to visualize the final form of the film.

The writer should remember the following guidelines during the writing of a screenplay:

1. He should make separate notes of minute details in every scene. It is not necessary that his opinions may be part of the draft but should be included in the final version so that everybody knows about them.

2. A screenplay should be clearly written and attractively bound for the presentation to the financiers, actors, distributors and other relevant people. This script is a trailer of the final film.

3. A detailed screenplay helps understand the sentiments and emotions of different characters.

4. The writer and the director must understand each other well and respect each others' creativity.

If the director does not prepare the notes of his constant downpour of imaginative ideas and innovative thoughts that keep on hitting him, it is possible that he may forget when he needs them most. This may force him to compromise with the concept or he may prefer to shoot the story in its abridged form. Both these situations are detrimental and the director would not remain the sole creator of its original work but be labeled as a mere translator of the original work of the author. In another likely situation if the writer lacks the knowledge of cinematic language, he would overload the screenplay with *dialogues* and miss out the visualization of scenes thus reducing the impact of inherent emotions and sentiments. The writers should know that film is a visual medium and should understand the intricacies of its presentation.

The journey to write a screenplay begins with an idea, short story, Novel or an adaptation of a literary work. They are the take off points from where the screenplay makes its first move forward. If the director himself writes the screenplay it becomes easier for him to develop it in the manners he conceives the film but it is not always possible. A director may have to work with one or more regular or temporary writers engaged by the studio or a production house. If the film is based on a literary work the director has to deal with the author and write the script respecting his sentiments. It is also possible that the story is a pure fantasy of the author. In this case the director is mostly dependent on the writer and his contribution in the form and style is negligible. It is ultimately the director's responsibility to present an attractive, innovative, imaginative and creative script to his financiers, distributers and the lead actors. An experienced director can accomplish the same with his original ideas or the salient features of the story presented without a proper and detailed script. To do it the director needs to have a clear vision about the film which reflects his own creative style and identity. Based on this preliminary concept the director may write a **synopsis** of the screenplay that has précised narration of the main story. If he is successful to convince financiers, producers, distributors and the main actors he can proceed to write a detailed screenplay in association with other writers. While writing the scenes writers and director should integrate necessary emotional, dramatic and technical details to continue refreshing and refurbishing the concept of the film in their mind.

Chronology of Screen play:

Normally outline, synopsis, treatment and the screenplay are written in present tense as a film or a play is always seen or heard in the present except the *flash back* where story moves back ward to explain certain previous events or moves to the future as character dreams or foresee things (*flash forward*) the way they would like to see it.. Even these flash backs and flash forwards are written in the present tense with proper indication to facilitate easy understanding to the readers about the past or the future. Afterwards the reader returns back to the present and moves forward along with the story.

The subjective view point of the writer should be reflected in first person-plural as '*we*' and not as '*I*' for the reason that from the beginning itself the writer must give an impression to carry everybody along with him. This creates a sense of belonging among the members in the film unit with the subject. This may be remembered that everyone in the film unit is also a film viewer so if they develop an affinity and the interest in the subject, it also means that the film has established its relationship with the audience. There are few chronological steps to proceed with writing a screen play for a fiction film which a director and the writer must follow with due earnest however for some convenience and necessity any of the steps can be skipped or reworked till complete satisfaction is achieved. In all these stages the coordination and the understanding between the writer and the director is of utmost importance. They should be on the same plane.

1. Synopsis: This is the first step to write a complete synopsis of the story as to be unfolded in the film. The main advantage of synopsis is to facilitate the reaction from main actors, financiers, distributers and the producers. If they appreciate the synopsis the first successful step is taken forward. If the story is adapted from a novel or a play or an idea, it may not be possible to narrate complete story in the same form in short time available for the purpose or it may not be grasped by others in the same spirit therefore a *synopsis* is the right form of narration that also depends on the style and effectiveness of the narrator. A synopsis does not require details of characters, situations, locations and development of the concept. This is written in the format of a short story where selected few characters and dramatic situations are developed in detail including the description of dialogues. It normally is neither a complete play format nor it is a shooting script.

2. Scenario: In *Scenario* writers have to develop and visualize every scene to include visual description, characterization, probable actions and dialogues. In this stage scenes are constructed according to the requirement of the story that leads to the development of the screenplay thereafter. *Scenario* while clearing the mist in the idea, provides an opportunity to some enthusiastic writers and directors to display their creativity and vision of their proposed film. A *scenario* can be defined as:

'The summery of outline or the treatment of a motion picture or television program, underlining the actions, the description of scenes and characters etc. in the order in which they would appear on the screen. Generally every scene is written in few lines in the chronological order.'

Climb the steps:

There is always a **purpose** for an action or event which forms a scene. A scene without a purpose not only obstructs the flow of the story but also becomes a hurdle in its narration. There is no formula for constructing a scene or deciding the purpose of it in the screenplay.

Flowing with the current of the story , writer divides his acts/sequences and events to create an interest. A scene is not effective if the writer does not feel the pressing need to include it in the script. It is true that the screen play writer has to work very hard to conceive each scene that not only takes the story forward but is also interesting to make the audience tied up on their seats without allowing them to go out for a puff. Every scene in the script is like a step which should climb the audience one after another to its climax. A weak stair will demolish the entire journey in the story and the film will fall flat.

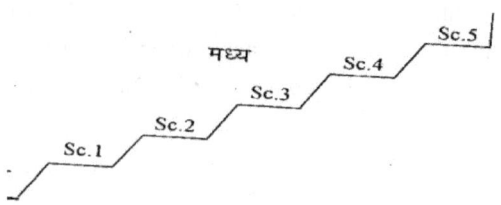

1. Climb to Climax

Purpose of the scene: why a character should come in and move out of the scene? It can be broadly defined with the purpose of his entry or exit, brief introduction, mental state, psychological and emotional reactions, twist in the characters and the situations, any other coincidences that require inclusion in the script. While constructing a scene or introducing a character the formula of 5 **Ws** and *one H* may be remembered by the writer to decide the inclusion. ***The Five Ws are 'What, Why, Where, When and whom' and one H is 'How'.***

3.Functional outline or Treatment: It is an extension of scenario in which every scene is described along with suggestions of dialogues and actors' performances. Many times writers combine the scenario and the treatment to save time and efforts.

The writer works on the *'treatment'* or an *'outline'* to develop it further. The treatment is not written in the form of short story or a novel but in the series of probable scenes in chronological order.. Every scene has to confirm to its cause, relationship, relevance, emotional impact and should be interlinked creatively in interesting actions like flowers in a garland. The treatment which decides a roadmap for screenplay should not exceed more than few pages. The writer should be aware of the technical limitations of shooting and should not write or conceive something that is not possible to be captured by a camera.

4. Master scene script: The writers who are not a director themselves write complete dialogues along with brief description of the scene in the *Master scene script*. It is not necessary that whatever is written at this stage may be included in the final version however this is the last but not the least important stage of screenplay writing which plays an important role to conceive the *Blue print* and the Master scene script. The master scene script also helps producer and the director to work on the detailed production plan simultaneously while the final version of screen play is underway. In fact this is a '**Guide script**' before a final screenplay is attempted.

5. Screen play: By the time writer reaches to this stage, his vision about the scenes attains absolute clarity regarding the film's form before the actual shoots take off. This is the version which includes detailed visualization of scenes, probable action and dialogues. It is normally provided in bound form to the actors, cameraman and the art director and other crew members to visualize the entire film to work out their respective roles according to the director's vision in the screenplay. The screenplay also provides a window to the actors to peep in to their characters. Few directors may find this process of distributing the screen play copies to others redundant but they should not take it as a compulsion. They should accept it as a process to create understanding and clarity with his unit members and the technical team.

6. Shooting script: Before the shoots director's main task is to divide the scenes in shots. This process is called *'Shot division.'* Unlike the writing of the screen play from the first scene to the climax, the shot division of the scenes in the shooting script is generally not undertaken in one go as it requires the details of the Shooting location/sets to decide possible camera and actors' movement for each shot which largely depends on the geography of the outdoor locations or the design of the sets. Therefore the shot division is taken up by the director in consultation with the cinematographer and the main actors before every shooting schedule when everything is finalized and director is sure of the locations and the set designs. Few directors take up shot division of the entire script and publish them in a book form for distribution among the crew members before shoots. This is practiced by many film makers abroad..

The shot division of a scene, from the film *'Toote Pankh'* directed by *Kuldeep Sinha* can be understood in the following example.

Film: Toote Pankh

Scene No.

Title: Back Home (as written in the script)
Location: A lonely rural pathway, exterior,

Day- Sunset.
Characters: Dayal, Cart rider

1.Sunset. A horse cart is moving forward on an isolated pathway of countryside. Dayal is sitting on the rear seat deeply drowned in his thoughts. Dayal returns home after many years.
Monologues: 'Such a transformation of this place in few years or nothing has changed at all except my perception of looking at things or it may be the time that has changed. From sunrise to the sunset there came the moment to light up a lamp in my life. In the process to light up others I forgot that I too would need some lights to drive away darkness in my home.'

2. Location: A Mansion- Exterior, Day.

The cart stops in front of an old mansion. Banvari , the care taker of the house comes to pick up his baggage. Dayal steps down and moves quietly to his mansion. Banvari opens unlocks the door and requests him to proceed but he looks around for few moments to recollect his past.

3. Location: Mansion- Interior, Day

Dayal enters after some time to see many pigeons that made this house their home in his absence flutter around . He switches on the light and observes lot of dirt and cobwebs hanging from the walls. It looks as if the house has not been cleaned since he left it. The wings of pigeons drop down when they flutter to escape out of the room. Main credit titles appear on the wings falling down. He recalls his hey

days with his family. Sound effects of pigeons fluttering and back ground music (Flash Back).

Shot division of the above scene:

1. Top angle, v/p cart, the pathway is left behind. The cart is running forward. Sound of horse hoofing.
2. Close up- Cart rider holds the reins of the horse.
3. Top angle. V/p of cart rider. Horse is running.
4. Close shot. Cart wheel moving.
5. Long shot. Cart is running on the pathway.
6. Close shot. Dayal in thoughtful mood.
7. Long shot Pan L/R. Cart running.
8. Top angle of the road leaving behind.
9. Close shot. Profile. Dayal is in thoughts.
10. Sunset.
11. Close shot. Dayal thinking.
12. Long shot Pan R/L. The cart moves out of the frame.
Monologue Dayal (from shot no.2-12): 'What a transformation of this place in few years or nothing has changed at all except my perception of looking at things or it may be the time that has changed. From sunrise to the sunset there came the moment to light up a lamp in my life. In the process of lighting up others I forgot that I too would need some lights to drive away darkness of my home.'

13. Long shot. Cart stops in front of the mansion. Caretaker helps him to step down and picks up his baggage. The cart returns back.
14. Mid shot. Dayal stays for few moments to look at his mansion where he spent major part of his life.

15. Long shot Pan L/R of the mansion.

16. Close shot. Dayal looks at his house from left to right.

17. Long shot of the Mansion from Dayal's view point.

18. Mid shot. Dayal moves forward to the entrance.

19. Dayal opens the door. (Door crackling effect).

20. Top angle. Long shot. Interior Mansion. Dayal enters in to a spacious Hall which had become home of many pigeons. They flutter around to escape. Dayal looks around the place that was unused for years.

21. Pigeons in the process to escape drop their wings. The credit titles are superimposed on falling wings.

22. Top angle. Dayal switches on the light by pressing a button on the side.

23. Close shot. A light bulb covered in a shade turns out of focus for **'Flash back.'**

Few new comers in direction shoot a scene in many possible variations of shots so the Editor does not face a crunch of visual material. This may sound to be a good strategy for a director but it has many drawbacks such as waste of time, money and raw stock to shoot extra length which may not be used by the editor. It also indicates lack of knowledge and experience of the director. In the high budget films which constitute very negligible share of raw stock in the total expenditure, it's wastage is not a concern as producers don't want to take a chance and the director too doesn't bother if he is sure of success of the film.

it is not only money that counts In a low budget film but also the professional reputation of a director which he would establish for himself during the course of the film. His lack of cinematic knowledge and technical indiscipline will be highlighted that may ruin his further prospects. He should take minimum and precise shots for a scene keeping editorial requirements in mind. The director may seek editor's cooperation in this regard. Few directors, who have an inclination for drawing, draw sketches of the first and the last frame of every shot. This brings clarity in shot compositions including their image size and the angles. These sketches reflect the requirement of the director from other unit members too.

No director prefers a screen play where shot divisions or minute details of the scene are predetermined where he has to forgo his creative freedom and own contribution therefore the director is always prepared to accommodate any opinion and suggestion for changes coming from anybody. It does not mean that director starts shooting without a scenario. Shot division of the scene is done as per the visualization of an action and is normally done on the set prior to the shooting in the presence and consultation with his cameraman and the actors. The shot division is required to facilitate the editor to reconstruct the scene in a continuous action. The advantage of having a scenario allows a director to peep in to the minute emotions of the characters and modify them if required before the shoot. It also guides the crew members to take technical decisions accordingly.

Normally there are two types of directors, first one are those who write each and every minute detail in the script before the shoots and others are those who have the mental sketch of every scene ready in their mind, rest of the decisions like shot division, camera placement, movements and angles, setting etc are taken on the set itself. I am of the opinion that the script is only a means to remind you of the continuity of the scenes. My grasp on the story and its every scene, development of characters and their emotions, creating an ambience for the scene etc inspires me.It boosts my creative energy and gives me confidence about the final result that would be better than my original vision. While writing the screenplay director should also involve the editor to make him understand about the rhythm of the film. It will avoid complications during editing process. If not, Editor may then have to resort to the use of cutaways and close ups to maintain the required pace.

A screenplay must be '**Homogeneous'** and **'Precise'**. The director must do his home work properly to ensure how he would shoot a scene. He may have extensive discussions with his crew members for a clear vision about their functional strategy, technical requirements, emotional effect and their expectations from him to avoid confusions at any level. While shooting director must behave like a leader and a guide to his unit members and not become their follower. An inexperienced director should hone his directorial skills instead of depending on others.

Everything in the nature takes place in a definite chronology and time. Its morning followed by the noon, than comes evening and the dark, a child takes birth, grows to be an adult and old before he breathes his last, we leave home, catch a train and reach to our destination. We cannot take a jump in our normal activities; whatever we do has a definite beginning, there is development in the middle and its culmination or resolution at the end. Our existence of life is restricted to the beginning, middle and the end. This principle of life is also applicable to a story that revolves around the life of some characters. Every story has a beginning that is independent which does not follow anyone or any situation but is followed by all the characters, events and the situations that develop the middle and proceeds to the end. Generally a story starts with the establishment of a problem or an issue along with the introduction of characters and the location and moves forward in search of a resolution of the issues or the problem at the end therefore the beginning of a story is just not a starting point but an opportunity for the writer to develop interest and involvement of the audience from the beginning itself till the end. The first scene of the story is a driving force in the train of scenes. More powerful is the beginning, more it will move its audience emotionally so writer must not hurry up to start the first scene but consume a considerable time and effort to work on it till everyone is moved by it. After the first scene audience must be curious to know what next and this sense of curiosity should not diminish in the middle till the end. The journey between the first and the last scene should not only be interesting but entertaining with different moods, emotions and sentiments so that memories of this journey linger on in the minds of the people for a longer time.

Fundamentally film making is a director's medium that's why he is called *'the captain of the ship'* so the director must never lose control over and actively involved while it is conceived by a writer. It is more important when the screenplay is not written by the director himself and he takes support of one or more writers in the process. If writers have functional knowledge of cinema techniques, it becomes easier for a director and writers to understand and coordinate with each other otherwise there may be occasional conflicts between them. Writers depend more on *'Dialogues'* than the visualization while director is more concerned about *visuals*. In such an eventuality the director must use his authority and convey what exactly he thinks about certain things.

The gap between the director and author:

The selection of an original story provides more freedom to the director and the writer to shape its presentation than an adapted literary work or a novel where the author has already detailed extensively in the body of work however there is always a gap between the concepts of a writer and the film maker. In case of adaptations the writer normally is not on the same page as that of the director who would like to take some cinematic liberties to revise an already accomplished work to suit the cinematographic presentation and the commercial viability. This happens due to author's lack of knowledge about technical requirements and economics of cinema. It is a great dampener for a director to accept a renowned or a published literary work as it is.

When a director decides to work on such adaptations he should be more careful, decisive and sensitive towards the basic sentiments of the story to avoid hurting the writer . In such cases the director must take the author in to confidence about the impending changes or modifications before he intends to start work on the subject. This will save lot of their time in unproductive engagements and also reduce, if not completely avoid, the conflicts and confrontations between them. The director must understand that as the film is so dear to him , the story is similarly close to the heart of the author however if working together, both of them must respect and accommodate each other. They should not be adamant to plough the field in different directions.

The mind as we all know never stands still even during sleep and so is the vision of a director when he is engaged in film writing, he is constantly on his thinking mode at any point of time. New ideas emerge and vanish; Some are useful and some are better forgotten. In such cases director must keep a note of every idea that strikes him related to the performance of the actors, special set design or setting, camera angles etc. This continuous flow of ideas and their notes help director to be more precise and clear in his concept.

The Act:

Football games are divided into quarters and, in the same way, plays are divided into **acts**. Each act is a major section of the play. Acts might be just ten minutes long, or they might be over an hour long. One-act plays are short plays that only need one section to tell their story. Typically, the opening act of the play introduces the characters and the problems they face. The middle acts further complicate the problems, and in the final act of the play, the problem is resolved. An 'Act' may be equated with a *Sequence* in Cinema.

Basically every story extends between the beginning, middle and the end. Generally the term *'Act'* is widely used in the theatrical productions or in the television shows to provide a *'break'* for the audience to return back. There is no technical significance of these breaks which are normally given for commercial purposes.

An *'Act'* is a significantly broad portion of a script which is divided in many sequences. There is a series of scenes in a sequence and a scene is consists of many shots and a shot has many frames

In the screenplay, all these segments are like a staircase that takes the story step by step upwards towards the resolution of the problem. The way a sequence has it beginning, middle and the end, every scene is also consists of a beginning, middle and the end which identifies the characters, main issue and the goal that is accomplished by the main characters. All the characters are linked and work with each other towards a goal till it's climax that provides final resolution of the problem or the main objective.

Characterization:

Every character in the story has a distinct personality, identity and emotions that is designed and developed by a writer and a director in their own styles. If the story is based on human relationship the director should first start visualizing his various characters and follow it to decide their behavioral pattern that look normal so that they identify with people as one among them. This is done with director's own or acquired experiences.

The process of characterization is one of the most important factors in film making where director must fully convince himself about their authenticity to convince his audience later. That's why it is more important for a director to prepare a mental sketch about his characters before he starts writing the screenplay. A new director may consult other experienced people in this task. An astute director who observes various characters around him in day to day life, is benefitted in long run to acquire sufficient knowledge and experience about their behavior, their living and their attitudes etc.

'Observation' is as important for actors as it is for a director who are benefitted by their minute behavior and mannerism. The knowledge acquired by actors reflects in their performance.

Conflicts and confrontation:

Conflict in the scene or a sequence is very important to ignite the interest of people. Audience must always be curious to know *'what next'*. The conflict is generated by two opposing groups or individuals who's objective is same and both want to accomplish it before each other. If there timing and the situations are similar there will be no conflict. They will achieve it separately as and when they want. When the path is narrow and two persons pass through in different direction then there will be a conflict when they come face to face to each other. If they don't change their course or the goal there will be conflict. If there is no resolution none of them will be able to achieve his goal therefore a resolution is as important as the conflict.

It is quite a difficult task for a writer to create a chain of such conflicting situations because in our culture we are always taught to avoid conflict to be a better human being . It is deep rooted in our personality. We are inspired by good things but ignore negative one. Still we have to experience such conflicts in our life and we try to find out solutions to them according to our upbringing and teachings. In a story, every character has his own distinct identity and cultural background and the writer is expected to develop conflict and find out their resolutions accordingly. When we are not able to achieve the fulfillment of our desires, it creates a conflict. Such situations are always prevalent in a story. The conflict here is not restricted only to fist fighting, chase or running away but is reflected in the mentality of each character. The writer has to discover and develop such conflicts. Arguments and difference of opinion don't come in the category of conflicts. Struggle in a story is not restricted to victory or loss. In fact there is no winner or a loser in the conflicts between characters, it is only a change in their attitude and ideology. Struggle is only a symbol of there will power that takes them to reach to their goals. Every character has an identity in this struggle that is displayed in their behavior from the beginning to the end.

During the *confrontation* one of them seems to be more powerful than other and he tries to nullify his strength. In case, both have similar strength, the conflict will be nullified therefore during a conflict both of them swing back and forth in to their power play to outdo the other which is important to create interest in the scene. There should be no stagnation in conflicting situation. Confrontation is an incident that must be followed by a resolution but it should not be an easy task for anybody. Characters should display their unflinching will power to overtake the other to continue their efforts till the end.

During the course of conflicts it may happen that mental and physical conflicts of a character undergo drastic changes when he feels that he may not succeed in his goal or he may find another cause or a sympathizer to share his plight, vent out his emotional outburst or there may be some inspiration that overhauls his entire perception, opinions and view points towards the situation or situation is completely reversed. Such incidents provide new dimensions to the character that may have to devise another strategy to reach his goal. This provides new opportunities to writer to create new situations and the scenes. This new strategy also brings new twist in the story which helps a writer to provide another form to the scenes.

No character behaves in linear or similar fashion from beginning to end as it is in real life when a person sometimes laugh, sometimes cry or he may be romantic, angry or violent in serious conflicts. Their behavior depends on the fluctuation of mood in different situation with different people. Their behavior is decided by the exigencies of the moments, mood and the interests that vary in individuals time to time. The mood is sometimes high or low; in conflict, the moods cross with others. If they have the same mood, there will be no conflict.

Self respect and ego of persons also play important role in creating conflict therefore while developing characters, the writer should define the limits of their self-respect and egos. Higher ego means more conflict and lower ego means less conflict. People of low self respect and the ego surrender to the situation sooner than the others therefore in such situations of lower ego conflict don't stay longer. The people with high self respect and ego are generally the savior of ideals, ideology and self respect of others. They have more mental strength to confront and struggle till end without being week.

It is not necessary that the main characters only have to carry the burden of the story in their shoulders. There is always a need to develop supporting characters to strengthen the main characters. These supporting characters as the name suggest appear in the scene occasionally like co-travelers in a train who just come and go when their journey is over. Meeting of supporting characters may bring a catalytic change in the situation. Some of these supporting characters may continue throughout the film while some may disappear once their purpose is served.

The writer should however remember that every character introduced in the scene has a definite purpose in the story. An isolated character will be an obstruction. Every character must be given its required length or duration on the screen not more..not less. No character should be stretched beyond its requirement in the story.

The originality of the story is not as important as its honest expression. Since film production is for public consumption there has to be an effort to ensure a continuous flow of emotions and sentiments of the characters in a unified manners to keep the audience glued to the screen till the end of the film. This helps audience to become part of the story and they start identifying them as the characters on screen. A success here is the success of the film and its director. Therefore the director should present its characters and various emotional situations in such a way that people identify with them and have the same sentimental feeling.

Every director has his own unique style to conceive a story and his characters which is generally influenced by his own upbringing, knowledge and experiences. Every film claims to be complete in itself but if the audience don't show there interest in it, these claims appear hollow.

XXXXX

'A plot can be construed as a single line concept of a story which needs to be developed.'

Act 4:

Behind the camera:

One should remember that a moving picture is a series of still photographs exposed in *film frames*. These still frames are given special meaning by the creative vision of a cameraman and the director. Everything in the frame is always not be seen, heard or felt completely by our eyes or ears. A film frame is much more sensitive than our senses. The composition of a shot is a reflection of what a frame contains. The frames are decorated by various means such as special lighting, property, set design, colors of the furnishing material, fixtures and the camera and actors' movement. For a cameraman or a film director a film frame is what a canvass is for a painter who plays with colors. Similarly on a film frame the director and the cameramen create a visual design which impacts our senses and sentiments.

It may be noted that nothing happens within a film frame without the knowledge and approval of director, even a bird can't fly across it without a purpose. Shots not only convey a new meaning when juxtaposed together but also offer different interpretation to the scene. Shots are a means of communication between the film maker and the audience to enable them to think on the same plane and wavelength as that of the director. When audience understands the same what a director wants to convey them through these shots, it is his success.

When we talk of *frame,* it means we are talking about still frame. The way the still frame is composed is reflected in the scene as these moving frames constitute a visual depiction of the scene. A frame can be equated with that of a canvas of an artist which is painted by colors and emotions visualized by the artist. Similarly a writer, a director and a cameraman work to create an effective *frame* that reflects an action, an emotion and mood. In cinema they are created by special set design, lighting, composition and performance etc. in the stripe of a film *frames* are the basic visual unit of a shot. During the shooting though we talk about a shot but we actually work on a frame as when these frames are projected in a particular speed than only they give us an illusion of a movement. Since the shooting is done by a cinematographic camera that runs in the standard speed of 24 frames/second. ***The length between the start of an 'action' to the end when director orders the 'cut' is called a 'shot'.*** The shot can be of any duration or length. Therefore it may be understood that a-

1. Combination of frames constitutes a ***shot,***
2. Combination of shots constitutes a ***scene,***
3. Combination of scenes constitutes a ***sequence,***
4. Combination of sequences constitutes an ***Act.***

Type of shots:

The distance between camera and the subject or an object defines various types of shots. This distance is decided to create different compositions, effects and emotions. The director and the cameraman divide the scene in many shots maintaining continuity of actions and dialogues. Every shot has different meaning and interpretation which is expressed in different size of images and angles of the camera placement. Every shot and camera movement has a purpose so a shot needs a great care while being composed. This is explained in the following pages.

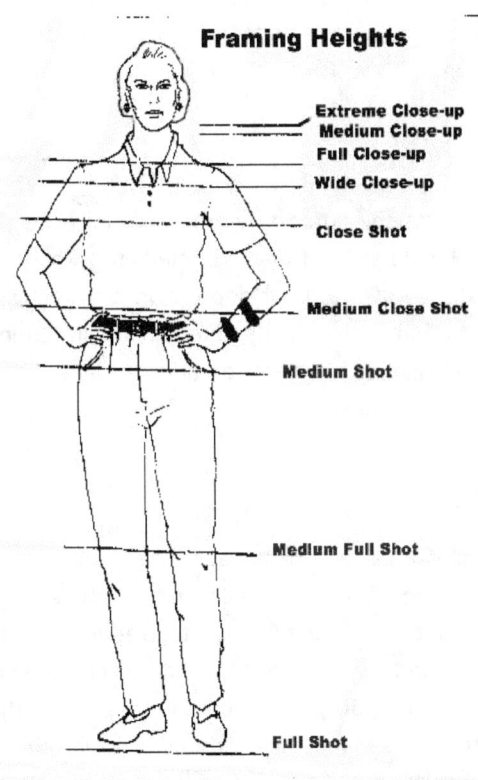

Framing Heights

- Extreme Close-up
- Medium Close-up
- Full Close-up
- Wide Close-up
- Close Shot
- Medium Close Shot
- Medium Shot
- Medium Full Shot
- Full Shot

2.Sizing of the shots

1. Extreme Long Shot (E.L.S.):

ELS are generally used to establish a wide spread outdoor location where an action is supposed to happen or the back drop of the story or a scene. This shot is also called *'Establishment shot'*. For example if the back drop of a scene is a dessert, a ELS will register an image of a wide spread desert in the mind of audience and they will understand that it is the place where entire story will be evolved. ELS can be taken from a top angle from the helicopter, airplane, hill top or a rooftop to show the area as wide as possible. War fields or a huge procession or density of crowd etc are established in ELSs.

Symbolically ELS is creatively used to establish isolation or loneliness, depression, inferiority or insignificance of a character etc. People in the theatre immediately know about his mental state, social status or depression of the character and identify with him. While a character is established in ELS, action is normally avoided because of its poor identification in the extremely long distances.

2. Long Shot (L.S.):

A *Long shot* clearly establishes place and an action on a location. Unlike in ELS, an action or a character has comparatively better visibility due to reduced distance between camera and the subject. LS too are used to establish the location or the backdrop of a scene. In LS less attention is paid to the atmosphere and the surrounding area but to the character or action, the background, ambience, setting or natural surroundings, properties. Undesirable people, characters or action are avoided in LS. Therefore long shot should be carefully composed with proper atmosphere, properties and lighting arrangements. Character movement in long shots looks slower so the length of an action should be short.

3.Long shot

It is normal for an actor to move from the distance to close or close to a distance during his performance. It is called '**long shot to close shot**' or vice versa in the same shot. In this situation the action, background, ambience, actors' actions and reactions can all be seen in a single shot. When a character comes close to the camera he gains importance and when someone goes away from the camera he loses it.

3. Mid Long Shot (M.L.S.):

It is the distance from head space (a margin between the head and the background) to the knees of a character.

4.Mid Shot (M.S.):

In this type of shot, objects and the area around the subject or the character is excluded. It is basically a '***Body shot***' where body of a person is kept in the centre to establish relationship between various characters without minute expressions and emotions. Mid shots are widely used in dialogue sequences.

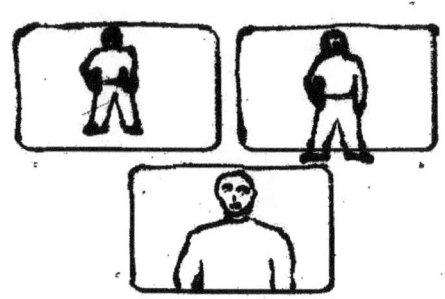

4.Long shot. Mid Long shot, Medium shot

5. Medium Close Shot (M.C.S.):

MCS covers the distance between chest and head and is generally used for conversations. MCS is easy to juxtapose with any other shots like MCS to CS or vice versa to bring variations in effects. During the conversation MCSs can also be taken from **over the shoulders (O.S.).**

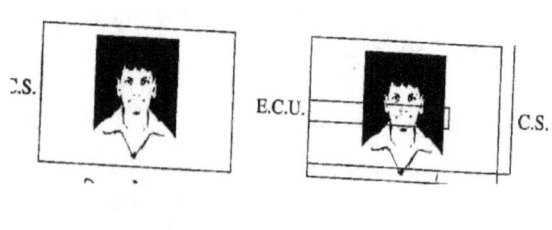

5. Close shot   6.Extreme close shot

6. Close Shot (C.S.):

Close shot is the most important shot in film making that takes the audience close to a subject or the object. It excludes everything around a character including the ambience or the background. Close shots are little closer to head and shoulders than the *mid shot*. It concentrates on the facial expressions where importance is given to emotions and reactions of the character. Variety in close shots can be obtained by changing camera positions and the angles. The coordination of moods, lighting and camera position is important while taking a close shot because of limited background and other details. Closer the camera- wider is the image size in a close shot in which other details are eliminated. Zoom or trolling to close shot creates better dramatic and visual impact. There has to be a complete coordination between camera position, its height, eye levels , tilting, lighting and the mood while composing a close shot to avoid camera consciousness . Director has to be extremely cautious when taking CS as they should not be taken if there is no facial expression. Close shots are effective in displaying emotions, built up of the climax and creating drama in the scene. Close shots can be juxtaposed with any shot as '*inter cut*' during the editing.

7. Extreme Close Shot (ECS):

They are useful to express minutest emotions, feelings and better dramatic effect. ECS are effective in creating suspense and mystery. Director and the actors must be sure of the needs and utility of ECS otherwise they will look unnecessary and forced in the scene. In ECS smaller and minute details of an object are magnified such as eyes, lips, finger thus it is used to create dramatic effects.

Different type of close shot creates different and deep impact therefore ECS are taken with extreme caution when required. One should avoid excessive use of '**close up**' which are also not related to preceding or following content (shots). Close shots are extremely useful for television due to its small screen size. Long shots are rarely used but even in television every shot should have a purpose and the meaning when used.

After discussing the type of shots the writer should also understand the methods to provide visual variations in the field of a frame of different film gauges. Normally a 35mm film is widely used for production which contains 16 frames/ft. when these still frames run in the speed of 24 frames/second , we have an illusion of speed and moving action and the location photographed in the frame.

Every shot, scene , sequence and the act has its own importance , identity and impact. When they all are joined together they make a film. A *frame* as a unit of a film is like a brick in the construction of a building or a *'word'* that is the unit in writing a play, novel or a short story. That is the reason why lot of hard work is required to create a beautiful and effective frame. Therefore knowledge of setting, and set design, lighting and composition, performers' look and the location is important.

Every shot has different area of field therefore a writer must get himself acquainted with various *fields of vision* by looking through the view finder of the camera to know the fields in a close shot , mid shot or a long shot. It does not mean that whatever is not seen is not important as the area, location, properties and other characters which are not visible in a shot may be visible in the next shot so in order to maintain continuity in the forthcoming shots placement of such invisible things may not be disturbed. If a writer understands the composition of a frame it is easier for him to conceive shots and create scenes within those limitations. After due practice and understanding writer is able to differentiate between the real field and the field of vision in a frame and visualizes his scenes as per the requirement of the frames.

Split frames:

Field of vision in a frame can be altered by some special visual effects. This can be done by *'masking'* certain area of the field as a needed.

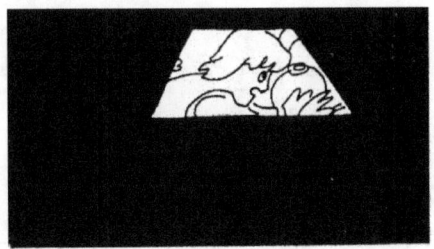

7. Masking

Multiple masking in a single shot is used to show different actions/visuals simultaneously. It is called *'split frame'*. Split frames are generally used to show characters in multiple roles. It is decided by the director and the cameraman, writer can also suggest it if he is conceiving the scene in such a way.

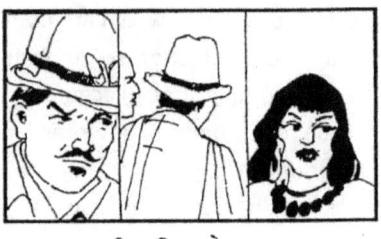

8. Split frames

The movement of an artist in a shot is decided by the director but the writer should have knowledge of the dimension of a frame. There are three types of *'Planes'* in a frame such as:

1. **Horizontal planes:** in this plane characters or objects move from left to right or right to left.

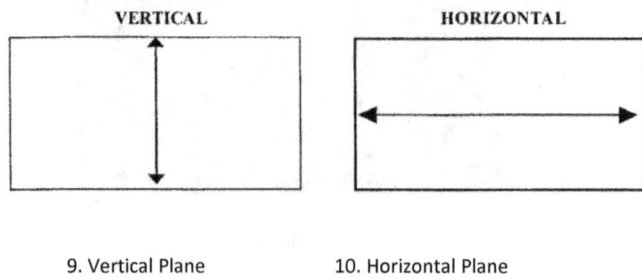

9. Vertical Plane   10. Horizontal Plane

2. **Vertical plane:** the movement in this plane takes from up to downwards or from down to upwards.

3. **Depth plane:** in this plane movement of objects and characters is from back to front or front to backward. When

the object is in the front it looks bigger and nearer in dimension but when it is in the rear, it looks smaller and it gives the illusion of distance. In this plane there are many more dimensions where objects and characters can be seen in detail.

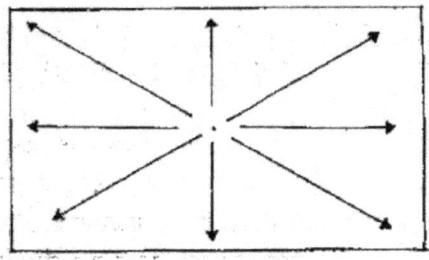

11.-depth plane

A frame should display only those objects and the characters which have some relevance and effect in the scene. It depends on the imagination and the vision of the director and the writer who sometimes play with symbolic objects, color scheme and special lighting to create better impact so that audience too is involved emotionally and feel to be a participant in the scene. If the writer and the director are able to create such an impact on the audience, the success of the film is presumed that is highly dependent on the acceptability of the audience who feel emotionally associated with the characters and the situations. It is the reason why we observe people laugh, cry, sing and dance with characters on screen. It leaves a long lasting impact on the audience till much after the film is seen.

Composition:

Every subject or object that is visible in the frame is a reflection of imagination of the director and the cameraman. It is similar to that of artiste who translates his imagination on his canvas. Cameraman and the director work hard to recreate their vision of the film on the canvas of celluloid film as attractive and effective as they can as we all want to see beautiful things around. Modern cinematic techniques and lenses help a great deal to recreate the visual magic in the frame.

There are many different *types of lenses* available such as *Wide angle lens, Telephoto lens, Macro lens, Zoom lens* etc in addition to the normal lenses varying from 16mm to 75mm that are part of the camera accessory to make the image more effective. Special lenses are available on demand while normal lenses come along with camera set up. Zoom lens generally takes care of most of the requirements of a cameraman in which one has just to change the focus.

Zoom lens is capable to take many varieties of shots from a single position by changing the magnification of the images. Shifting focus multiple times in a single shot may be a creative urge of a director or a cameraman , it should be practiced only when it is absolutely required as it is not only time consuming but risky to have multiple focus in a shot. It may result in blurring of shots if the assistant involved in follow focus is not confident and experienced enough.

The type of lens to be used in a shot is purely a cameraman's prerogative considering the concept and setting .The director generally should not interfere in his discretion so the director should concentrate on the composition of shots instead of deciding the type of lens or lighting etc. Composition of a frame depends on the creativity of the cameraman and the art director. If the director himself is operating the camera, it is he who should do it otherwise director must leave the operative cameraman to do his job independently.

While composing a shot decision about an angle that gives specific image magnification and the effect is another crucial task before a cameraman. The image size and its effect jointly give an identity to the shot therefore the selection of an angle and image size has to be done very carefully to complement the desired impact that the director and the writers have envisioned. It may be noted that every size and the angle has different effect and purpose therefore their selection should be such that displays the specific emotional expressions. Selection of a lens, an angle and an image size reflect creative and professional merits and maturity of director and the cameraman.

Many of the directors and the cameraman indulge in unrestrictive use of a zoom lens to save time, raw stock and to speed up the pace of the scene without considering the character of the shot ; It should be avoided as the excessive use of a zoom lens neither enhances the impact of the scene nor it serves any purpose but has another danger of being stressful to the eyes. Zoom lens has a specific purpose to highlight a characters emotions and the expressions which should be appropriately understood by them and used whenever it is require

The Real time and Screen time:

What is *time*? It is believed if there is no time there will be no discipline in our life. It is the time that manages our life in hours, minutes and seconds. Everything takes place at a particular time for a definite duration likewise the sun raises and sets at a fixed time of the day, darkness engulf us in the night at a time and it is morning after the night. Days extend to weeks, weeks to months , months to years, years to decades and the centuries and the time moves on in its own discipline. It never stops. It is the time that becomes an identity of important events of our life and we keep on remembering them in future. If there is no 'time' it will be difficult for us to keep a track of events in our life time. The time moves on in chronological system such as there will be morning after a night, than noon and the evening before it again becomes dark. This system is never broken and continued since the evolution of human kind. Time has its own schedule of seasons, summer, rains, winter and spring. It comes in this chronological order at its scheduled time. Following the time chronology our life also moves on similarly. It is birth that is followed by adolescence and youth to middle and old age. Our schedules are managed in similar chronology such as we sleep in the night and rise in the morning, we work during the day and spend the time as per our requirements, moods and the needs.. It is the law of nature where everything takes place as scheduled in chronological order. Our activities are timed on *'real time'* factor. This real time cannot be stretched or reduced as per our convenience. Whatever time has to be consumed by an activity, it is required, we can only reduce or increase the 'speed' of performing it, however it depends on individuals capacity, strength and the merits but time moves on its own speed that cannot be changed.

An entire gamut of events taking place in the story may take more than few decades and generations in *real time* which is contracted within two to three hours of *screen time.* It may be done in such a way that audience doesn't feel the distortion in real time. While doing so unnecessary events are deleted and only those are kept which have some bearing and relevance to develop important characters and take the story forward. Care should be taken to ensure that all the characters, events and the scenes are emotionally, aesthetically and physically integrated and have logical relationship and continuity with the plot, inherent sentiments and proper timing. The timing can be reduced or increased as required in the scene for example action scene have to be faster than the emotional ones but every scene has to be developed in such a way that every event has an illusion to be happening in real time. There is no mathematical calculation to determine the duration of each scene. It depends on the director's vision and requirement of the story. This reduction or extension of time to project events on the screen that gives an illusion of real time is called '**Screen time**'. In television serials we have the liberty to extend span of a story indefinitely till it continues to be popular however this liberty is restricted on cinema screen where a story has to be wound up within the limits of exhibition slot. While we have no control to temper with the real time of events , we can conveniently manage the screen time of an event or a scene.

During the narration of the story there is a possibility to move back and forth in time when a character narrates his experiences or recollects past events of his life **(Flash back)** or he may dream something to happen in future **(Flash forward).** Such probability gives writer more freedom to design his narrative style when he either may decide to go for linear or straight narration or he may have a character narrating the story that allows him to move back and forth in time conveniently. But shifting in time should not happen without a reason or the purpose.

Flash back and *flash forwards* are generally used to reduce or increase *screen time* to establish changes in the situations, to disseminate some information about a character or the situation that occurred in the past or something foreseen , anticipated or dreamt to happen in the future. Screen time must be managed with the above devices very carefully so that they don't interfere in the flow and they contribute in the development of the story otherwise such device will just become an ornamental tools which will not benefit in any ways. There is also a risk of losing interest in the story if they are used as gimmicks. Flash back and flash forward should be used with suitable transitions including dialogues to avoid confusion and ambiguity. People should know it clearly whenever there is a flash back or a flash forward.

Film; Zubaida

Scene No.

Time: Day

Location: House of Heera

Characters: Heera, Riyaz, Suleiman, Rose and others.

1.Riyaz knocks at Heera's door. Riyaz introduces himself and enters in the house. Heera is taking drinks. Riyaz sits nearby him.

Heera: 'who is there?'

Riyaz: 'Heera lal ji...'

Heera: 'Who is that...?'

Riyaz: ' Are you Heera lal ji ?'

Heera: 'Yes, I am Heera Lal.'

Riyaz: 'I am Riyaz, a Film journalist. May I come in..?'

Heera: 'Come in my son. Have a seat."

Riyaz: 'Do you know film actress Zubaida...?'

Heera: 'Who...?'

Riyaz: 'Ms Zubaida.'

Heera: 'Zubaida baby...Zubaida. How can I forget her.' (Flash back starts. Heera moves in the past.

2. Location- Studio where some film is being shot.

Heera continues: 'once upon a time her father was the owner of this studio. Suleiman Seth was very strict. He had a wife at home and another... Zubaida baby used to visit me after the school. In the evening her father picked up in his car to home. What a car it was...such a long one.' A long car enters in the studio. Flash back ends. Heera and Riyaz talk to each other sitting face to face.

Heera: 'Zubaida baby was interested in Dance. Flash Back starts again.

Heera, Zubaida and other dancers are rehearsing their item in the studio. Heera feels very happy with their performance. 'Good ...very good.' Suleiman gets out of his car and enters in the studio where Heera is training girls and Zubaida,' Ta...ta thai...ta ta thai. Its excellent...I am so happy.' Zubaida wants to leave seeing her father.

Suleiman calls her,'Zubaida...'.

Heera: 'very nice... now you come every day Zubaida ji you have qualities to be number one heroin of India.

Suleman wishes Rose,' Hello Rose.'

Rose: 'Hello.'

Suleman: 'How is everything/'

Rose: 'Fine.'

Suleman: 'are you dancing well?'

Rose : 'Yes , everything is tip top....going on.' Heera greets Suleman. Zubaida joins him.

Heera: 'Adaab.'

Suleman: ' Adaab. Is everything fine Masterji?'Let's go home my child.'

Zubaida: 'just a minute...'

Suleman (to Rose): ' so you remember...?'

Rose: 'ok.'

Suleman : 'ok.'

Suleman , Zubaida and Rose walk towards the car. Rose and Heera see them off.

Heera: " Madam'.

Rose: 'Bye...'   Flash Back ends.

Heera: 'Suleman Seth then sold off his studio to Nand lal Seth. Suleman was a wicked person otherwise Zubaida would have been a top heroin. She played some role in a film, it is that Poster. What nuisance Suleman created when he came to know about it. It was a filmy scene...' Flash back starts again. A song is being shot on Zubaida and other dancers....

Zubaida is an excellent example of *Flash Backs*. It could also be called a flash back film. Flash back is not used to provide information about a character or a situation but different characters provide some information about the main character of the film therefore flash backs are not enforced in the screenplay but they create a distinct style of story telling where there is a realistic approach of a documentary imbibed with dramatization of the fiction. The frequent to and fro movements do not keep the story stagnated in a specific period or the place but move it forward by pouring a new information every time.

Time lapse:

The most important factor in managing time is *'time lapse'* that takes place between the transitions from one scene to another. The time lapse is indicated by various means like a *'dissolve'* in which a scene **fades out** and another **fades in** simultaneously. **Dissolve** is the most popular device that is understood easily by the audience. Day and night scenes can be easily identified so there is no need for any direct indication or special effect.

It is not necessary that time lapse should always be indicated if not required, by a clock or a calendar as most of the times audience can make out time lapse taking place in the flow of the story. Another popular method to inform about the time lapse is through Dialogues where characters give an indication about the time and the place following transition to the next scene. Similarly when the transition time is short, this can be shown by direct entry and exit movements from one place to another.

Parallel action:

Other devices to manage time include *parallel actions* in different scenes taking place simultaneously in different locations. This method is considered to be more entertaining and interesting; it is used to increase tension and curiosity.

There is more scope for managing screen time in this method as for example; two different actions in different locations may appear on screen for about two minutes but in reality that action might take more than ten minutes. So in parallel scenes contraction and extension of screen time can be done more conveniently and smoothly without disturbing the sense of real time. This authenticates the saying that *'a film is not a reality but a realism'*.

Editing:

The life is a series of events and happenings since the time of birth to the death which we may not recall after some time until and unless the experience of that event leaves a permanent imprint in our mind. The events that occur in normal cause are not very important for us therefore we don't remember them after some time even if we try hard to recollect them this facility of segregating memories and the experiences is a special gift of nature to human kind. The power to remember or forgetting something is only human being are privileged off, non humans don't have such power. Just imagine if we would have possessed the power to remember everything in life, our mind would a clutter box where all the experiences desired or undesired would have been stored, it would have been very difficult to pick up, choose and reject something if we wanted to do so. It is similar to a house where everything is kept and nothing is disposed, it would be impossible to find something if it is required for use immediately. In real life this process of deletion of unimportant material from our mind space may be called 'editing'. In this process we store and remember only those things which have very intimate relation and connection with us that we want to remember sometime later in our life without confusion or misrepresentation. Whatever is to be stored our mind carries out a minute and an in-depth analysis with reference to our past experiences, studies, social and economic background etc. before taking a decision to store it or not for future recall. It is this principle of editing that guides a writer to discard or accept certain events and experiences in the story which may be of interest to the audience and start his work from this point onwards.

Our eye sees something happening only once. It means we may not see the same thing again in the similar form. We also see things in entirety that means entire event happens from beginning to end without a cut but in cinema a scene or an event may take place in fragmented form. We can experience an event or an action split in many parts (*shots*) or may be dispersed in different chronological order along with other scenes taking place in other locations at the same time (*parallel action*).every shot has a different meaning but when it is juxtaposed with other shots, it has a different meaning which gives extension to the story. It may so happen sometime that a shot A has no meaning but it gets a meaning in the company of other shot B, it means A+B= C. This could be understood in the following illustrations-

1. Shot 1- Two man walking left to right
2. Shot 2. A Police station
3. Shot 3. A temple

In different shots, in shot 1 two characters are goving to an unidentified place and in shot 2 and 3, we see an image of a temple and a police station respectively, individually these shots have no meaning. when shot 1 is joined with other; this juxtaposition not only conveys a meaning but also gives an identity to the characters. the characters in shot 1 who walk towards a temple in shot 2 can be easily interpreted as devotees and characters in the same shot 1 juxtaposed with shot 3, can be identified as criminal. This juxtaposition also extends the meaning to the next level of the action.

Similarly when the images blooming flowers, butterflies and birds flying along with a shot of sunset are juxtaposed they convey the meaning of a pleasant evening When another shot, the close shot of a girl, is added in the scene, it conveys the her pleasant mood and happiness . it gives a meaning to the character of the girl. Individually this girl in a separate shot has no meaning and identity of the girl in the evening, she could be anyone. Therefore a writer can visualize a scene to create a special meaning in the scene that extends the story further. Example-

First chronology-

1. Shot 1- A food plate
2. Shot 2- Close shot of a man
3. 3.man is eating

Second chronology-

1. Shot 3- food plate
2. Shot 1- he is eating
3. Shot 2- man is waiting for more food.

Third chronology-

1. Shot2-man is hungry and is looking to the plate full of food
2. Shot1- food plate
3. Shot 3- man is eating

With the juxtaposition of the above shots in different chronology, a different meaning can be created otherwise these shots individually have no significance. Just by altering the order of shots, the meaning can be altered. The writer should ensure that while watching a film, audience doesn't interpret a different meaning than what the writer wants to convey. If it happens there will be a communication gap between a writer and the audience that may misrepresent the content. Thus the audience may move to a different track. It is a serious failure of the writer therefore he must avoid inclusion of unnecessary interpretation that may spoil the meaning of a scene.

Cinematic Space:

Whatever we see on cinema screen is not true, whether it is real time or real space or places; we create an illusion of reality. we have discussed how screen time is managed. Similarly the place where a scene takes place is called **Cinematic space** or **place.** This place is completely different than the real one because when a story is developed in our imagination, we have to develop an imaginative place where it takes place. Whatever objects or things are kept or displayed in this place is called 'Property'. None of these properties can be put to use by us in our life. The way cinematic time is managed, cinematic space is also manageable like a devotee may travel many pilgrimages in the duration of few minutes of screen time. It is possible only in cinema..

Real time with cinematic time or real space with cinematic space, though they are different in character, cannot be separated. While Screen time gives us an impression of an event lasting for this duration on the screen, cinematic space tells us about the occurrence of a scene in that *place*. The arrangement including setting and interior decoration, are managed in the location where the shooting is planned according to the requirement of the shot. Here only those things are given importance which are visible in the composition. The placement of the properties, movement of the actors, interior and exterior decoration and lighting is done in such a way that entire place gives us an illusion of real space. Sound effects and the ambience sound support the action to enhance the illusionary effect of reality. In the absence of the sound effects neither the place nor the action will look real.

Space in Theatre and Cinema:

A theatre audience is fixed on a particular place to view a limited area; *the stage*. Their field of vision is restricted to the area of enactment. The distance between the person and the stage is also fixed therefore they can watch a theatrical act from a definite angle, distance and magnification only. It also restricts overall impact of a theatrical performance in the mind of the audience. Actors have to make special efforts to impress and reach to the last man sitting in the auditorium but in cinema a person sitting anywhere in the hall may experience the action and the activities on the screen from every possible angle, distance and the magnification while sitting on his seat.. He can watch it from near to afar and from low to top angles, therefore the emotional connection of the audience with the actions and the characters on the screen is more intense than the theatre. The distance and the angle of the on screen actions is managed by camera technology. A film camera can take its audience emotionally to the close of a performer whose emotional outburst is reflected by his tears in close shot while he can feel parted with a character moving away in a long shot. The close shot enables an audience to feel the emotions of the character and is attached more intimately with him to have better interaction.

The audience has a neutral point of view in a Long shot where he can see everything but does not feel connected and involved therefore Long shots are used only to establish a cinematic location to enable them to travel to the place in their imagination. A crane shot takes people to the top angle. Symbolically a crane shot reflects the weakness and the helplessness of a character in a dramatic scene by reducing his magnification. In contrast a Low angle shot of a character reflects his strength, superiority and power. In low angle, his magnification is increased. The *eye level* is considered a 'Normal view' which has no special impact. Eye level shots project the actions on the screen as they are seen normally from the view point of the audience. Eye level shots are generally taken in mid size magnification.

In the above explanation we have observed that **Visual area** can be changed and managed by placing the camera at different angles and distance which is not possible in normal life. In addition, there are many more cinematic devices such as wide angle lens, Telephoto lens, Zoom lens etc for different visual impact. We can also change the view points by placing camera in top angle or a low angle for the audience to see the images from these angles. Therefore it is clear that whatever is captured by the camera, audience sees the same to relate, associate and experience with the characters. People become a participant in the action with similar sentiments.

While writing the screen play, it is not important to explain, except in special cases, all the angles and placements and magnification of the shots as it is the responsibility of the director and the cameraman however it is the responsibility of the writer to establish an association with his audience in his script that is carried forward by the director.

Point of view:

Through the angles, placement of the camera and magnification of the images, we decide the visual area or the **Field of vision** and take the audience to the place of action by the use of different lenses. This becomes the view point of the viewers. There can be two viewpoints-

1. **Subjective view point:**

When a person places himself with the character and starts looking from his view point, it is a *subjective view point.* Here the person thinks, speaks and acts and walks like the onscreen character. He sees what the character sees from his eyes therefore the person himself becomes the character.

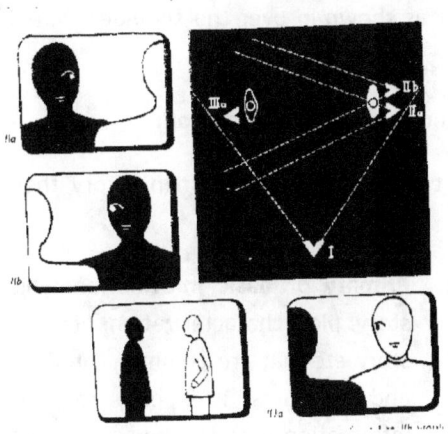

12. View point/ over the shoulder shot

2. Objective view point:

Here the viewer sees what is shown by the camera. It is not necessary that camera always shows the view point of the audience. When we move in a public place like market or on a road, there are many things happening that are not important for us but they are important to create an ambience. These are generally common and routine activities of the place such as two person talk face to face as in the above sketch. They may or may not be part of the scene but we see them in objective manners. They don't make any impact on our mind but they are helpful to break the monotony and maintain continuity in the story.

Objective point of views are used in the scene to establish a cinematic location or neutral activities to create an ambience while *subjective point of views* are used in conversation scenes where characters view point becomes the viewers' view point as shown in over the shoulder shots in the above sketch.

Primary and secondary Information:

There are two types of information in a story, they are-

1. **Primary or basic information** which include a story, plot, characterization, development of the story etc that are communicated through action and dialogues. It is easy to identify primary information because they are *'direct'* and can be understood through actions and dialogues. Primary information provides depth to the story.

2.   The other one is **Secondary information** which is about the atmosphere or ambience. They are *'indirect'* information. In addition to this, many time a writer innovates secondary information to dramatize the scene and creates special effects by using special actions, symbolic dialogues, properties, color scheme and lighting or expressive sound effects. Behind the scene dialogues, narration, monologues, commentary. Unusual costumes, hair style and make up play an important role in creating secondary information. The direct and indirect information both together contribute immensely to interpret a meaning effectiely. Therefore secondary information is to be conceived carefully.

Juxtaposition:

Juxtaposition is the Transition from one shot/scene to another in order to arrange the events or the action in the story. Juxtaposition may be carried out in many different methods which is suggested by the writer in his script for the guidance of the editor who assembles the shots/scenes in the chronological order in the screenplay .It is a normal process however there can be many other methods for juxtaposition such as visual similarities or phonetic similarities that can be decided by editor and the director to make the scenes more effective.

A writer must write the screenplay in the similar form as is going to be presented on screen. Therefore he must determine the content including the scenes and the shots along with their placement in the predefined chronological order that will be followed by the editor. Loose and jerky editing pattern in the script will be carried over in the final editing too. This will spoil entire efforts of a director and editor on editing table and they may end up scratching their heads without a solution as the film is shot according to the written screenplay. Any flaw in the script will be reflected in the film.

Editing of a film cannot be confined with the role and responsibilities of an editor but it begins at the moment a writer picks up his pen to scribble the idea of a film . it extends to the director, cameramen, sound recordist and sound editor to other technicians in the crew. No serious efforts have been made in the past to define the exact scope of editing for other technicians therefore the entire process of editing has been confined to the editor's table which is aesthetically not correct. Delinking the process of editing from other technicians including the director is not only an injustice to the poor guy called the *'Film Editor'* but it also wrongly absolves others to share their legitimate responsibility putting an unnecessary burden and onus of making a good film only on the Editor.

Continuity:

The pre-requisite for an uninterrupted flow of a visual action and emotional expression when projected through the series of scenes is its **'Visual continuity'**. A moving action of the scenes after divided in shots is captured in the form of still photographs of celluloid frames. When these frames are projected through a film projector in the prescribed international standard running speed of 24 frames/second or 25 frames/second for digital projection, these still photographs come alive. These frames run one after another in the prescribed speed to complement its previous and preceding movement to take the action forward from one frame to the next. It means that every action in the frame has a direct relation with its previous and the subsequent movement. If it is not so then the scene lacks the continuity of the idea and the flow in physical action as envisaged in the scene . It may be remembered that a screenplay consists of many scenes and a scene consists of many 'shots' so a *shot* is the primary unit of a scene, that's why we discuss the *'shots'* and not the *'frames'* with reference to a scene. But if a frame is meaningless and irrelevant, the shot too will be meaningless and irrelevant thus making a scene ineffective as a scene is the end result of the *juxtaposition* of many shots. It is the reason why a cameraman and the director concentrate more on the composition of a frame that forms the visual content of a scene therefore the director and the cameraman should be very careful and attentive to maintain continuity while composing and designing a frame.

When screenplay is in the process of being written, it should be ensured that every scene has a definite meaning and the dimension. It should be expressed by proper juxtaposition of shots. A slight deviation from it may spoil the entire scene. In the suspense or mystery films, directors have some freedom to deviate while taking few shots not confirming to defined continuity but it should be relevant to create drama or deepen the mystery.

Film: Zubaida

Location: House of Mehboob

Time: Day

Characters: Faiyazi, Qazi, Suleman, Zubaida, Mehboob, Zenub.

1.Everybody is assembled to materialize divorce between Zubaida and Mehboob

Qazi: It was decided to pay rupees one lakh as Mehar. It should be paid before divorce.

Suleman: ' The girl forgives this money.

Qazi: ' then divorce can be immediate say it.'

Mehboob: 'I, Mehboob Alam, in my full senses agree to free Zubaida Khatun. I give you Talaq...Talaq...Talaq.'

Zubaida starts crying after Talaq. She hugs her son Zenub. Faiyazi asks Zubaida to leave for home. Zubaida continues to cry with Zenub on her chest. Everybody sits in the car and the car moves.

Cut to...

Scene No...

Location: interior, Zubaida's room

Time: Day

Characters: Zubaida, Rose, Faiyazi

1.Zubaida puts her wedding photographs/memories and clothes on fire. Rose comes in and talks to her when Faiyazi too joins them.

Rose: 'Happy Birth day Zubi..happy birth day to you. Oh my God,these are your wedding photos, what happened?'

Faiyazi: ' oh what are you doingTalaq is complete but don't burn your wedding attire.'

Rose: 'Talaq is over, any way it was to happen. Don't worry my dear Mehbbob Alam was not suitable for you.' Zubaida cries.

Faiyazi: " A husband is a husband after all. whatever you say.'

Rose: ' don't cry my dear. Spineless man like he is not worth it.' You need a real man like your father.'

Faiyazi: ' let's go Zubi.'

Cut to...

Scene No.

Location: Interior, Hall

Time : Day

Characters: Riyaz, Faiyazi

1.Riyaz and Faiyazi are in conversation. Riyaz feel sorry on Faiyazi statement. Faiyazi tries to change the subject.

Riyaz: ' How father could leave us like this. Did he never care for us?'

Faiyazi: 'leave it now. Don't talk about your father If he was concerned of you he could have come to see you.. He has not written a letter in thirty years.'

Riyaz: (On the Dining table), ' what was the relation between Nani, Mom and Rose?'

Faiyazi: If Rose was not there, your mom would have been alive and stayed with us.'

Riyaz: ' but what Rose has done right? If you don't tell me I will ask her .'

Faiyazi hides facts about Rose then Riyaz leaves the food to go out to rose's house. Faiyazi attempts to restraine him.

Faiyazi: it is not good to waste food allah has given . You have to give account of every grain on the doom's day.'

Cut to...

Scene No.

Location: Rose's house

Time : Day

Characters: Riyaz, Rose

1.A cat roams around the room of Rose, Riyaz enters. Rose call for feeding milk to the cat. Riyaz asks someone about the room of Rose. The person guides him to her room. Riyaz asks her but Rose continues to feed her cat.

Rose: ' Mom has enough for all of you. Come on.

Riyaz: ' Excuse me. Can you guide me to Rose's room.

Man: ' I t is there.' He indicates.

Rose: 'what ever you sell, don't need it. Now you go...go.

Riyaz: 'I have not come here to sell anything. I am Riyaz Massod...Son of Zubaida.

Rose : 'Zubaida..? who ...Zubaida.'

Riyaz Presents her flower. She feels happy and thanks him.

Riyaz: 'Suleman seth was my father.'

Rose: ' oh that...'

Suleman: 'It is for you.'

Rose: ' Thank you.'

Riyaz: 'Roses for Aunty Rose.'

Rose: ' so you are Zubaida's son...?'That's the same smile...you motherless boy. Come and take your seat. What do you want from your Rose aunty..........?.'

In the above illustration from the film *'Zubaida'* while arranging scenes in chronological order, dialogues and flash backs are also used for transition like Riyaz leaving food on the dining to go to Rose's house is cut to next scene where Rose is seen calling her cat to drink milk *(food-visual similarity)*. Similarly in dialogues when Riyaz desires to go to Rose's house, the next transition is to Rose's house *(Phonetic similarity)*. There can be other similarities as that of properties , actions, colors etc for example door closing may be cut to door opening in another scene or thumping on a table with anger may be cut to a bang in next scène. Such visual and phonetic transitions may be meticulously planned and suggested by the writer in the screenplay. Such transitions not only save screen time but also ideologically connect the audience immediately to the next scene. Any other scene in between would delay and break the action continuity therefore it must be ensured by the writer that no cut is abrupt and the transition is smooth.

Cinematic Motion:

Movies are called 'motion *Pictures'* therefore it is implied that there will be *motion* and it is true that without a motion there cannot be a motion picture. It is similar to our real life experiences, where nothing occurs without motion so people tend to ignore *motion* in a motion picture. Earlier we have discussed management or manipulation of *'time'* and *'Space'*, similarly the *cinematic motion* can also be managed or manipulated the way we want.

Motion in cinema provides a *definite speed.* There is no scene that's motion is cinematically not manipulated to provide desired speed and emotional impact to make it more effective, intense and dramatic. Motion is also managed to achieve a definite *'Rhythm'* and *'Mood'.* Writer must develop an understanding of different moods and motions in different situations. To begin with the he must keep on observing and identifying various actions , activities and events around him and minutely analyze, compare, categorize and describe them to understand them in terms of their motions and effective expressions because normally only those motions, emotions, situations, characters, expressions are used in cinema which we normally experience in our real life.

Motion in itself is very effective in nature but when it is used creatively in cinematic expressions, it becomes more effective. When the motion is used as a tool, it itself becomes attractive and obstructs the flow of the film so it should be avoided. It is the responsibility of the writer to create *'Motion'* in the scenes. This process is called *' Motion of action'*. Whatever happens in a scene is an action. Since no action can be static, it is called *'Motion of action'*. An action is the process of interaction or communication. If there is no action, there will be no communication. These actions express characters' emotions and ideology and thus become their identity. It is not necessary that there should be description for every action in the scene as they are normal actions; therefore only those action require description which have some relevance and identity with the plot and the characters. Such actions provide a distinct dimension to the character.

Natural Motions;

The writer must be aware of the fact that all the motions are not natural. *Natural motion* is the motion that takes place normally in our daily activities. They don't require conscious efforts, creativity or imagination. Natural motions are shot by camera in normal speed. Natural motions can be created for various reasons. They are of three types-

   1. **Primary Natural Motion:**
      This motion is generated by the actions or objects to describe about the character and the forthcoming events. They also inform about characters' thought process, ideology and their personality. Primary motion helps the plot move forward.

2. **Secondary Natural Motion:**

   Secondary motions are derived from the primary motion. Sometime secondary motion becomes so important in a scene that they replace primary motions. Generally secondary motion is the reaction of the primary motion so it can also be termed as *'counter action.'*

3. **Induced/created Motion:**

   It is a privilege in cinema that we have the liberty to create certain motions in addition to Primary or secondary motions such as in animation caricatures or characters drawn on a sheet of paper which are given movements. Motion of animation characters is different than natural motion. We know that a film runs in 24 frames/second and shot in the same speed but in animation, camera shoots in single frame at a click and all 24 still frames with their induced motion are shot separately. The back ground and other movements are created separately. There is otherwise no action or movement in the still characters of animation therefore the movement is created to give a feel of motion in an animation film.

Film: Guide

Time: Day/night

Location: Rozi's room, cave

Characters: Raju, Rozi, Marco

Raju is taking rest out of the room of Rozi who is not well . Raju enters in to her room.

Raju: ' Do you need anything...? He helps her to lie on her bed.

Cut to-

Parallel action: **Digging is going on in the cave.**

A man: 'Run...run...'People run here and there shouting. Marco looks at them. He comes in the cave

Time: Sun rise.

Rozi gets up and is shocked to see Raju.

Raju: 'You have woken up. How do feel now?'

Rozi: ' what are you doing here?'

Raju: ' At your service...' Rozi gets up and sits on her bed. Raju comes near to her. Rozi asks him about her husband,

Rozi: 'where is he?'

Raju: 'he is....'

Rozi: 'He did not return in the night?'

Raju: ' There was some more work tonight...'

Rozi: 'what was the work that was more important than my life?'

Raju: 'He does not know that you….

Rozi: 'don't know. It is not a threat . what I say will do it.'

Raju: 'it means that what you told me….'

Rozi: 'but how it affects him/ it would have been good if I die.'**Raju:** 'You have not heard completely what I said. You could have asked why I returned. When I reached there, Marco sahib got excited and said,'Raju, what a donkey I am that I am sitting with a sad face. It is so sad that you are not with me. What a forest ..What caves…what a Dak bungalow and what delicious food Josef cooks. There is only thing I miss. If we would have brought Rozi too, it would be nice, It could be a nice picnic. I am so lonely at heart. Rozi would have been been nice being here.' Believe me. Ihave just added some poetry, rest are his words. Do you think I am lying?'

Rozi does not believe Raju as she knows her husband well. H never cared for her. Raju gives her medicines.

Rozi: ' and you think that you are talking truth.'

Raju: ' take the medicine. I will send tea for you'.

Rozi: 'no need.'

Raju: ' yes , it is needed. I will bring it myself.'

Cut to…

Scene No.

Time: Day

Location: Rozi's room

Characters: Rozi, Raju, Dr, Vegga

Dr Vegga laughs after her check up. Raju stands nearby,

Doctor: 'Everything is fine. Continue the medicines.'

Raju: 'it is better if you only give her the medicines because his cup of tea in the morning was used to wash cloths.'

Rozi:' I will take myself.'

Raju: 'Doctor, is it ok to travel because she is going to her husband by car.'

Doctor: ' no harm. In fact it is good. Raju leaves the room with the doctor. Rozi is annoyed with reference to her doing to her husband. She asks Raju to explain. Rozi bursts in to laughter with his response.

Rozi: ' who told you that I will go?'

Raju: 'you did not say so but I am thinking of Marco sahib. If he comes tomorrow and you consumed tablets. If you do not go today , he might take the tablets.'

Rozi: ' I f my husband could make me laugh, I would never disobeyed him.

Raju:' and you are disobeying me because I am making you laugh.

Rozi: ' Are you married?'

Raju: 'No, God has saved me till now...why...?'

Rozi: ' she will be happy with you.'

Raju: 'it is your opinion. I am very strict person. I will make her prepare bread, serve me, press my legs and if she creates some nuisance, I will slap her three four.'

Rozi: ' But will you love her or not?'

Raju: ' I have to love her.'

Rozi: 'then there is no problem her life will be a success in preparing breads, pressing legs and being slapped.'

Raju feels bashful. She refuses to go her husband with him.

Rozi: ' I will not go Raju but you promise me that you will not tell him anything till he asks about me.'

In the scene from the film *'Guide',* there is absence of any physical action but emotional actions conveyed through dialogues move the story forward. *Natural actions* and *reactions* establish relationship and emotional connection between different characters. The scene reveals the hatred between Rozi and Marco, separation, disappointment and complexes, her loneliness, carelessness and detachment of Marco for her etc which take both of them far away from each other physically and emotionally. This loneliness brings her close to Raju. She finds a lovable husband material in him. She tries to fill the void created by Marco's deficiencies with him. She is even ready to forgive Marco for his excesses because for her, husband's love is important.

Raju is sympathetic to her but tries to narrow the gap between them. Perhaps Rozi is impressed by his efforts; She starts sharing her emotions with him when he is not directly concerned with her. He is only a guide who brought her husband to these caves but this short introduction becomes an intimate relation. So it is not necessary to have events in every scene to take the story ahead. Introduction of characters, their sensitivity, and their relations and ideological connection is sufficient to develop a story. They are natural actions which are important ingredients of the story.

Natural Camera Movement:

It has generally been observed that sometimes camera is used static as artistes perform in front of it. This placement does not distinguish between cinema and stage. Camera should move according to the movements of the actors and not vice versa where actors act according to camera movements. It is not natural. The camera movement must be used for communication and not for the sake of the movements. Such movements are not only ineffective but also without purpose. A purposeful camera movement helps in the narration of the story. The camera must follow the action of the actors to look them natural in their activities.

The static camera fixed on a stand can pan from left to right or right to left (*Horizontal movement*), tilt up and tilt down *(vertical movement)*. If you peep through the view finder of the camera or a peep hole on a piece of paper and move horizontally and vertically, you will clearly understand the difference in effects between these movements. If you move faster than normal speed, you will experience a blurred vision. You will also experience the objects near to the camera are larger in size than objects in distance that look smaller.

If you tilt up and down, you have the sense of *exploration* of new objects. Forward, backward, sideways movements give us a sense of *following* an object. When we tilt down we see an smaller object which reflects the *weakness or inferiority complex* of the character. Opposite to it when tilt up we see object in low angle in larger size that reflects *power, strength and dominance.*

While in a trolly, train or any other moving device if we, move forward, backward or sideways we can follow a subject and the object. A trolly can move camera forward, backward, sideways, it gives a *feeling of traveling.* When a subject or an object is followed, the motion becomes subjective which is generally used in action like chase or race sequences.

On an elevator when we move upward, we feel *optimistic and energetic* but when it is downwards, it reflects a sense of *dejection, low energy level* and *negativity* or *running out.* In cinema such effects can be obtained by placing camera on a crane to move up and down.

All these movements can be undertaken either separately or in combination with other motions. It is observed in all the motions that each of them has its own purpose and effect to create better interaction, intimacy and impact. The dramatization achieved with these motion is more interesting and natural.

Expressive Motions:

While Primary, secondary and induced motion push up the story forward, there are other motions which have their own affects. They not only express but interpret them too. Some camera movements have their specific meanings so these movements become part of the scene. Some motion take the audience far away **(trail away),** tilt up or ascending movements fill up the audience with **energy and optimism,** Revolving movement reflect **happiness and excitement,** Diagonal movements indicate forthcoming hurdles, Descending movements express **sadness, danger** and being weak or powerless, Pendulum motions break the **monotony,** cascading motions reflect **relief, flexibility** and spreading motion is an indication of **growth and development**. Effect of these movements can be felt through a view finder.

Structural Motions:

A screen play is the blue print (*structure)* of the film drawn on a piece of paper which is divided and shot in fragments *(shots).* The shots are an integral part of the story. After the shoots ,it is the editor's responsibility to join them to create a structure. If a screenplay is the structural plan of the film then the editor builds up the structure as planned by juxtaposing and editing the shots one after another in the chronological order . The exposed material is the raw material for the editor. The quality of film however depends on the quality of the exposed material. If the exposed material is good, the editor will be able to make a good film. But even if the exposed material is good, an editor has to work hard to create a *movement* for the film that is called *structural motion*. Structural motion includes Tempo, pace and the rhythm of the film which an editor has to create according to the mood of the scene or the entire story.

Editing is the culmination of the process that starts with the writing of screenplay therefore editing of the film cannot be termed as an isolated process but it supports other process of film making that have already taken place earlier. A good editor can make a good film out of the good raw material but a weak editor may spoil a well shot material. By joining the shots editor has to create *speed, rhythm and pace* in such a way that audience are glued to their seats till end therefore structural motion have a very deep meaning and interpretation for the editor.

In fact process of editing begins or must begin with the writing of screen play which is executed during the shooting and culminated on editing table therefore a writer must have sense of structural motions while writing screenplay.

Tempo:

Tempo of a scene is determined by the length of the shots used in a scene, when the mood of the scene is somber, serious or monotonous, the shots will be lengthy. Longer the length makes the scene slower. If there is a scene that expresses excitement, curiosity, happiness where scene requires speed, the length of the shots is reduced. While cutting the shots special attention is given to maintain continuity, screen time and space. *Tempo* in a film can be equated with the tempo of music which is increased or reduced when required. In cinema, *mood* of the story decides the Tempo that has to be created by editor by increasing or shortening the length of shots. In the absence of a proper tempo, the scene becomes ineffective.

Rhythm:

Rhythm in the film has the same importance as it has in the music. Rhythm in music is created by the arrangement of different musical instruments. Repetition of certain notes and beats create a pleasant musical effect. Similarly the rhythm in cinema is created by the repetition of dramatic actions, special sounds, objects and the style. In the visual medium like cinema imagery and sounds are equivalent to musical rhythms. The combination of theme, melody, orchestration, beats and intervals create rhythm in music, similarly repetition and proper juxtaposition of different shots, actions , objects, properties, set design and setting, dressing, special lighting arrangements, different camera speeds create cinematic rhythm however there is a different meaning in each repetition. The repetition in a film is what punctuation is in grammar that provides special effect, meaning and interpretation to the scene. That creates special rhythm in the film.

Pace:

The speed can be increased or reduced to the requirement of a scene. *Pace* is created by actors by their performance; slow or fast, which is decided by the events and dramatic requirement. They are the guiding factors for the director and the actors to determine whether a scene has to be slow or fast. There is no parameter to decide about the pace. Different writers may pen a scene in different style but they have to take care of proper tempo, tone and pace, similarly a scene can be enacted by actors in various moods and speed. Therefore pace can be interpreted as the speed of action or event in a scene which is decided by its mood.

Motion of Cartoon characters:

Unlike the films shot in 24-25 frames /second which is the running speed of the camera (The standard speed for film camera is 24 frames while for digital it is 25 frames/second) the animation camera runs on *'single frame exposure'* at a time shooting a series of still drawings or caricatures which have inherent continuity of movements in their characters/objects.

One might have noticed in a film stripe which have number of still photo frames and every frame or a photo has some action. When the same is projected in normal speed, there is an illusion of a continuous action. All the actions are recorded in normal speed of 24 frames /second In live shooting while in Animation or cartoon films every action is created and shot in single frame. When the animated film is projected in normal speed, we see a continuous action created in each drawing or a caricature.

Creating animation on celluloid is very complicated and time consuming as an artist has to draw hundreds of drawings manually which means he has to create 24 designs for a second of film time therefore preparing thousands of designs for an animation film of few minutes is not a mean task. Dozens of artistes are engaged for making these sketches, caricatures or designs manually. It takes months or years to make a full length animation film. These designs are prepared on transparent cell papers. Every character is designed in separate sheets and every design must have some movement of the character. There are separate designs for the background which also requires having some actions/ movement such as movement of the tree leafs in the forest, birds flying etc.

The movements of cartoon characters are determined before shoots in the drawing process which is based on the **story board** that is prepared according to script. *Story board* is prepared by professional artists as per the director's vision.

Now of course, with digital technology animation is created faster in computers. In fact Animation has taken multiple leaps and revolutionized animation techniques which did not remain confined to just drawings and caricatures but has expanded to create *special effects.*

In fact the **special effects** created by digital technology, have become an independent genre in filmmaking paving the way to produce full length fiction and nonfiction predominantly with special effects. While the computer animation has eased out the labor of the artistes, the process has more or less remained the same except that the designs and action of the characters can be created in computers faster than the manual ones. The special effects and computer animation has become an inseparable ingredient of any film or television production that has revolutionized the *'action'* in cinema.

The audience continuously follow the characters while being static on their seats in cinema hall These movements are created by different camera angles, distance, image magnifications, special lighting and characters' movements. A camera can take its audience to any place and come back to its original position. Distance of the subjects and objects from the camera creates special impact in the minds of the audience.

A writer's job is to create **psychological motion** in the script. It is created by the writer and the director by managing different physical and cinematic motion. Physical motion is the effort and time taken by performers in the scene, cinematic motion is created by editor in the cutting room while the psychological motion is the cumulative impact of the scene in the minds of people. Visuals and audio play important role in creating these motions to involve audience in the scene.

XXXXX

Act 5:

Image and Phonetic symbols:

What we see and hear creates a visual image in our mind that we identify and name it. This is a **symbol** of the image that we always recognize, for example when we hear the word 'Tree' images of trunk, leaves, branches etc appear in our mind and when these images come in front of us, we recognise them as a 'Tree'. Similarly when we hear the sound of a 'temple bell', images of deity, devotees, worship appear that we associate them with a temple. In the ancient times, men inscribed the symbolic language on the rocks which gradually developed in to letters and words. Every word has been assigned a meaning. These *words* later became important tool for communication. It is not an exaggeration to say that these words not only identify subjects and emotions; they have become essential for existence of our life. We are dumb without these words. What we *see* are *'visual signs'* and what is heard is called *'audio signs'*. Both these signs affect and decide our actions and reactions. We are happy sometime but get upset on something. Anger, love, sympathy, hatred and other emotions are created due to many actions and reactions coming from different visual and audio signs spread around us. These signs are widely used in cinema to make audience feel the same that is reflected. When these signs are appropriately used, they effectively transmit the right message and emotions. It is called *'effective communication'*. When they are inappropriately used, they confuses the audience and wrong messages and emotions are transmitted. It creates a *'communication gap'* therefore a writer must be very careful to pick up and use such signs that transmit the right and intended message and emotions.

When given an identity and a meaning, these signs can also be creatively developed with our perception and knowledge. Everybody interprets different signs based on his personal experiences which have different meaning for different people but there are signs which have common meaning and interpretation for everybody that cannot be misinterpreted.. Such signs are linked to individual emotions so the writer should understand what a sign means for someone. If a sign transmits a meaning other than what is intended by the writer, it may not be correct. So only those signs should be used that conveys the right connotation and generally accepted interpretation.

Visual symbols: They are those that either create a visual image or provide an interpretation of a visual in the mind to register a definite *identity* and an *emotion*. There are many visual symbols such as:

1. Words, 2.Picture, 3.Natural/Conventional,

4. Semi conventional, 5.Similie, 6.Metaphor.

7. Related symbols, 8. Associated Images, 9.Setting.

1. **Words**: it is mentioned above that a sign may have a different meaning for different people; similarly every *word* may have different interpretation for different people. It depends on the experience of an individual person for example a *lion* may signify 'terror' that can horrify a person but for some it may symbolize 'masculinity', brave, power, bold and the king. Similarly color *'red'* may symbolize *blood* for someone but for someone else it may mean an 'affectionate son'(Lal; in Hindi) or any other interpretation like *Red* may be a warning sign for some danger so a word has different interpretation for different people in different circumstances therefore a right *word* may be used which is acceptable and understood by everybody with the same meaning and interpretation.

2. **Picture:** The picture symbols in comparison to the words present more accurate communication because what is seen and understood is the same so there is negligible possibility to misinterpret them. There are some common symbols which mean the same for everybody like moving head left and right means 'No'. Moving head up and down means 'yes'. 'Red Cross' for medical services, white flags or white pigeon are symbol of peace.

3. **Natural/Conventional symbols:** such symbols present a subject in its natural shape, form and color which have no room for misinterpretation such as Pen, Tea in a cup, Glass, Idol of a deity, Temple, Church, Temple bells, train etc. Such symbols cannot be altered by any photographic technique. Some

words in combination with picture symbols provide a common meaning such as showing palm with stretched hand means 'stop'. Such symbols may be called *'conventional symbols.'* These symbols are widely used in motion picture to make people see and understand as they are. If a subject is constant, it will be seen constant or a moving object will be seen moving. So natural symbols are seen and understood as they are. They are also called *Conventional symbols.*

4. **Semi-conventional symbols:** These symbols are generally full of similes and adjectives which are used in literary work or scenes related with literature. Such symbols reflect a specific identity, character or an institution in the form of *'**Logo**'* or *'**Monograms**'*. They may be created in combination with natural and conventional symbols which may not have a single meaning and are open to individual interpretation.

5. **Simile:** when a poet or an author compares a subject or a character with another, it is *'simile'*. A writer underlines the importance of a subject to make it more effective by the use of similes. Similarly a screenplay writer creates **'cinematic similes'** like *Lion arms in a chair* or *spreading lion skin on the ground* to show the power and influence of a man sitting on the chair. When similes are used there is no need for other symbols.

6. **Visual Metaphor:** The subject is not compared here but it becomes something else. They reflect an

emotion or experience instead of direct explanation. There is an attempt to understand the situation and emotional expressions through non conventional symbols.

7. **Related symbols:** They are the reflection of individual's emotion and have a direct relation with the subject, situation and the character. Their meaning is known when they take place like *a lady is shedding tears in the light of a melting candle*. It symbolizes lady's sadness and sentiments that she is too melting like a candle within her. The juxtaposition of object and subject gives a different meaning and effective interpretation. In this process an object is selected which has a special meaning and effect. It is established early in the scene to maintain continuity and to avoid its sudden appearance. Then it is juxtaposed with the character to express a specific emotion. The related symbols provide a special emotional meaning to the subject. They also analyze the past, present and the future and a decisive situation. It is called 'Poetry' in literature so we can also term *related symbols* in cinema as *'cinematic poetry'*.

8. **Associated Images:** These symbols are based on *'similarities'* with that of similar visual images on screen. Though it is the job of a director and the cameraman to create them but a writer can always make creative suggestions.

9. **Setting:** Setting has an important place in theatrical production to create *'Mood'*. Everything placed in the background, lighting, color scheme, artistes' movement creates an appropriate ambience. In cinema the area shown in a shot is considered the *'stage'* which is designed and decorated by art director, in coordination with the director and the cameraman. Some of the suggestions may be provided in the screenplay. The writer, in order to create more effective scenes visualizes everything including background, lighting arrangements, color scheme, property, costumes, makeup and hair styles and movement of artistes that is to be seen by cameraman through his camera. This arrangement is called *'setting'*. It creates suitable ambience for the scene.

Most of the setting for a shot is carried out very carefully with full awareness of the outcome. Setting varies as per the requirement, sometimes it can create horror, or religious feeling or it may reflect peace or war. Every expression and emotion necessary in the scene is considered minutely to ensure a proper ambience. There can be different ambience like that of a court, a temple, a meeting hall, a palace, factory, green fields, a township etc or seasons like summer, winter, rains or spring, harvest, cloudy or clear sky, morning, day, evening or night, lunch time, breakfast time or dinner time. Characters too have a role in creating a proper ambience reflecting their profession like a businessman, a doctor, an engineer or a nurse, openness of characters in sea beach or garden, specific machines and tools being used in a place like a tractor, plough, bulls, water wheel in the agricultural fields, machines in factories, employees and staff, reception in an office, special colors on special occasions create proper atmosphere.

Initially it is the responsibility of a writer to create an ambience and suggest appropriate properties which he can visualize and include it in the scene as screenplay writer is the first man who sees a complete film in his imagination. It is he who later inspires a director, cameraman, art director, dress designer, actors and others to translate this imagination in to reality therefore more accurate and detailed is the screen play, easier it is for others to translate it in to cinematic images. It does not mean that a writer should give details of everything in the scene; he should describe only those details which are necessary. The setting conceived by the writer should relate to objects and the characters, their dialogues and the movements to facilitate right communication. The writer creates a scene in *'words'* which are recreated by the director and his team on celluloid therefore scenes created by the writer should be complete in content, expression and emotions, transmit proper effect and create similar mood in the minds of audience. A screenplay should never be a shopping list of items required but there can be suggestions for specific composition, lighting, color scheme movements etc if required in the shot.

Phonetic Symbols:

The beginning of cinema was with silent films. Camera used to capture images without sound. There was no recording facility available. Camera captured live events, characters' movements and different emotions. The dialogues were conveyed through *captions* inserted in between the scenes to make people understand the story however actors moved their lips. It was the same experience as if we close our ears and look around to see different actions and activities. Importance of sound can be understood by closing the ears once and then open your eyes to see around. Thereafter, Analyze different sounds and audio symbols and their impact while eyes are shut and ears open. Generally there are two types of phonetic symbols-

1. **Synchronous sounds:** These are the sounds that emanate from an action or an activity while it is being performed. They are called *'incidental sounds',* like sound of footsteps when someone is walking, sound of door opening or closing, telephone ring etc. A writer need not suggest them until they are required to create some specific effect and those can be imagined by the writer prior to writing a scene.

2. **Non-synchronous sounds:** These are *Non synchronous sounds* that are spread all over in the atmosphere which don't come out of any specific action or activities but are generated by general activities such as traffic, wind, waterwheel, floor mill, train, birds chirping, dogs barking, humming in crowded place etc. They are not related to any specific action or activity but to the *ambience*. The *non synchronous sounds* provide realistic feel to the scene. the scene is life less without these symbols. They are very important in cinema as they make an audience

experience the same ambience as they have in real life such as dry wind blowing in a desert takes them psychologically to a desert or sound of bullets and firing makes them feel to be in a war zone.

The way composition, motion, imagery, location and many other things together send a definite communication, sounds too communicate at various levels. It depends on the type of sounds used to generate an effect which include ambience sounds, incidental sounds, and dialogues, music and other symbolic sounds to complement a visual. The visuals and sounds both create a special meaning, feeling, effect and emotions when they are integrated. In this process sometimes visuals become more effective than sounds and some other time sounds become more powerful than the images. This continues till the end of the film however any of them can be manipulated when required. After the shoot the recordist along with the director and editor prepare a *sound plan* to list different phonetic symbols to make a scene as effective as possible. Thereafter these sounds are recorded in studio or procured from other sources to ensure that the they are clear and noiseless. Sometimes they are recorded on location if they are not available to record later.

Dialogues:

Dialogues are an important tool for the characters to communicate and express their emotions, opinions and philosophy in film and television fictions. The dialogues give a distinct identity to every character differentiating their style of delivery. In a stage performance, the dialogues have to be heard by the last man sitting in the extreme corner of the auditorium therefore they have to speak them aloud in high pitch and volume. The characters speak with their natural emotions due to technological advancements in cinema and television. One can say that in theatre the dialogue are forced to *hear* but in cinema they are spoken to *express* normally. In cinema camera captures the minutest expressions on the face of an actor by placing it at various angles and distances from close shot to the long shots therefore the dialogues are spoken as per the emotional requirement. While watching a play audiences sit in fixed position, at the fixed distance and angle from the stage so the dialogues are delivered in different style. The dialogues must complement inherent emotions and the expressions of the scene, relevance and relationship, ideology and beliefs and should avoid unnecessary details. The language and the style of delivery of dialogues is an expression of characters, personality, background, culture, educational background, nature and his emotional state. Similarly the language of dialogues should not be too complicated and tough to understand but should be simple and effective. It sometimes can be touchy to make audience feel the similar emotions as that of the characters. Actors may be permitted to do minor alterations in the dialogues to suit their performance. Many times it happens that an actor in a comedy or negative roles or in an actions scene, may prefer to write his own dialogues to complement his unique style. Where there is a need to provide more information the use of background commentary or narration may be useful. Writer should avoid writing lengthy and long winding dialogues but write short and to the point. The lengthy dialogues if required may be interrupted by aural reactions to break the monotony of the scene.

Film: Devdas

Scene No...

Location: Chandramukhi's house

Time: Day

Characters: Devdas, Chandramukhi.

1.Devdas lies on his bed with empty bottles of alcohol and glasses scattered around. Chandramukhi looks at him. Devdas pours liquor from the bottle in to his glass and throws the bottle away. Chandramukhi comes to him and he hangs down in hangover.

Chandramukhi: 'Don't drink more Devdas...'

Devdas: 'Why?'

Chandramukhi: 'You started drinking since few days. You will not be able to bear this much'.

Devdas: 'who the bastered drinks to bear'. I drink to breath. I have no strength to move out from this place that's why I am lying here and keep looking at you, even then I don't lose my senses. Some consciousness is always left. Tell my senses that I should never be in senses.

Devdas comes near to Chandramukhi.

Chandramukhi: 'There are people coming here who don't ever touch the liqueur.'

Dev stumbles. Chandramukhi lends her support to him. He

sits down.

Dev: 'They don't even touch it...? If I have a gun; I will shoot them. They are greater evil than me chandramukhi. First I will not leave drinking and if at all I leave it then I will never return back to this place. I have a cure but what about them who don't drink and still come here. **Chandramukhi tries to hold him** Don't touch me chandramukhi, I still have some senses left'.

Devdas gets up and throws the glass on the floor. Glass pieces scatter around

Devdas: ' You don't know how much I hate you people and will continue to hate them but still I will keep on coming here , sit beside you and talk to you. What else is the remedy but can you understand it? People commit sins in the dark and drink here in the light.'

This scene is one of the best examples of not only dialogue writing but also of a fine delivery. The simplicity of the language and the short length of dialogues straight away hit your emotions therefore they should never be stretched beyond the acceptable limits.

Dialogues are just not the medium of effective communication but are also an identification of writer's ideology, principles, introduction of characters, means to move the story forward and a process of effective presentation. Dialogue is not a series of different expressions and interaction but they are the mirror of a character's personality. A writer can create wonderful entertainment and impact by appropriate arrangement of visuals and dialogues therefore the selection of *'words'* should be made very carefully complementing the character otherwise dialogue will not only be ineffective but a block in the proper flow of the story.

Dialogues are useful to reduce or increase the length or the duration of an event or activity besides expressing about the past, present and the future events, plans, true or false information about any character. They are the vehicle to carry forward a story, character, and the scene. They can intensify the effect of an event, action or emotion while creating laughter in a comedy scene or bringing tears in a tragic situation. Dialogues also provide motion, the rhythm and pace to a story. Sometimes repetition of words creates *beats* as in a musical composition, by their specific delivery style. The *tempo* of a scene can be managed by shortening or increasing their length or by fastening or slowing down the *delivery* or increasing or decreasing the *tone* of dialogues to louder or soft ones.

To understand different effects of dialogues, the writer must observe and analyze different people talking and expressing them in different styles or they can be recorded to hear later. This method is good to study impact of *'dialogues'*. It may be remembered that dialogues spoken in real life cannot be replicated in a screenplay because they are spoken without a thought as part of an instant action and reaction while in the screen play they are part of storytelling, characterization, situations and circumstances, impact, emotions and sentiments that are written after careful thought and consideration. It will help a writer to study dialogues of pre written screenplays.

writer should avoid repetition of an information or statement which has already been conveyed earlier in any scene, dialogues or action. If it is necessary to repeat it, it should not be without a reason. The Dialogue should not be long in the form of a lecture or a speech as it becomes monotonous and boring. The audience feels compelled to listen when they are least concerned with it. Such dialogues in the form of a lecture or speech lose their spontaneity therefore information conveyed indirectly has more impact and acceptability.

Film: Pakeeza

Time: Night

Location: A tent in forest, interior and exterior

Characters: Sahibjaan, Salim

Salim keeps his gun aside and looks at a shadow moving behind a white tent and thinks about it.

Salim: (to self) 'what a co incidence as if someone is narrating a story.'

Sahibjaan greets Salim after seeing him from inside the tent, ' Sahibjaan: Tasleem…not there, this side…'

He sits on a chair kept outside it. She too sits there. Salim talks and she listens. Salim recognizes her.

Salim: I am surprised to see you here in this distant forest. Who brought you here in the loneliness of my camp. Tell me something…that you are ?' **Sahibjaan stands up when she comes to know that this tent belongs to Salim. He asks her**

name.

Salim: 'what is your name?'

Sahibjaan: 'My name....my....'

Salim: 'You did not respond.' **Sahibjaan turns her head to other side. Salim stands on the entry of the tent.**

Sahibjaan: ' who am I and how I am here...I don't know.'

Salim: 'This night will make me crazy. Do I remind you something... perhaps something may come out of the depth of your memories.' **Sahibjaan tries to recollect him from his voice.**

Salim: (continues) 'it was a rainy night. You were travelling in a train. Incidentally I entered in your compartment. You were sleeping. You continued to sleep but you your feet were awake and they started playing with my senses. You must have got a slip kept on your feet that I wrote in praise of them. You must have read it...remember,' saw your feet...they are beautiful. Don't keep them on the ground, they will become dirty.' **Sahibjaan remembers Bibban's voice who told her.** -

Bibban: *'Sahibjaan, this message is not for you.* **'Sahibjaan remembers her own response to him when she told him.'** 'What?..No...no... it is for me only got it on my feet.'

But Bibban contradict it saying,' may be but you may not be wearing ankle bells on your feet.' Salim asks her again.

Salim: ' Did you remember anything?' **Sahibjaan closes her eyes Salim goes out.**

Cut to-

Time: Sunrise.

Sahebjaan comes out of the tent hearing Salim.Salim stands there.

Salim: 'Please listen..'

Sahibjaan: 'hoon.'

Salim: ' I will be leaving you for some time.'

Sahebjaan: ' why...where?'

Salim: 'not far away...just across the river. Bur I will send my man from there, He will take care of you till I come back.'

Sahibjaan: ' when you will be back?'

Salim: I will return before the dark.'

Sahibjaan: 'Please do return before the dark. Listen.'

Salim turns back on his horse and looks back to her.

Salim: ' you want to say something.'

Sahebjaan: ' Please do return back before the night sets in.'

Salim: ' sure.'

Salim leaves on his horse. She continues to look at him.

The dialogue in the film *'Pakeeza'* left an indelible imprints in the memories of people. They are recollected even after five decades of its release. Every word in the dialogues is full of sentiments. Beside the dialogues, the concept of this scene is remarkable too.

Salim is surprised to see an unknown shadow in his tent. He cannot believe his eyes when he recognizes Sahibjaan that it was the same women whose feet made him lose his senses. Sahibjaan does not recognize Salim as she was asleep in a train compartment when Salim entered there. In praise of her beautiful feet Salim leaves a note on her feet which reads, *'Looked at your feet...they are beautiful. Don't keep them on the ground, they will become dirty.'* This happened in the train during a rainy night. These words are repeated in the scene to remind Sahibjaan about that eventful night. If he would not remind her , she would not recognize him. These are the words which connected him with her and with the train in the night. She preserved these words in her memories, in her heart and in her loneliness, that's why she waits everyday for the same train in the thick of quiet mid night. The memory of this event unsettles her. She continues to wait for the man who made her crazy but can't believe when he really appears in front of her.

When Salim wants to leave for some work, she insists him to return early before the night sets in. Repetition of her words again is an expression of her love for him as if she wants to inform him that she has been waiting for him till this time. Dialogues in this scene not only introduce the main characters to each other but also link them romantically. It is an indication of the beginning of their love story. The intense desire to meet each other can be observed in their heart touching dialogues which still miss out few heart beats.

Narration:

The characters in a scene express them through dialogues while concentrating on each other. Normally dialogues are spoken directly by the artistes to convey a message. *Narration* in contrast is information coming from the background without *narrator* being seen on screen. The tone of narration is generally *neutral* as it is meant to provide information only as it is practiced in documentary films, *Narration* is a supplement to the on screen images. It conveys information when juxtaposed together with visuals. The words in the narration are incomplete without the other.

Monologues:

An expression of personal emotions by an individual character is called a *'monologue'* that comes out from the background in a scene. Monologues are used to convey personal information, sentiments, background, a specific situation, and description of a character or the story, expression of an anger or love, description about a past or the present event without dialogues.

Narration, commentary or monologues are non synchronous sounds so they can be associated with any mood such as serious, comedy, romantic etc and in the forms like poetry, prose, reporting or any other form to take the story forward. The background words are also useful to manage screen time. Following example is a combination of monologues and the dialogues which complement each other in a scene taken from a film' *Toote Pankh'* conceived, written and directed by *Kuldeep Sinha.* It is a story based on the dejection and loneliness of a senior citizen Mr. Dayal ,a retired a govt. officer whose hopes are dashed when he finds his son and daughter in law indifferent to them.

Scene No.:

Time: Day

Location: Abhay's home.

Characters: Dayal, Sunanda and her children.

Dayal climbs up the stairs of his building heaving a sigh with his knee pain to reach his son's apartment on the third floor. He presses the button of the doorbell. Sunanda opens the door.

Monologue: 'The age has started showing its impact on my body. Due to Knee pain I faced problems in normal walk and other activities at home.' **She picks up the bag of purchases. Before he could rest for a while, she asks him to get some potatoes too from the market without considering his age and knee pain.**

Sunanda: ' Babuji, just a minute. Please go to market and get some potatoes too so that I can fry them for snacks.'

Dayal: (tired) 'ok , I will get it.' **He returns back quietly.**

Time lapse

Dayal is playing with his grandson and the grand daughter on a bed. Children ask him to tell a story.

Children: ' Daddaji...dadaji...say some stories, Dadaji.'

Dayal: ' ok , I will tell you a story. There lived a lion in a forest cave. He was very strong and powerful. All the animals were scared of him so they used to bring food for him. After some time the lion became old. His authority was reduced. Animals were no more scared of him and stopped bringing food for him. He remained hungry...'

Baby: 'Dadaji...dadaji... have you also grown old?'

Dayal: 'who told you this?'

Baby: 'Mom was telling papa that you have become old so what do we do. We are also burdened.'

Boy: '..and also that from where we bring money to take care of them.'

Baby: '..so she has terminated the services of house maid.'

Dayal feels upset on hearing this bitter truth coming from the innocent children. Tears fill his eyes. He starts cursing his old age.

Monologue: 'It is the first time that I felt being old and our burden is so unbearable that my son's shoulders cannot lift it. We don't know where we went wrong in their upbringing. we distributed everything we had to our children. we failed to understand them. Perhaps they have themselves become a machine leading a mechanical life of a city. They have just become a part of the machine devoid of love and emotions.'

Time-lapse

Dayal is reading news paper in his room. His ailing wife Janaki lay nearby him.

Monologue: 'All the decision was taken by my son and daughter in-law. Our job was only to accept and comply with them.

Sunanada tells something to Ajay who later comes to Dayal.

Abhay: 'papa...'

Dayal: 'hoon...'

Abhay: ' Papa, you can shift to the smaller room so we can arrange their study in this room.

Dayal: ' ok why not...'

Abhay: ' Thank you papa.'

Dayal accepts his proposal. Abhay returns back to his room.

Cut to

Location: store room

We see house hold stuff stocked and scattered in this dingy room which hardly has space for a cot. Seriously ailing Janaki is crying with pain on a cot. Her condition worsens.

Monologue: 'and thus we too became stuff in a store room. May be it was our destiny. Janaki's condition was deteriorating every day. Not to be more burdensome on my son, I tried to manage her medical expenses within the meager pension that I received every month. Then there was a demand from my younger son Chhotu who was studying medical and wanted five hundred rupees for examination fee. Janaki's medical treatment…Chhotu's fee.. I had no income other than my pension.'

This scene from the film *'Toote Pankh'* is one of the brilliant examples of a dialogues combined with monologues. They both complement each other not only in the development of the story but also portraying inner feelings and emotions that are not visually shown in the scene. While *monologues* are an expression of Dayal's dismay, disappointment, frustration and tribulations in his life, the *dialogues* are the reflection of events, indifferent attitudes and disrespect of a son towards his parents occurring at home. The story of a lion is a catalyst to the information innocently revealed by the children to their grandfather about his being old. It leaves the old couple benumbed. It takes the story forward. They have no words to react on this situation. They realize that their old age has deprived them of their self respect, dignity, status in the family and mainly his voice. What remains is their helplessness, few tears in their eyes and a long wait for breathing their last.

The turmoil within and the events taking place outside have been chronologically expressed by alternatively used monologue and dialogues that makes the scene very effective and emotional. Since such things invariably happen in our life and we react on them instantly therefore alternative use of monologue and dialogues does not look unnatural but the audience start walking along with Dayal in his turbulent journey.

Situational Sounds:

There are different sound symbols for different situations which inform us about a particular situation. These symbols are also as important as words and images which give information about a scene. This information is vital for the development of the story. Situational sound symbols provide us many information such as where we are (*place*) someone's entry or exit *(action)*, morning, evening or night (*Time of the day*), Mood, seasons etc. Every scene takes place at a particular time morning, noon, evening or night and place which may be a village , a town, a home (*interior or exterior*).characters movement shows their mobility. The sound symbols related to time, place, actions, seasons and mood such as following symbols give the following information about a scene:

1. Traffic sound- Roadside, town, city
2. Heavy traffic noise - noon time
3. Less traffic sounds- morning , evening or night
4. Call bell- someone arrival, door closing- someone left.
5. Cooker and utensils- cooking activity.
6. Dog barking- someone unknown arrives
7. Crowing of a cock- morning
8. Cloud's thunder, lightening- warning of rain
9. Raining sound- rains and rainy season
10. Dry wind- summer
11. Leaves falling- spring or fall season
12. Clapping- appreciation or applause
13. Long clapping-more appreciation
14. Ploughing, floor mill, water wheel, cattle's howl, oxen bells-village

15. Sea waves-sea side
16. Train, hawkers in the station, travel announcements-railway station

Above are few of the examples of situational sound symbols. There are unlimited number of such sounds that provide different information about the scene. These symbols take the scene to its depth. It is not necessary that such symbols are always heard along with the visuals, they have their independent significance therefore it depends purely on the creative merits of a director how he makes use of these symbols to enhance the impact of the scene.

Special Sound effects:

Any of the natural, secondary, situational symbols can be used to create a specific mood, warning about an event or action. expression of emotions and depth etc. The sound of shoe tapping in pin drop silence may create some chill, falling water drops may create suspense, mystery, howling of an owl or dog barking may be a warning sign of some improbable. The quiet before and after a sound symbol, may reflect peace or seriousness.

Contradictory sound symbols:

With different meanings, they do not endorse the visuals. Generally such symbols are the combination of idealism and realism such as a leader tormenting a helpless man through his goons with the overlapping of his speech on human rights followed by clapping; it reflects the double standard of the leader. In motion picture where images reflect reality, the sound symbols used with them are generally subjective expressions which in combination with visuals provide an emotional expression of the past or the present. Creatively and deliberately used such symbols along with the visuals involve the audience subjectively and objectively. Since their interpretation may differ, extreme care should be taken to avoid their misinterpretation in the scene.

Symbolic sound effect:

The way with proper arrangement of visuals; similes and metaphors are created, similarly with the combination of different sounds *special sound effects* are created.

A dacoit comes out of a temple and sees a child crying. He picks him up and tries to calm him. The child's cry combined with a cat's meow reflects the dacoit's softness. When a man shouts along with dog barking in the back ground, it creates a sound metaphor. The man is compared with a dog who barks on anybody without reason. In the popular Indian television serial *'Chandrakanta'* the crowing sound is overlapped whenever the antagonist 'Krure Singh' appears in the scene, it signifies his shrewdness and manipulative nature.

Whenever a character tries to look what he is not and he uses things or voices which presents him in different personality, then the sounds used in the process function as *special sound symbols*. In the film *'Sholey'* Gabbar Singh is characterized as a normal man but his shoes and their metallic tapping reflect his cruel and insensitive personality. The metallic tapping of his shoes is special sound symbol. The qualities of sound symbols such as echo, hollow, metallic or wooden provide a definite characteristic to the subject. While the use of sound symbols is the discretion of the director , writer can make his suggestions in the screenplay.

Music:

When the cinema was silent the sound of projector was a terrible disturbance to the audience, the background music inspired by the theatrical practice, was played live by a group of musician sitting in the back of the screen to overcome this problem. This was the beginning of background music in cinema. Musicians used to play music according to their understanding of the scene like soft music during a love scene, loud music during a war or confrontation scene, special music on special occasions such as an action or special events. When the sound came in cinema, music attained a special status to enhance the effect of the scene. The responsibility for providing suitable background music fell on director and music composers.

When two shots are joined together give a meaning, sound symbols with back ground music also create special impact to involve audience. Music and sound should always be used with a reference and effect and not to fill up the silent spaces in the track. This dilutes the impact of the scene. Audience should *not just hear* the sound symbols but they should *feel the effect*. They should assimilate with the scene like water in the milk but not like oil on the water surface as every sound has its own character, affect and importance.

XXXXX

Act 6:

Characterization:

The most pertinent question is; what is more important - a *plot, a character or a theme* or which has a priority. The answer to this question is that all the three are important in the form of a story. They are integrated with each other and cannot be segregated. They walk and develop together. The way we cannot separate seconds from a minute and a minute from an hour as they complement each other and help their growth from the smallest unit to the full-fledged development, similarly plot, characters and the theme move together in tight fists. A character is developed with reference to a plot., a plot is developed with characters, situation and conflicts and the theme is the objective that is achieved by the development of a plot with the involvement of characters. It means a theme is conceived with the change in the situations and the metamorphosis of characters. The changes and the growth creates conflict between characters therefore plot, characters and the theme have no significance in the absence of other. Without their integration and story cannot be developed.

Every character in the story has a distinct personality, identity and emotions that is designed and developed by a writer and a director in their own style. If the story is based on human relationship, the writer should first start visualizing his various characters and follow it to decide their behavioral patterns to look them normal so that they identify with people as one among them. This is done with writer's own or acquired experiences.

Characterization in cinema is different than that of a story, a novel and a playwriting. In these genres characters are explained in *'words'*. The words are a tool to express their emotions, activities and conflicts. in theatre they are expressed in dialogues and actions by the artistes but in cinema which prominently is a visual medium, every action, emotion and the conflict is *'shown'* through moving images. Therefore in cinematic scenes, characters, situations, conflicts, moods, places etc should be visually dominant. Every idea and imagination in a screenplay must be visual- oriented that's why *characterization* in cinema is difficult and challenging.

A character is   limited   screen presence so his behavior , habits and other personality traits have to be concise. His avoidable qualities and habits may be removed and only those traits must be developed which are important for the story. A communication without dialogues is an effective way of expression when performers express their emotions, actions and their personality. It is comparatively easier for a writer to work on voiceless characters who can communicate freely without using words. Description of the personality traits of different characters is an important ingredient of screenplay. This can be acquired by minute observation of people and the situations around us thereafter a particular habit, behavior or mannerism of a character may be highlighted.

Most of the characters in cinema resemble real life people so they should be conceived keeping this factor in mind. No character should look unnatural, though it may have been created by writer's own observation, conviction and perception however their presentation must be objective so the audience see and think what he wants them to see and think, otherwise there will be a communication gap between them. Characters don't realize that they are being watched When looked through a peep hole but the audience continue to relish their actions, activities and their onscreen- life experiences, more so in the process audience become part of their existence therefore they don't have to explain everything they do and feel on screen.

Most of the performing arts are based on dialogues and action as it is in theatre where actors have to perform in a limited space of a stage. They are not seen appropriately from every angle and distance however in cinema we see and hear everything minutely. In theatre dialogues and actions are dominating factor, the screen play writer should integrate both of them in cinematic explanations and expressions.

Creating a character:

It is the main task of a writer to create characters which not only take a story forward but also prepare a blue print or an outline of the film. All the characters together create a path for the story. In the process, the writer describes the name, profession, address, future plans, his likes and dislikes, details about his family members and their relationship, their social and economic standard and status, his personality, culture, objectives, ambition and his efforts to achieve them, creating and resolving conflicts to reach at the end of the story. In fact he tries to discover the reasons which connect one character with another during the course of their growth. His observation and experiences help him in this pursuit. Every character has a different identity, tastes, needs and necessities, behavior and mannerism, different reactions to different actions in different situations. The writer's imagination should be very fertile to invent a new personality for every character who together takes the story towards its culmination.

Creating characters in the screenplay is akin to meet new persons who are not only different from real life but they are larger than life. They are more interesting and enticing unlike their natural counterparts. They have their definite image and they live in their own world where many of their personal information are known and unknown. They have their weaknesses and strength, golden moments, success and failure, hopes and despair, , time or place which they have lost or deprived off, their efforts and struggle to get them back. Their power and determination is different than normal persons. They don't create sensation but they are the one themselves. They are not anarchist or a revolutionary but they are the revolution.

Such characters imbibe with those qualities and characteristics are created with specific reference, reason, society or the world. They are not one among us but they look like us. They are not realistic but close to reality. Human behavior is the result of his past memories and experiences so it is not sudden or accidental. This past decides the present and future of human behavior therefore their actions look as authentic as in real life.

The Growth:

The growth of a character means the development of their personality because they are not just a piece of an imaginative fiction but are living human beings. They have the same sentiments as we have. While developing a character writer should acquires the knowledge of the process of a personality development, changes that take place, ambience, emotional impact, social and economical effects on the character, relationship, dramatic effect of their actions and reactions etc as these factors impact a personality. In this process the writer analyzes *cause and effect* along with the self awareness of a personality which also starts influencing the writer himself. He becomes minutely aware of and sensitive about the events taking place around him in the family, in the society and in the world. It helps him to develop a distinct personality of a character. It is important to have a strong character. A person upholding the truth may not be an *ideal* as such a person would like to keep himself aloof from all those things and behavior that taints his personality. He accepts the situation as it is. In the screen play such characters are considered *'weak'*. The on screen characters continue to deny and defy accepted norms, discipline and the truth. They analyze their guilt, conflicts and confrontation, love and hate, competition, introspection to have their distinct image which can be positive or negative. The writer should be aware of why a character behaves or should behave in a particular manner.

Development of a personality:

The personality of an individual starts developing the moment he/she takes birth that continues till death. The person continues to move forward facing various and innumerous problems, challenges and opposition at every stage of his life. The experiences that he gains in the process provide a definite direction and dimension to his personality.

1. **First year and the child development:** From the time of birth, the *first year* of life of a child is very important in terms of his *growth*. It draws an outline for his future. In this year, he develops the feelings of trust and the mistrust. He finds out if there is someone to take care of him in the world around or not, is there any one to feed him when he is hungry, is there any one to sooth him when he is in pains or injured, if there is any one to love or cool him down when he is crying, is there anyone to play with him or is there anyone by his side in the times of his loneliness.? It is the time when the child identifies and differentiates between his *own* and *other* people. He understands to trust his own persons and mistrust others. Sense of security and insecurity becomes stronger. Those who feel secured are answerable to their family and the society.

Those insecure grow in the atmosphere of mistrust and are not accountable and answerable to anybody. They develop in isolation and can indulge in anything for their necessities and pleasure. They lack sensitivity and are aloof towards any relationship. Anger and complexes become their permanent traits. Nascent state of a child is completely dependent on others therefore others' attitude towards him becomes a foundation of his behavior. Whatever emotions he receives in this age become his personal identity.

2. **Second & third year:** The first year onwards the child grows toward *self dependence.* The quality to understand things, thinking and decision making develops. He learns to walk, talk and play. If he is given freedom to take decisions, make commitments and improve upon his mistakes with guidance and affection, it is possible to develop him independently and creatively.

    In a rigid discipline in a caged atmosphere at home where the child is restricted, he is fearful, scared of a punishment. In the absence of guidance for his mistakes ,he not only develops complexes but also becomes arrogant, obstinate, untrustworthy, ashamed and full of guilt. He is very conscious of his dignity at this age. His surroundings are the mirror of his image that lays a foundation for his attitude and habits. He tries to find acceptance for his actions, if it is not available he gets irritated and angry. He develops inferiority complex when others of his age are pampered and appreciated.

3. **Forth & fifth year:** In this age the child is *curious* to know about his identity, he explores and is eager to know different things, he begins to be creative, develops imagination and day dreaming. He tries to understand what he can do or not do and should do or not do. At this stage of life, he should be given absolute freedom to learn from his mistakes. He should be encouraged and inspired.

    Rigidity damages his decision making quality and kills initiatives to do things which affect his further growth, therefore the first six years of his life are very important to shape his personality. In these years, the person develops his personal qualities, independent identity, trust and ambitions that are the foundation of his opinion formation about the self, the family and society.

4. **Six to eleven years:** During this phase of his life, *'learning by doing things properly'* is important. He develops the sense of cooperation and propriety. He identifies self in others' behavior towards him. Right and positive behavior encourages him to do positive things while negative feedback takes him towards negativity. In short our reactions and feedback becomes his mirror.

5. **Adolescence:** In this age he discovers his strength and weaknesses, what he is, what he wants to do and what he can do. It determines his direction for the future. He becomes inquisitive and needs answers to many of his queries. The absence of right answers and response to above questions may result in many personal aberrations. It is also the age when he experiences many physical and anatomical changes. A sense of lack of depth in relationships and humiliation creeps in such cases. He expects others to accept all his actions and reactions as a sign of his *independent identity*. The absence and non-acceptance of his *identity* becomes a hurdle in establishing intimate relationships.

6. **Adult:** The intimacy and affection in relationships inspire *creativity* in adults. He starts giving

importance to emotional and physical exchanges. He connects with others beyond the self in search of new relationships. In the last phase of development there is an intensification of the sense of integrity and unification. He starts feeling responsible towards society . The feeling of cooperation and interest in different places creeps in. He attempts to defend 'his' people from an external threat. Those who lack such qualities are isolated in the society. They become abnormal and confrontationist.. They live life of a defeated, drudgery, disaffection, and dissatisfaction.

It is not so that destiny does not have a role in this process but it is also not correct to infer that those unfortunates cannot move forward to another direction and form leaving their past behind . The difference between a child and the adult is that children cannot take a decision being under the authority of adults while an adult can independently work for creating better situations and opportunities within his rights with a new thrust and new support system. Discovering new opportunities, new responsibilities, new relationships and a new objective or ambition fall within the rights of an adult that may create a new ground for him which is different than his past experiences and accidents. It is the change which leads him to further development. It is in the similar vein that a character grows in a series of changes taking place during the course of his exploring self. The writer should identify and understand who are his characters , how they are affected by the changes in different situations and how should they move on realistically while remaining important and illusionary.

An ideal character:

An *ideal character* does not mean to be without vices because in real life there is no one who does not have negative qualities besides having some good ones. It is rare to find a person who is perfect in all respect or have all negative traits only. Everybody is combination of good and bad qualities. Normally we consider an *ideal character* that is motivated to grow to achieve something in life and works hard in that direction however he should have those sparks, possibilities and merits to grow. He works out a plan of action and direction according to his knowledge, education, culture, familial background and experiences based on the outline of the story. Cinematic characters take their decisions according to their roles on screen which are determined by sentiments of trials and errors, swim or sink, put up or shut up and do or die. An *ideal character* undergoes some metamorphosis in different times and places, from one decision to another and this metamorphosis is the crux of storytelling.

An *ideal character* possesses all those qualities which are universal and possessed by a normal human being. He has sentiments of love and hate, strength and weaknesses, likes and dislikes. He desires to acquire all the materialistic pleasures as we all desire. In addition, an ideal character does not easily bite the dust or defeated. He falls and rises again and again. Even after rendered helpless, he conjures up his energy to fight back with same vigor and valor. None of the hurdles can distract him to achieve his goals. While an ideal character struggles mentally and psychologically, he is physically strong too. The conflicts reflect his determination, ambition or *inner goals*.

Outer goals are *plot objective* while inner goals are his *personal determination* or ambition. Sometimes they contradict each other. Some time a character cannot attain his personal goals due to lack of strength, resources, social restrictions, economic conditions and relationship. Such contradictions make a story interesting and dramatic. Attainment of personal goals is very important which is true in real life too when a person struggles to achieve them even if he is not capable but he does it to prove to others that he can do it. The great men have great goals or to say that they become great by attaining great goals. Their strong will power takes them to the place where it seems impossible to reach. In dramatic situations, an *ideal character* functions very mysteriously to keep the audience guessing about his next move or how much is left of him. He comes up with new strategies, fresh energy, extra strength and new methods to attain what he wants. His behavior is always sensitive and sensible. He carries some unpresumptuous methods under his sleeves to carry out his actions.

In the screenplay all the characters have a definite *purpose* and *goal* to take it to its logical conclusion. They work to meet their objective but their every move and behavior is according to the story that is guided in the screen play.

Types of characters:

1. **The Protagonist:** It is the main character of the film that represents *'idealism'* to the people and the society. The hero or the heroin works as an *ideologue*, *intellectual* or an *opinion maker* who is accepted and followed by everybody. The protagonist is an ideal example of change, growth, honesty, sincerity, and

righteousness. His will power and determination is so strong that he breaks through his goal in spite of many hurdles in his path. He always moves forward on the lines of changes and development drawn for him in the story. People identify protagonists as their icons and follow them. They are the medium to transmit human values that are considered important by the screenplay writer. The decisions taken by the protagonists catalyst a constant change and the growth. They say and do what script writer wants them to say and do to convey to people.

In the film 'Damini', the female protagonist of the same name stakes her relationships and the society to uphold her principles and the truth. Her fight is directed towards her brother in law and his friends; the rapists of Urmi, a domestic maid. She is left alone in her fight with them when her husband also turns his back in favor of his family's dignity and leaves her to fend for herself. Then comes Govind, a professional lawyer who believes in upholding the truth, assures her to bring Urmi's rapists to justice. Damini breaks down in the court when she is asked obscene and undignified questions by the Public Prosecutor Chaddha. She realizes as if she is herself being raped in full public glare in the court of justice. Her hopes to get punishment to the criminals' are dashed. Govind gives her confidence that she will definitely be successful.

Scene No.:

Film: Damini

Time: Day

Location: court room

Characters: Damini, Govind, Shekhar, Public Prosecutor Chaddha, Judge.

Govind and Damini are in the court room. Damini is furious and taunts the judge saying *'Now she has no hopes to get justice.'* **Govind consoles her and assures her that she will be successful. She exposes public prosecutor, press and police who all have been hand and gloves in the crime.**

Govind: ' Damini, I am confident that only you will win...you will get justice.'

Damini: 'What justice...whose justice. I don't want anything now. Let me speak Govindji, let me speak. I have seen a lot and heard a lot. Urmi's rape has been declared an accident. They have sold Urmi's ruin in installments to the press by concocting spicy stories. Her destruction became a source of money for the police. We decorate a stone idol with silken clothes in the temple but remove clothes of women. They bare her shamelessly. I don't want to prove my truth to them...not now.' The court listens her in pin drop silence. She vents her ire and disappointment in words. Govind, Lawyers, the judge and the people in the gallery are silent. She continues,

Damini: 'I have seen nobody had sympathy with Urmi. She was raped in every lane and places...sometimes by the police, sometime by the enforcers of justice... where has she not been raped?' She turns to Public prosecutor, 'and you the public prosecutor, your questions were important but the way they were asked from her and from me in such a lusty and obscene manners, where were those brothers who tie a band on their wrists for their sisters safety and defense?. Now I ask you... please reply Mr. Chaddha, you call the place below the neck that is breast? You hear less so now I say it loud so that you all can hear it clearly that the place below the neck is called a breast. Mr. Chaddha, It is the first introduction to a human being. A mother feeds her child from her breast only,' PP Chaddha listens quietly, 'you also must have had this milk but did you ever asked such questions from your mother or sister that you have asked me? No, I don't want truth now. Let Urmi's soul rest in peace. I think I was mad ..I am mad.. You please send me to mental hospital. I think I deserve that place. I will be fine there. I am mad... I am mad...'

Damini cries in tears. She is disappointed. She is losing her strength to fight further. Everybody in the court room is quiet. Shekhar her husband enters in the court. People look at him. He comes and stands in the witness box. Damini continues to look at him. Shekhar disposes and judge looks at him.

Shekhar: 'I am a culprit... I am a criminal. It is a fact that Urmi was raped. I have seen it. My brother and his friends have raped her. This fact has been hidden by me and my family for its honor and dignity. Urmi is also murdered. In this conspiracy Mr. Chaddha and my father is involved. I have reached here in this shameful situation after many hurdles. I have confronted with my death. If there is a power behind it, it is she who stands there (to Damini) 'Damini , I am proud of you.' (Back to Judge) 'My Lord, she is my wife. I am proud that I am her husband.' **Damini starts crying hearing Shekhar.**

In this scene when Damini is portrayed as a bold and truthful woman who wants to revenge for injustice committed on Urmi but later rendered helpless when she is faced with uncomfortable questions in the court. She not only feels humiliated but realizes that entire womanhood is humiliated by such questions. She hates double standards of society. She is heartbroken to accept that she cannot fight with the society. She has grudges with those who have sadistic pleasure on others' subjugation and take advantage of the situation. On other hand Shekhar a well meaning and kind hearted person is not able to decide his role as a husband while knowing that Damini is fighting for truth and justice. He does not know to whom he should support , Damini or his family. He ignores his ideals in his indecisiveness and objectives are different, it creates conflict but later he surrenders to her and decides to stand by her. Both these characters represent human weakness and strength in pursuit to be an ideal character and convey a message of the power of truth and fight against injustice.

2. **The changer:** There is a continuous process of change and development in the story. If it is not there the plot will not move ahead. So there is a need of a *changer* to provide a push to this change and further growth that pursues the antagonist to change his course and the goal. Since their methodology and objectives are different, they come in conflict with others. This conflict is important to create dramatic situations. Normally a *changer* does not *'change'* and remains the same till end however some situations may change but not his character. They also don't lack *inner strength* and *determination* like the

protagonist while their objective is decided in the plot.

As explained above , the objectives and methodology of both changer and the protagonist are different so in all likelihood there will be conflicting situations between them as they both want to achieve their goals with a strong determination. It is not an easy task as only one will make his way to the goal post until any one of them changes his course and the goal. Since the changer is not to change, it is protagonist who has to change. The protagonist has to face many challenges and hurdles in the course of his growth. He has to break many barriers, resist neutralizing opponents and objections, knowledge and power to convince and bridge the gaps. These hurdles force the protagonist to embrace new decisions and choices that change his behavior. This new behavior is the beginning of his further changes and development. The *changer* is an important contributor in this process.

3. **The Antagonist:** An antagonist may be a hurdle in the path of a protagonist but he is not the only one. There may be many other characters to oppose him and create many conflicts and contradictions that the protagonist has to face. These conflicts are important for the plot and not for a character. The conflict open opportunities for the character to take new decisions in the new situations to change his behavior which is a normal process for a protagonist.

The relationship between a changer, the opponents and the protagonist depend on the final outcome in the plot. Their struggle compels all of them to change which is a necessity for the development of protagonist. Normally no one is defeated at the end. Everyone is a winner only situations change and everybody accepts them however audience may feel about someone defeated while other is a winner. Both the situations and inferences are important in the screenplay. A changer and the protagonist represent different characters due to difference in their goals and methods to achieve them. The writer must clearly understand the difference between them for a convincing characterization.

Film: Waqt

Time: Day

Location: Mansion of Chinay Seth

Characters: Raja, Chinay Seth

Raja and Chinay Seth enjoy a drink in the garden.

Chinay: 'Raja, have e you ever thought of the distance between you and Meena?'

Raja: 'what distance?'

Chinay: 'you are a law breaker and her father is a savior of justice, you are an anonymous identity whose family is not known and she is rich and belongs to a status family. You are a thief and she is a judge. If they see your real characters then just imagine what can happen.'

Raja: 'who can show them my real self?'

Chinay: 'your deeds.'

Raja is disturbed hearing what Chinay said. He presumes that he can be black mailed by him. Chinay laughs on sensing his dilemma.

Raja: 'That's why I have left everything.'

Chinay: 'But what about you're past that is chasing you. If some day it reveals its face then...?'

Raja: 'So what do you think is that my life is in your control?'

Chinay: 'No.No. In fact my life is in your control. You do know Raja how much I adore diamonds and the queen is coming to the city tomorrow. She is a diamond mine. You only can do it.'

Raja: 'And what if I don't do it?'

Chinay: 'Then I can hate you as much as I love you.'

Raja: 'Love and hate...Chinay Seth. Those living in a glass house don't throw stones at others.'

Separated from his family in his childhood Raja of *B.R. Chopra's* film 'Waqt' is fostered by Chinay Seth who is the don in the world of crimes. Raja too becomes his accomplice in course of time. After falling in love with Meena, the daughter of a judge, he decides to denounce everything. He wants to reform for her but Chinay Seth does not allow him to do so as he is fond of Raja's intelligence and strength. When he refuses to steal diamonds, Chinay blackmails him but he too shows him the mirror.

In this scene while Raja tries to *change* to be a good and ideal man, Chinay Seth does not relish it. This contrasting role of two negative characters creates conflict and confrontation between them. It brings out many questions in the mind of the audiences to let them find the answers till the end. The audience walk through this path along with the writer, they want to know; how much Raja is influenced by Chinay's pressure tactics, if Meena comes to know about his past; how is she going to behave, if their love story will continue or will be terminated, if Meena continues to love him, whether her father, a judge, will accept a criminal to be his son in law because he is a rich and dignified man?' This small scene provides many information and contradictions, many question with no definite answers. It brings new conflicts and new situations to the fore. When it seems certain that a criminal is on the verge of change for better, the negative character of Chinay throws a stone to create waves in the calm water for a short while. Thus in the entire screenplay there can be many opposing situations and the characters to prevent protagonist to change by creating many hurdles and compulsions in their path of success.

It is not necessary that a character will always be negative or an antagonist. Such negative characters play the role of opposition to the protagonist. It may happen due to many reasons and unpleasant experiences in their past. Antagonists are very important to spice up a screenplay. They have the capacity to make a turnaround in the story such as, a momentary selfish motive of Kaikeyee in Indian mythology *'Ramayana'* makes her an *antagonist* for a brief period and the immortal Ramayana is created. If there would be no Kaikeyee, there would be no 'Ramayana.'

It is explained above that an antagonist does not mean that he should always be an antagonist or he should meet his fate at the end though it is a general notion that there is necessarily an end to the antagonist either in terms of elimination or surrender to the protagonist based on the mythological belief about *'victory of good over the evil'* but sometimes it may so happen that a protagonist turns to be an antagonist due to some tragedies or past experiences in his life. Though he may not behave crudely like an antagonist but some where he nourishes a strong desire to take revenge with those who either tormented him/her or their closed ones.   Amitabh Bachchan and Shahrukh khan in the film 'Deewar' and *"Baazigar'* respectively may be clubbed in this category. In both these films the character they portray is not a conventional antagonist but his actions and activities are not socially accepted. He behaves like a common man with all the human sentiments, sensibilities and emotions.

Film- Baazigar

Scene No.

Location-Exterior, Day

Characters: Ajay, SeemaC.U. Ajay talks on a public telephone

Ajay and Seema are in love but cannot marry due to opposition at Ajay's home. He informs her to marry with the man of her family's choice or commit suicide. Both of them write a suicide note to prove their love. But later he tears the note calling it a prank.

Ajay-'Seema, Try to understand my compulsions. You know well that I have no status or a position to face your father.'

C.U. Seema cries on phone other side.

Seema- 'I don't know. If you cannot talk to Daddy then I will tell him everything about you and convince him.'

Ajay- 'But Seema….'

Seema- 'Ajay, we have only a weak with us.Daddy has fixed my engagement next week.'

Ajay- 'Ok. Seema, meet me tomorrow. I will find some way out.'

Ajay keeps the phone back.

                                                        Cut to..

Scene no.-

Location: Garden, Exterior, Day.

Seema is crying. Ajay turns to the camera and moves forward

Ajay- 'Seema, You marry where your Daddy wants.'

Seema is shocked, 'what are you saying?'

Ajay- 'I thought a lot about it. There is no other way.'

Seema- 'Ajay, I don't want a way. I want a destination. And my destination is you. I cannot live without you'

Ajay- 'then there is only one solution which can unite us forever.'

Seema- 'What?'

Ajay- 'suicide.'

Seema- 'Suicide?'

Ajay-'Do you agree?'

Seema- 'if death is the way out of our love, I am ready to die happily.'

E.C.U. a letter enters in the frame where it is written that... In the same frame another letter comes

Ajay- 'I, Ajay, write in full consciousness...'

Seema- 'I, Seema writes in full consciousness ...'

Ajay-'...that without pressure from anyone in frustration with life...'

Seema – '...that without pressure from any one in frustration with life...'

Ajay and Seema sit under a tree.

Ajay- '...is committing suicide.'

Seema- '...is committing suicide..

Ajay- '...and nobody are responsible for it.'

Seema- 'and nobody are responsible for it.'

Ajay and Seema sign on the letter.

Ajay- 'Put your signature here. Seema signs on the paper.'

Ajay laughs and moves out of the frame.

Ajay-'shit…'

Ajay tears off the note signed by him. Seema stands behind.

Seema- 'what happened?

Ajay- ' you are passed with hundred percent marks.'

Seema- '..Hundred percent marks?' **Ajay walks towards her.**

Ajay- 'I was testing you for your love and for your trust on me.'**Ajay throws away his note.**

Seema- 'then why this suicide note?'

Ajay- 'only cowards commit suicide and Ajay is not so weak that he will lose the battle of life so easily…we will have court marriage tomorrow. Come to marriage registrar's office at one. I will wait for you there. Now are you happy?'

Seema smiles. Ajay looks at her. Seema moves out of frame laughing.Ajay looks at her going away.

Cut to-

Location: Exterior

Ajay moves forward and see Seema who looks away. Romantic duet song.

Cut to..

Scene no.

Location: Seema's room,

Seema takes out her Wedding necklace from her drawer. And looks at it with smile.

Cut to-

Scene no.

Location: Marriage Registrar's office.

Time: Sun rise, Next Day.

Exterior of a building. Marriage Registrar's office.

Ajay and Seema looks at the board. It is lunch time.

Seema (complains to Ajay),' See, it is lunch time between one and two.'

Ajay- 'How did I know that in every office people feel hungry only between one and two?

Seema- 'Now what do we do for half an hour? If somebody notices us...'

Ajay- 'can't do anything. Let them take lunch and let's too go and have air.'

Cut to-

Scene No.

Location: Terrace, Day.

Top angle from the building. We see everything tiny. Seema looks down.

Seema- 'Oh my God. People look like ants from here.'

Seema stands with her back to camera. Building is in the back ground. Seema turns back scared and touches her chest. Ajay cleans his specks.

Seema-'Ajay. Our wedding is so unique.. There is no procession, no band... no dance.'

Seema: 'Ajay, tell me. What is that gift a husband gives to his wife on their first night?' **Ajay scratches his head.She comes to him. He looks at her. When wedding necklace comes in to frame.**

Seema... 'I knew, you will forget. No problem. I have brought it.'

Ajay- let's see what it is.? Ajay opens the locket and finds photos of them on each side. It is very beautiful as you are.'

They stand on the edge of the terrace and talk holding each other. He lifts her to sit on the wall.

Seema- 'Oh.'

Ajay- 'Do you know Seema. I want to take you to the heights of the sky like this.' **She is scared on the height**.

Seema- 'what are you doing? I have vertigo. I see circles when I look down. Please take me down.'

Ajay- 'when you have held my hand then why are you scared.'

Ajay-'I am mad to take you away from your world after marriage.'

Seema- 'Every girl has to build her new world after marriage...'

Ajay removes his specks and sits down. He looks at her feet.

Ajay-'...And walking on these beautiful feet she is relieved from all her ties and gets freedom from them forever...' **Low angle. Seema looks down. Ajay lifts her feet up saying-**

Ajay-'...I am giving you freedom. Forgive me Seema.'

Seema falls down on her back. She shrieks. Ajay gets up and lifts her feet. Seema rolls and falls back from the boundary.

Long shot. Top angle. Seema is falling down.

She falls dead on the ground.

One of the trend setters in thrillers in Hindi cinema, which earlier depended on clichés like scary music, horrifying visuals, surprises and shocks, the horrible looking antagonists, needle of suspicion shifting from one character to another, shadow play etc., was a great hit of its time *Abbas-Mustaan's 'Baazigar'* not only turns its protagonist to an antagonist but catapulted its lead actor Shahrukh Khan to become a super star.He established that an *'antagonist'* could be a lead character of a film, the concept which was taboo years back. The antagonist of the film is a serial killer. He hooks beautiful girls in to his love charm to win their blind trust and kill them later. In the above scene Ajay traps Seema in to his love web. The scenes provide a chronological development of his evil design to kill her without getting legally involved and suspected in the murder. Knowing well from the beginning about his modus-operandi, the unsuspecting audience enjoys their romantic relationship giving him benefit of doubt without adverse presumptions. Their intense love gains support of the viewers who keenly wait for them to get married. Their reaching to Registrar's office for court marriage signals their seemingly unflinching love for each other. Ajay's dictating a suicide note to her has another twist when he confesses that it was just a prank to test her trust. Nobody could suspect anything wrong in his actions as such pranks are very common in relationship between a boy and a girl in love. Even in the last act when he lifts her feet and compliments her beauty, no one has inkling that something wrong would happen till Seema is finally pushed to death from the edge of the terrace by him. A pure romantic scene followed by a romantic duet song in between takes the audience to a nostalgic height. While people are aware of Ajay's mischiefs, it is difficult for them to anticipate that he would kill her. It is more or less a writer and Director's scene . Throughout the film Ajay behaves like a gentleman with unscrupulous thoughts that no other character in the film is aware off. The audiences are kept aware of his evil designs but they are not sure of his probable intentions. This keeps them on their toes till end of the film when he confesses his crime and justifies his revenge connecting it to his past. Ajay adds another dimension to the characterization of an antagonist mixed with a protagonist with grey shades.

4. **Catalyst:** There are many characters in a screenplay who create new situations, new problems and new behavior, they are *'catalyst'* who may not be directly involved or be part of an action and a conflict nor they have an issue with the protagonist or other important characters. They only provide new information and situations to dramatize them by their response. The main characters react to the situations created by him.

Film: Aankhen

Location: Training centre for blinds

Time: Day

Characters: Neha, Rajput, Agent

Neha is training a blind boy while Rajput observes her. Few other blind children are playing games. Rajput asks Neha.

Rajput: 'whose child is he?'

Neha: 'he is my brother Rahul.'

Cut to..

Rajput is in the office of a news paper agent to flash an advertisement for a workshop for blinds. Agent feels happy when this ad will be published?'

Agent: ' day after tomorrow.' and agrees to give an advertisement.

Agent: ' It is a chance of a life time for the blind. A workshop for blinds are you sure it will reach to the blind and what it is.'

Rajput: ' when this advertisement will be published?'

Agent: 'day after tomorrow.'

Neha comes running to him. Rajput comes to her and sits nearby. Disturbed Neha is searching for her brother who is missing. She enquires from Rajput about him.

Neha: ' you...? Where is my brother...where is Rahul..?'

Rajput: ' mortgaged.'

Neha: ' what? '

Rajput: 'you brother is mortgaged with me. If I give you Rs fifty Lakh then I need some valuable security to keep with me. It is business and for you what can be more important than your brother.'

Neha is disturbed hearing it form Rajput. She does not understand what exactly he wanted.

Neha: 'what...what are you talking about..? I don't ...'

Rajput: 'not understood yet... will know it soon. I will give you Rs. Fifty lakh. You will train three blind people for me using your skills.'

Neha: ' for what...what for..?'

Rajput: ' for one of the most unique and unusual bank robbery.'

Neha: ' what...what../'

Neha is surprised on his proposal. He talks about a bank loot by trained blind men.

Rajput: ' don't you believe me?' no one else will believe it. Who will accept that three blinds may loot millions of rupees of a bank in broad day light? Who will? But it will happen because truth is stranger than fiction.'

Neha: ' see it is not possible. Please don't make a prank with me.'

Neha suspects that her brother is in trouble but she feels it is impossible to carry out his plan. Rajput explains her.

Rajput: 'I have planned a special workshop for blinds and given an advertisement to invite them from all over the country. The advertisement says that they will be provided training of all kinds.

Neha: ' see... please listen me...'

Rajput: 'they all will be given a scholarship and employment after the training.'

Neha: ' why are you doing it with my brother?' He does not listen to her and continues..

Rajput: 'and they may get lot of money if they tell me what is their ambition and to what extent they can go for their ambition. This will be the criteria for their selection.'

Neha: ' stop it...stop it...'

Neha helplessly wants to stop him but knows she has to do what he wanted because he has kidnapped her brother.'

After terminated from his job in the bank, Rajput plans to loot the same bank for a revenge. He gets an idea to train blinds by Neha, a trainer in a blind school. He kidnaps her brother Rahul to compel her to train three blind men for the execution of his plan. He explains the entire plan to her.

In this scene Rajput is a *catalyst* who uses Neha for his ulterior motive. She works on his plan and he only observes her in her job thus catalyst works to change the main characters and divert the course of the story. In *Ramayana* Character of *Manthara* is a catalyst that insists Kaikeyee and diverts the course of story that sends Lord Rama to an exile for fourteen years.

5. **The revealer:** They are those who hide many secrets, information, mysteries about himself or other characters, situations or previous events etc and reveal it at an appropriate moment. This revelation brings another twist in the story and changes the behavior, ideology, a long held notion about something, thought process, relationship and future events. The revealers are capable to introduce a new twist in the story.

6. **Supporting Characters:** In addition to main protagonist there are many other characters that give him a dimension, an identity and help him in his

development, metamorphosis and achievement of the goal. They are *supporting* characters who contribute a lot in the story, they have their own identity, importance and dignity and objective. They take their own decisions to move the story forward. Sometimes *supporting* characters are completely different with each other. Their difference highlights their qualities as in the film *'Deewar'* ,two brothers are diametrically opposite to each other. Vijay is a materialistic, practical, less emotional and atheist while Ajay is a sentimental, a theist, caring for his family and a savior of family values. Their interaction on opposite lines provides a peep in to their personality traits and analysis of their persona to give another dimension to the characters. Sometimes there may not be any difference between main and the supporting characters who prepare an ambience or special atmosphere along with the main characters such as a *commentator* during a match, presents an insight of the game.

The characters of six of Gabbar gang in the film *Sholey* who obey his wishes and orders to the hilt to carry out his loots in the area. Though they could not take control of Jai and Veeru, who resisted hard during one of their robberies in a village, it was their defeat and humiliation. It was not uncommon in such operations when robbers have to run and return back to their dens empty handed but it annoys Gabbar Singh who takes it as his personal defeat. Though he is aware of their sincerity he wants them to be punished for their insult. These gang men provide Gabbar an opportunity to introduce his personality, fear and scare in the area, his insensitivity and his inflated ego, uncompromising attitude. He also laughs with them when three of his bullets misfire and they are saved. It shows his occasional light heartedness. The presence of his gang men not only establishes them as his *supporters* but also introduces Gabbar to the audience with peeling out his various personality traits. Supporting character can either be positive or negative depending on whose side they are, are they with protagonist or with antagonist? However a *supporting character* may not be an antagonist or an opponent, his job is only to support the main characters.

7. **Small Characters:** There are innumerous actors in the film who play different small roles. They are generally meant to create atmosphere during the occurrence of an event. They are required for a definite purpose in the scene. Their presence is useful to create an illusion of reality. They normally have no independent identity or significance therefore the writer must identify such characters that can be part of a scene but their presence or entry should not be without reason.

8. **Extras or Junior artists:** As the nomenclature suggests they just come and leave the scene such as a crowd of people required for ambience for a market place, a fair or a match, a congregation, a celebration, an audience etc. The extras can be vendors, hawkers, buyers or other engaged in minion jobs in the back drop of the scene. The number of junior artists required and for what job is decided by the director according to scene. They create liveliness in the scene with their presence.

Integration:

In the game of chess every pawn is given a name and each of them has its definite direction to move. Their movement decides the goal and strategy of other pawns. In this course, they all face many problems, opposition and hurdles before they attain their success or failure in the end. This contradiction and conflict keeps the game engrossed till the game is over. If there is no conflict and every bead moves in the planned direction, the game itself becomes monotonous and boring. It is similar to an orchestra where different musical instruments of different nature, tone, beats and character harmonize to create an interesting piece of music. Sometimes they sound the same and some time they sound opposite but they all have a common goal to create a melodious musical harmony.

It is same in a screenplay where all the characters big or small, male or female, old or young, protagonist or an antagonist, friends or enemy, they all works for a common goal to make the film interesting and entertaining. Their contrast provides turns and twists to the story otherwise it will be a monotonous narration. Therefore the writer after identifying their characters must give them an *identity* and a *name* before they are blended together . Every character should lend his support to others so that they form a family or a society and become a part of every event in the script. To attain end, writer must keep observing different activities, characters, anthropology of different geographical areas and communities, actions, reactions, culture, traditions, people of different economic stature etc as our personal experiences may not be sufficient in the matter. *Observation* must be a continuous process that helps him to design, devise and decide the direction of different characters according to the story in realistic manners. Nothing should seem to be concocted, artificial and forced.

Inspiration:

1. Generally there is no formula for writing a screen play. Similarly there is no formula for creating a character. A character can draw inspiration from anywhere as there can be a *person* who you know well with his back ground, social and economic status, his struggle, his success and failures, his nature and sensitivities etc who can inspire an original story. He is the person who you know thoroughly so you have to create a character who resembles with this person to the maximum. We imbibe the qualities of that person in the character to take him to the end with a message that we want to convey.

Film: Saransh

Time: Day

Place: House of Pradhan

Characters: Pradhan, Vishnu, Parvati

In the nursery Parveti gives Pradhan some money. Vishnu stands nearby.

Parvati: ' what is the matter?'

Pradhan: ' I need some money.'

Parvati: ' what for?'

Pradhan: ' can I not ask money from you?'

Parvati: ' why you say it but what is the issue?'

Pradhan: ' I will tell you later. And listen...don't go anywhere to buy the medicine I will get it.'

Vishnu: ' where are you going?'

Pradhan: ' Airport custom.'

Cut to...

Scene No.

Time: Day

Location: Airport custom clearance office

Characters: Pradhan, Vishnu, Agent.

Pradhan and Vishnu are in queue for their turn along with others. An agent comes to him Pradhan and Vishnu move in the queue.

Agent: Hello sir, do want to clear the TV?'

Pradhan: yes but there is something else that is to be cleared first.

Agent: 'please give this bill to me; it is not your job.'

Pradhan: ' Thank you but in which department do you work?'

Agent: 'No, I don't work here but in a way I work here only. I am a clearing agent.'

Pradhan: ' clearing agent?'

Agent: 'yes. Lot of material comes from abroad and there are very few officers so it takes time. I know all the tricks of this place. I can get your work done in few minutes. I charge only two hundred rupees but why do I take more from you senior citizens. You pay me only hundred rupees.'

Pradhan: 'Thanks.'

Agent: ' ok then pay me only seventy five rupees. If not then keep standing in queue till death.'

Vishnu and Pradhan move a bit further. After a man leaves office calls for the next. Pradhan comes to counter where a custom officer attends them. Pradhan gives him all the documents.

Pradhan: 'if you don't mind please do it fast. We have been in queue for long.'

Officer: I am not here without work.

He looks at the papers. Pradhan and Vishnu stands there.

Officer: ' where is the letter from Indian embassy?'

Pradhan: ' I don't have it.'

Officer: 'come back when you have it. Please move.'

Pradhan: 'But at least you listen to me.'

Officer: 'No if and buts when you have all the document, you will get your TV.'

Pradhan: ' I don't want Tv. I want this.'

Officer: 'please go .will you clear the queue?'

Pradhan: ' Please listen to me.'

Officer: 'tell A.C. whatever you want to say.'

Pradhan: 'I will directly meet AC.' People are waiting in the queue to move ahead. Pradhan and Vishnu leave the queue. They encounter the Agent.

Agent:' Hello sir, your work is done? You have been in queue for three hours what did you get? Just no, I would do your work just in seventy five rupees. Now, you go to AC. You will whirl for three days.'

Pradhan and Vishnu go to AC's chamber. AC is on telephone. Pradhan and Vishnu enter in to his rom.AC fires them seeing inside. AC holds the phone and asks him to leave irritatingly. Then he recognizes Pradhan and becomes sober. Pradhan was his teacher.AC asks them to take their seats.

AC: 'yes, it is necessary, tell them...follow it...yes.'

Pradhan: ' I want to talk to you.'

AC: 'who allowed you to come in? Please leave and meet the public relation officer.'

Pradhan: 'I have come to see you and tell you that your people have no manners to talk. They think everybody is cattle. I have come here to collect my things and not to beg something.

AC: 'see Mr.....everyone wants his TV... oh Mr. Pradhan I am seeing you...I am Shinde, please have a seat.'

Pradhan and Vishnu beg him with tears in their eyes. He wipes them out.

Pradhan: ' I have not come for Tv. I have come to collect the ashes of my departed son. Whether a father has a right on the ashes of his son or I have to bribe even for that. I hope you have this mush time to get me those ashes.'

AC keeps the phone down on the receiver when he looks at Pradhan in tears. He takes the documents. AC hands over the ashes to him.

AC: 'I will talk to you later(to Pradhan) please give me your papers and have a seat.'

Peon: 'Sir, David Saheb...'

AC: 'later. (turns to Pradhan) I am sorry; you are troubled because of us. We actually work under lot of pressure so we become rude sometimes other things like Tv,, refrigerator, VCR etc will be cleared once we receive letter from the embassy.'

Pradhan: ' I am not in hurry for those things. Excuse me my son. I think I have been a bit arrogant. In fact, there may be some deficiency in our education .We may have not given the right coaching.

AC: 'Please come.' AC sees them off to the exit.

Pradhan: 'Thank you very much...Mr. Shinde. Vishnu what do I tell his mother?'

We all must have experienced similar plight that is faced by Pradhan in the film *'Saransh'*. This scene is not a reflection of his pain only but is a satire on the system that has lost its sensitivity for human emotions. People work like puppets in the system that is plagued with many deficiencies like bribes, lethargy, menace of middle men who is a link between corruption and the common men. He knows the tricks to lose the red tapes. Pradhan refuses to accept his offer to get the work done in few minutes for Rs seventy five only but an honest teacher does now bow to his allurement. He meets AC who initially behaves arrogantly but after recognizing him as his teacher, helps him to get his son's ashes. It proves that in this system no work can be done without money or high contacts even if it is a matter of someone's sentiments. Such incidents are part of our life from obtaining a Ration card to driving license, passport, school admission or a train ticket. There are touts everywhere who play the game of money for every work. The character of *Pradhan* is inspired by such common incidents that form the base for the story. His helplessness reflects common men's struggle that he continues every day. There can be many more such experiences that can inspire a story and a character that's why it is important to keep observing minutely the happenings around us. Based on real life stories and characters for a film attract people's attention and emotional connection easily and intensely.

2. Another inspiration may come from an ***incident*** that compels to think. A character for such stories should have maximum resemblance who can present the incident identically in the similar form with the same conviction. Since the events and the people connected with it are well known,

any variation in its presentation will make it unconvincing and unbelievable therefore a detailed research, investigation and analysis of cause and effects about the incident and the connected persons is very essential. The writer has to create harmony between the past and present incidents and references when creating situations which carry forward the message that he wants to convey at the end. The development of the script depends on the proper interpretation of the events, characters and the situations, causes and effects and the mental states of characters.

3. A *'theme'* can also inspire a story . You require characters that can portray a personality suitable to the *theme*. The end becomes very important factor in such screenplays so it is the end that guides the creation of new characters and situations to arrive at the desired end. The main characters begin the laying of foundation for other characters and situations accordingly.

There may be other different sources of inspirations but strategy to attain the required end is same. In all these options writer has to understand characters and situations according to the built, life, opinions about the world and the society, moral values, the nature and temperament of the main person who has been part of the real life incident.

Attributes:

While creating a character we know about his physical appearance, age, cast and religion, weight and height, his strength and weaknesses, his behavior and habits etc. These personality traits inform us about his merits and demerits. It includes his cultural heritage, moral values and his objective opinions on an issue. A child may look at a problem from a different perspective while an adult will have another view point. It even varies from males and females. A woman will have her point of view that may be different to a man. It is not important to have different opinions but it is important as how such differences in characters take the story to its logical and desired end affecting each other.

We now know that after the birth of a child it takes few years to formalize his identity and perceptions therefore it is necessary for a writer to underline a character's identity and perceptions, changes and affects in the development of his personality in his formative years. Imprints and experiences of his childhood are always carried forward in his life till the end therefore writer must define his birth place, family background, his relationship with his siblings, his country or the area where he is brought up, his home and neighborhood, his interest and ambitions etc. in addition , it is also important to know about his parents and their background, business or occupation, socio economic conditions, their educational back ground, atmosphere at work place, timing or extra- time working, whether he is under pressure, his standing and contribution in the society, his political lineage and activities, his opinions on various issues, his priorities in life, his cultural inheritance and upbringing to his offspring, all these information help develop a character. Writer should also find out in the story the details about the character's siblings, their relationship, behavior, age and sex, respect for elders, their opinions on different issues concerning family, whether they are together or live separately, their harmony with other family members, favorite member in the family who is a constant support, their joint activities at home and outside, friends etc prepare a social and economic background of the character.

The information gathered from above questions takes to other specific qualities of the character such as whether his needs in his childhood were fulfilled, if he has played with any one as a child, if he was made to realize about his mistakes or punished, if he has struggled as a child. These details decide about a character's future behavior, view points, habits and how he rates himself in the society to accommodate with them or he has some anxieties, mistrust on people, if he will be able to accept his situations, If he deserve affection and respect of others, if he is required or is a burden in the family or society, if he can move forward with confidence independently and also decide about his strengths and weaknesses. Thus the character gets his identity.

It may be remembered that if a character has been brought up in a healthy and supportive atmosphere, he will be able to live life positively and creatively. He will behave responsibly with his family, society and peers. His mental development will be faster that will lead him to the path of development instead of being defensive. He will mould himself to the needs though it does not mean that everything comes to him easily because life is not a bed of roses. He has to struggle to get everything on his plate but his thinking, direction and activities will be creative and positive. He will be full of self confidence,, flexible in his behavior, capable to resolve issues etc. in contrast a character brought up in negative atmosphere will suffer with inferiority complex, anger, lack of confidence and always confronting with the society and self. Different characters in the screenplay may behave differently such as -

1. **Adolescent:** The experiences one gains from his childhood to the adulthood decide the direction of his life as they affect him in positive or negative manners. The series of questions coming out of this phase contribute immensely in the writer's efforts to develop a character. He understands about behavior with his parents, teachers, peers, if he is popular among them...can he accommodate others in a group or he is a confrontationist, his achievements in his early phase, is he a leader or a follower, does he follow rules and discipline in his school or home or he is an anarchist, does he participate in extracurricular activities or not, if he is competitive, is he a drug addict or not, is he interested in higher studies or not, his subjects of interest, does he confirm to his gender qualities, at what age he was attracted to opposite gender, about his future plans and his relationship with his friends and others?.

2. **Adult:** Answers to the above questions give a name and an identity to an adult. With this he develops a definite *image* that confirms to his name. if it is normal or abnormal, is he attractive or not, has he got any identification mark on his body, his physical or mental disability if any, his sense of dressing, if it is cleaned and ironed or untidy and dirty, clarity of his speech or stammering or a reluctant speaker, his style of walking, talking, movements and other

mannerism, any peculiar habit, is he sober or a rowdy? etc.

3. **Professional interest:** after the formation of an identity the next phase of development is related to his *interests* in financial status and professional leanings, social and political activities, educational and religious faiths. What does he plan to do to improve his economical conditions, is he interested in minion job or some specialization, source of his regular income, his working conditions, is he a learner? It is also important to know about his friends and foes, his modes of entertainment. His interest in music, literature, sports or spirituality, where does he live and with whom, if married; how many children he has, familial relationships, his life style and status, what category of people interest him, is he a pet lover or not, what vehicle he drives and what is most important for him?

4. **Value system:** an adult character is developed with the above traits and qualities along with a *value system* he inherits or wants to follow. This value system distinguish different characters from others. It is a parameter to make the judgment on a personality to define his social status. How he wants to live if it is on his own terms or under social discipline, what is his philosophy of life, his priorities and ambitions, his respect for truth or untruth, his behavior with

others and his expectations from others, conflicts with values and struggle.?

5. **Emotional response:** The next step towards the development after attaining a *value system* is the development of *'emotional'* response in a character that allows him to express emotionally with others. This emotional sensitivity is important to bring life in a character without it he will merely be a hard rock so it is important to know how a he expresses his positive and negative emotions, Why he gets angry or cries? Is he afraid of something or jealous, his response in success and failures, can he enjoy or love someone or is he compatible with others or he is full of hatred and negativities or revengeful? It may be remembered that an *emotional response* is the mirror of a personality.

6. **Nature:** In addition, we should know about his *temperament* as no two characters have the same temperament nor it should be so, it makes them seem different than others. It is necessary to know about a character if he is open or closed, share others grief and happiness or confined to self, if he is of submissive nature or an autocratic in others' company, is he energetic, working or workaholic or lazy, conservative, conventional or practical, can he take risks or not, is he self motivated or needs others to push, support and assure, his trustworthiness and sense of responsibility, is he of suspicious nature, timid or

a manipulator and shrewd?. These traits affect the common behavior of a character.

7. **Secrecy:** There is always an element of secrecy in a person that he does not want to share with anyone how so ever closed another person may be. He keeps them close to chest. It is better to know about the *secrets* of a character or an object which he likes to hide from others, his behavior, habits and mannerism that is restricted to his family.

The characteristics detailed above reflect multiple shades of a human being that are important for the development of a personality therefore writer must work out a sketch of every character from the time of his birth till his entry in the screenplay. In fact the writer must live all those characters himself to understand about their metamorphosis, problems and issues that crop up at different age and stages, their solutions etc. These details inform the writer about their special qualities. It helps him to draw an image of a character which he translates in the screenplay later. Though it may still not be enoug but it is the first step to begin the characterization process. Once the process takes off it is the character itself who guides the writer about his further moves and development. The writer just has to follow his instincts with logic of *cause and effects* as there are certain moves and events involving different characters that follow automatically on the basis of their action and reaction leading them to decide about their objective and the next move. The writer has only to ensure that his characters move to meet the desired end of the story. They should not go haywire in their approach so creating a character is a process for the writer to learn, to practice and to think meticulously and deliberately. There is no mystery or a miracle in the process. More he learns and practices, more he widen the scope of his characters as he discovers, studies and learns about human psychology, society, culture, family and different personalities as they are all imbibed in each and every character of the story.

Film: Sholey

Time: Day

Location: Ramgarh Railway station, exterior, road

Characters: Basanti, Jai, Veeru

A train stops at the Ramgarh railway station. Jai and Veeru come out to Basanti who waits for passengers with her Horse cart 'Tonga'. They look at her and her Tonga.

Basanti: 'Hello Babuji, where will you go? Belapur, Rampur, Fatehgarh, Ramgarh.. Where you have to go? Hello, have you not seen a Tonga earlier? It is village Khera. You will not get a car to sit and drive fast. It is only Basanti's that Tonga runs here. See I don't have habit to talk nuisance. If you want to come tell me yes we go.'

Basanti is a chat-machine, young and beautiful village dame and she does not allow Jai and Veeru to say anything.

Jai: ' yes we do have to go.'

Basanti: 'if you don't want to go, it's fine with me. You will not be an enemy of Basanti. When you came out I thought you need a Tonga so I asked you. Anyway it is a compulsion to sit in the Tonga. It is Basanti's Tonga. It is not a slavery of a land lord that you have to do it when you don't want to do. It is like saying....'

Veeru tells Jai to get in to the Tonga. Basanti stands there. Veeru sit in the rear and Jai in the back side of it.

Veeru: 'why should we not go, we have to go. Get in yaar'.

Basanti: ' ok...ok..Then come in. when I said no to you. See I don't talk foolish so it is better to tell you before we move. I will charge Rs two for Belapur and Rs one and half for Ramgarh. Don't crib later. What Basanti said is said.'

Veeru: 'ok, it's all right. We only....'

Basanti: 'yes I understand, now you will ask me 'Basanti, why two rupees for Belapur and One and half rupees for Ramgarh so you ask me where this Tonga is from? Ask...ask me.'

Jai hears Basanti's chats and Veeru enjoys her talking.

Veeru: 'which is the village?'

Basanti: ' It is from Ramgarh..But it is also to be seen that if I take passengers for Belapur then there will be two rounds from here to Belapur and from Belapur to Ramgarh, if I go to Ramgarh then I go only to Ramgarh. Although this Tonga is from Ramgarh and me too is from Ramgarh so it is all about me, now you tell me where will you go in Ramgarh?'

Veeru: ' we too will go to Ramgarh.'

Jai takes out some cotton from the seat cushion to block his ears.

Basanti: 'Ok then go. When did I refuse it but whose house you want to visit in Ramgarh. You have to tell me that Basanti take me to this house or that house because if I don't know where do you have to go, where will I stop my Tonga? You should know that who is moving the Tonga? I am doing it and if I only don't know it...'

Jai: (interrupts Basanti to say) 'we have to go to Thakur Baldev Singh.'

Basanti: 'ok ok when did I say no to you go then say that you have to go to Thakur Baldev Singh's house. Move Dhanno Move. It is like that ....' Basanti continues her gossips, 'who does not visit Thakur's mansion is either mad or an outsider. So you know that I did not have my parents earlier and them there was Mausi after my Mausa then tell me who had to shoulder the responsibility of this Tonga. People ask me why being a girl I run a Tonga so I reply them if Dhanno being a female horse can pull it, why I being a girl cannot run it? Tell me ...tell me.'

Veeru: ' yes why not.'

Basanti: 'you are from the city but seem to be intelligent. Whets your name?'

Veeru: ' Veeru.'

Basanti: 'you did not ask me what my name is.'

Jai opens his eyes and asks her name tauntingly.

Jai: 'what is your name Basanti.'

Veeru: 'he always talks nonsense.'

Basanti: 'though I was not talking to you but since you have asked me I will tell you. My name is Basanti.'

Jai: ' I have heard it for the first time.'

Veeru: 'Its lovely name.'

Basanti: 'why my name is Basanti there is a story.'

Jai: 'what is it Basanti?'

Veeru: ' you keep quiet.'

Basanti: 'it happened that when I was a child the mother in law of my Mausi's brother in law said...'

Veeru: 'what she said?'

Basanti: 'Everyone has a name but it should be thought why that name should be given...?'

The Tonga passes through a village.

Basanti in the film *'Sholey'* is different than the normal characters. She is a carefree, talkative and lively girl. She has a habit to escalate a reference which has no concern with others. She even forgets what others will think about her foolishness and nuisance talking. Since this character does not leave a negative impact and in a way entertains people , it is acceptable. Her innocence is touchy. She also does not have an inferiority complex or insecurity of running a *Tonga* being a girl. This character in fact brings a relief in otherwise tense moments in the film and audience feel relaxed for some time when she appears in the scene. The long drawn dialogues of this character are its specialty as she does not allow others to speak except her. It is difficult if not impossible to conceive a character like this that leaves its impact in the crowd. It is the reason that even after five decades of the release of the film Basanti and Dhanno are still alive in the memories of people.

Action:

An *action* is a mode of expression by a character to express his internal and external emotions and desires. An action reflects a change in a character in chronological order. ' I hate him' is expressed by tightening his fist, banging on a table, wall or hitting his fists strongly. A person may suddenly start running when he sees a transport arriving because he wants to catch it. A person drifts apart when he gets a current. One feels happy to hug an affectionate person or may get angry when he looks at his opponent. A desire to have a glass of cold water takes him to the refrigerator. When he is sad, tears roll out, looking at other side means he does not want to talk to anyone. An action is a *visual activity* that has some movement, time and space and it creates some sound. Action are generally of two types:

1. **Plot actions:** They take place according to the requirement of the story at a given time and place in which the character moves from one incident to other such as a thief runs and Police chases him, the thief stumbles when exhausted and he is caught by police. Running of a thief and police chase is the requirement

of the plot. If the thief is not caught, there will be a gap in the story and some important personal emotions and experience will be missed out.

2. **Character action:** The expression of characteristic traits, behavior, mannerism, emotions and experiences by a character is *'character action'*. In fact these actions are his identity. There are two types of character action –

   a: They are the action which are performed for others to know their reactions and

   b: They are his *personal action* which are restricted to the character he plays. He hides them from others to know about his personal emotions and experiences. They are the signs of his insecurity, conflict or scare. It is difficult for a writer to discover such actions as the life is full of innumerous experiences.

Both the above actions are different in nature but they are integral part of a screenplay except few special mannerism like scratching his head regularly, straitening the moustaches etc. No action is without an expression of an emotion or a thought as it happens in real life. We try to hide them when we are not sure of other's reaction but in theatre or cinema, it is necessary to convey them to the audience. The actions convey the compulsions and the intimate emotions without expecting a reaction. An action draws a line of growth according to the story.

There are some important *objects* which are used by a

character during the course of an action however these *objects* should match with the character such as nailed boots on the feet of a soldier reflect his confidence, valor and determination. An long and uneven beard is a sign of depression and internal turmoil. A static pen means steadiness but a pencil with an eraser is a reflection of insecurity and indecisiveness. A cigar is a sign of riche but a Bidi reflects poverty.

The performance of an action indicates a character's mental state and psychology. Banging the phone after a conversation shows disrespect and dislike for the person on the other side of the phone. It is similar to that of banging the door on the departure of a person as if the character waited for him to get out. Intermittent lighting of bulbs displays mental conflict, helping a patient to move shows a caring attitude but rebuking him is an indication of the nurse's strict and dominant personality.

Those who have seen film *'Sholey'* may not have forgotten the character of Gabbar Singh who is different than his peers. He does not shout like others nor does he move in the country sides in a group of gun wielding henchmen on horses' back. He is a simple looking, illiterate, tobacco chewing common man hiding a cruel and insensitive devil within. Shielding himself in hilly terrains, Gabbar runs his business through his assistants and henchmen so many of them have not even seen him.

The scene is an introduction of the antagonist who is also the main character of the film. The scene comes after the gang men of the dacoits Gabbar Singh , which is a terror in the area, are hauled out by two young men Jai and Veeru when the gang members went to a village for their routine loot. Jai and

Veeru assured the villagers not to worry and be scared of Gabbar Singh. They single handedly without arms hound them away and warn them not to visit the village again with their nefarious designs. Gabbar Singh feels insulted and challenged for his authority in the region. He is annoyed by the defeat of his gang men samba and Kaila. Following scene from *Ramesh sippy's Sholey* is reproduced in edited form to give writer an idea of shot division.

Film- Sholey :

Scene…

Location- A hilly terrain,

Time: Day

Characters-Gabbar Singh and his gang men

Camera pans from left to right and shows three dacoits. The feet of Gabbar Singh enter in the frame and move on a rock. Camera follows his feet on a trolley .Metallic effects of shoe steps. He asks- 'How many people were they?' (voice overlapped)…only two. **C.U.Zoom in to the face of Gabbar.**

C.U. of three dacoits.

Gabber- 'They were two and you were three.. then also you came back empty handed. What did you think that boss will be very happy…will complement you… true? Shame on you. You have spoiled my dignity.'

M.S. To L.S. Zoom out. Camera follows Gabbar from the back of the three dacoits. Gabber sits on the rock.

Gabbar- 'O Samba, how much head money government has fixed on Me.?'

Cross angle, three dacoits

Samba- 'full fifty Thousand Boss'.

M.C.U. Gabbar mixing tobacco on his palm.

Gabbar- 'full fifty thousand. Heard everyone?'

L.S. Samba dacoit.

M.L.S. Composite shot. Gabbar faces the camera and each of the dacoits from the back.

Gabbar-'Full fifty thousand and this reward is for the reason that fifty miles away from here in a remote village when a child cries then his mother tells him to sleep otherwise Gabbar would come....'

Combined shot. Three dacoits

Gabbar-'You will be punished for it...reasonably punished.'

M.S. Gabbar stands up with his pistol.

M.L.S. scared dacoits look at Gabbar.

L.S. Gabbar moves to one of the dacoits.

Gabbar- how many bullets are there ... how many in this pistol?

A Dacoit- 'six, Boss'.

Gabbar- 'There are six bullets in it. Six bullets and three men. It is not judicious.'

Intercut from the view points of the dacoits. Gabbar takes out his pistol when he reaches near them. Gabbar fires three shots in the air.

Gabbar- Its ok now. Now there are three bullets in its three houses and three are empty. Now I will roll it. Now I don't know where the bullets in its three houses are. Which house has bullets and which does not have, I don't know....

M.C.U. to M.S. Gabbar wheels down the mill of the pistol.

E.L.S. all the dacoits are scared. Zoom out. Gabbar keeps his revolver on one's head

Gabbar-now there are three lives and three deaths in this pistol. Let me see who gets what?

Combined shot, Gabbar press the trigger on a dacoit's head.Sound of empty pistol.

Gabbar- 'bastard is saved.'

Trolley shot. Gabbar triggers on another head. He moves to third dacoit and keeps the pistol on his head. He presses the trigger.Sound of empty pistol.

Gabbar- He too is saved. What will happen to you, Kalia?

Kalia-Boss, I have tasted your salt Boss'.

Gabbar- 'Now have the bullets. (Sound of empty pistol)

Gabbar- it is a miracle.

L.S. all dacoits are laughing

L.S. Samba Dacoit.

M.L.S. all three dacoits laugh.

C.S. two dacoits are laughing

Back shot of Kalia laughing.

C.U. two dacoits laugh cautiously

M.S. Gabbar Singh

L.S. one of the dacoits laughs.

M.S. Gabbar is laughing.

C.S. Kalia laughs.

C.U. separate shots of three dacoits laughing.

L.S. Two dacoits laugh.

Combined shot. All three and Gabbar laugh together.

E.L.S. All are laughing.

Combined Shot as in 30.

M.S. Gabbar suddenly fires at all three of them.

C.S. They fall one by one.

E.L.S. The last one falls.

Zoom. Gabbar spits on his left and goes out.

Gabbar- 'The one who is scared is deemed dead.'

This scene from *'Sholey'* is considered not only a marble of editing but one of the best ever conceived in Indian cinema. Whether it is the dialogue writing, or dialogue delivery, direction or cinematography, sound effects or back ground music, characterization or acting, the scene is distinct in all angles. It is mentioned earlier that most of the dialogues are influenced by theatrical techniques where all the characters deliver their dialogues standing in one position with little movements. Camera too concentrates on their faces in close or over the shoulder shots making it static. Directors too don't make a sincere effort to go to the depth of the characters and the atmosphere.

In the above scene, three dacoits return defeated by Jai and Veeru. This maddens Gabbar Singh with anger. He accuses them for their weakness and narrates a story about his terror in the region saying 'those fifty miles away when a child cries, his mother tells him to sleep otherwise Gabber would come.' The audience too now thinks that the bandits will not be spared by him. This is an introduction of Gabbar in the film. The scene shot in hilly terrain amid rocks is a reminder Chambal which has been a safe haven of dacoits for decades. The feet in close shot moving on the rocks with metallic sound effects create the right ambience. In reply to Gabbar's question,' how many were they?' Samba's reply,' only two.' reduces the gravity of unforeseen consequences and lightens the atmosphere giving a bit of relief to the viewers. After that Gabbar's rebuke to their failure is not more than a display of ego, power and authority which is necessary and normal to keep it's flock intact. his reference about the reward on his head presents him like a common man with his wide spread terror and power. It is not unusual for the viewers to be aware of it. His talk about six bullets and three men does not seem to be more than his fear tactics. When all three bullets are fired empty saving their lives , the scene seems to be over .By their laughter it is attempted to establish that he is after all not that inhuman as people thought. By this time everyone is assured that worst is over when suddenly all three bullets are fired at them and within moments the three fall prey to his bullets. The tension grips the atmosphere once again. Sudden change in his behavior reflects his unpredictability, insensitivity that he could kill anyone unsuspectingly even his loyalists. Gabber is unique comparing to other plunderers conceived so far for Indian screen. He is not horse riding gun tottering dacoit who would only order his men nor does he indulge in routine robbery with his people. He is a normal looking careless man with unshaven beard, tobacco mixing and chewing man spiting anywhere, without thunderous dictates. He is humorous and jovial with others but one can see terror on his face.

Generally, people have notion that for all the enactments, the responsibility lies on the actor as to how he decides to portray it, how he expresses his emotions and opinions and how he tackles his internal conflicts. If so the actors must be rendered complete freedom to present his character. In most of the instances, an actor portrays what has been briefed, imagined, visualized and written by the writer in the screenplay therefore it is necessary for him to give his characters a definite identity and prepare a *performance guide* for him by describing his actions and dialogues so that the actor knows his character in detail without ambiguity to enable him to discover suitable actions for a convincing portrayal.

In the Film' *Wapsi'* (The home coming) directed by *Kuldeep Sinha,* the introduction and the development of a character has been made without taking support of dialogues through *Monologues.*

Film: Wapsi (The Home coming)

Time : Day

Location: A busy road of c city

Character: Kishan

Kishan is strolling goods in his hand cart on a busy road of a city. He is breathless and sweltering. He feels exhausted after the daylong labor but continues his work. He reaches back to his dingy home only after the dark. Background poetry is an expression of his compulsions to migrate to a nearby city to get a job.

Poetry: In a beautiful village there was a holy fig tree, underneath it there was a bestowed shelter, that was a small house .I left that village, I left that dense shade of the tree for the city but lost in the crowed.

Time lapse

Time: Evening

Location: Kishan's room

Character: Kishan

Kishan returns back and unlocks his home in the dark. He tries to find a matchbox and lights up a lantern. The room is lit up. He takes out a letter from his mother and starts reading in the dim light of the lantern. Few images emerge on the letter.

Narration: 'There is a letter from mom in the village. This time too she got it written by a neighboring dame Saloni, *'My son, now you come back to village at the earliest. I am not well in this age. My body too is not cooperating with me. It is either cold or fever. Saloni keeps coming and helps me in house chores. Your younger brother Kanhaiya takes care of other external activities. The village head gets him some mean jobs. Day before yesterday he told me to call you back from the city. There is a new opportunity for unemployed where he can accommodate you so you come soon. It is better to have a dry bread in the village than having ghee bread in the city. You have suffered with lot of kicks for many years. Now Kishna you come back home. Kanhaiya too has grown up. Both of you now can manage home. When you return, I will bring Saloni as my daughter in law so you come soon...will you...?'*

It is evident from the above piece that without taking support of dialogues not only the main protagonist Kishan but also his relationship with his mother, brother and Saloni has been established. All other information about the family, the village, their poverty and intention to marry him with Saloni have been conveyed effectively. The monologue has conveyed the reasons for kishan's migration to the city, he not getting married with Saloni, unemployment issues in the village, Kanhaiya's growth by indicating that when kishan left the village, kanhaiya was a child and was not in the earning age but now he is ready to earn a little. sympathy of the village head towards the family, feeling of kishan's absence in the home, misunderstanding of the mother that he is enjoying city's life with the metaphor of ghee bread compared with dry bread of the village. This notion is proved wrong when Kishan is seen strolling goods on a hand cart..How helpless he is. The letter from his mother gives him a little happiness endorsing the fact that he too is lonely in the crowed of the city. Saloni's reference deepens his loneliness to establish his feelings for her. The introduction of the characters, their situations and their miseries is like filling the sea in a pot.

The management of screen time is a brilliant exercise in the scene in such a small scene lot of information about characters, their background, their development, drudgery of a city life where so many things are spread all over that have been bundled in few shots. In fact many years of the real time in the story has been concise to few minutes of screen time without letting people miss out anything. It could have not been possible if there were dialogues.

XXXXX

'Shot – The smallest unit (or building blocks) of the unbroken film. Shots are separated from each other by simple cuts and other kinds of transitions.

Act 7:

On the desk:

When the form of the story and the film is ready in the mind of the writer with the detailed images of all his characters, he is only one step away to descend his imagination and the visualization on paper. In this process he has to explain all those things in *'words'* in such a way that the readers understand the same that he wants them to understand, they should see what he wants them to see, he should hear what he wants them to hear, they should feel what he wants them to feel. Though a writer has the freedom to choose his format, major details are common. It may be remembered that that 'words' written in screenplay are completely different to that of a story or a novel. In the screenplay *words* are used to express the *'visuals' and 'sounds'*. The screenplay is a link between the writer and the film which is first read by the producer, director, financiers and other crew members including actors and technicians. They should understand what a writer wants them to understand. The screenplay is the foundation to realize his imaginative film on the screen therefore every scene has to be very carefully written in few words explaining necessary details.

It is also possible that the script changes few hands in the process of approval. In this situation the first page of the screenplay is very important and its comments may be crucial for *the approval* or *rejection* so it is imperative that the screenplay with its attractive presentation provides maximum information about the scenes that are required for an effective picturization..

Page Designing:

Page designing is the time when the first draft of the script is ready and it is to be attractively presented. It is the *Page design* that is more important than the film at this stage so it is appropriate to work on its standard format. It is a general habit of readers to first look at the number of pages to have an assessment of the duration of the film. There after scanning few initial pages   of the script, he will try to assess professional merits of the writer. This is the first impression of the writer which may be the last too, that he makes on his readers therefore the page designing gains importance. The presentation of the script keeps on changing as and when required however there remain many common information such as Number and the title of the scene, time- Day, night or evening,, location-interior or exterior and characters, page no. etc. these information are given along with the title of the scene for an easy readability.

> *Name of the scene:*   *Scene No.:*
> *Location: interior/exterior*
> *Time: Day/Night*
> *Characters:*

Generally a full length film contains about 100-150 pages and the duration of a page is considered to be about a minute so. It is an approximate assessment of the duration of the film with the number of pages of the screenplay.

It is writer's responsibility to narrate the story with in the limited screen time therefore he must make his own first assessment of the *duration* of the film. If no control is applied on the duration from the beginning, there is a probability of the film duration going hay wire and then it becomes difficult and costly to reduce it later. If a character has to stay on the screen for just half a minute, he should not be given more than half of the page space in the script. Unnecessary details about him may be discarded and the scene should be written well within its stipulated time. The writer develops this sense of timing by practice. It is easier to assess the screen time in dialogue scenes by reading them along with the action involved in it. The notion of a page for a minute makes it clear that there are no long winding dialogues or speeches. The characters in a screenplay communicate with each other precisely and effectively in the bare minimum words and actions. Lengthy dialogue reflect unprofessionalism of a script writer. If there is need of lengthy statements and the dialogues, the paragraph should be broken in to pieces to look smaller.

The purpose of designing a page is to create reading interest. A *congested page* creates revulsion for reading. The blank space in a page not only looks good but it also makes it easier to read. One can study few of the advertisements in a news paper or a periodical to find out how they display their important messages or information, what type of fonts or colors they have selected, the placement of photos and sketches etc as the main objective of an advertisement design is to attract people to read it. There is no definite template for a page in the screenplay. It depends on the imagination and the creativity of a writer.

It may be remembered that no producer or director reads the script verbatim; they just scan it quickly. A congested page full of words and the dialogue doesn't appeal to them therefore it is important to place vital information about the scene in the central position where they can be seen easily and assess the effectiveness of the screenplay.

Page No.

Scene No.:

Name of the scene:

Time: Day/Night

Location: interior /Exterior

Characters:

Visuals :

Dialogues:

1.Normally in screenplay of a **fiction film** visuals and dialogues are written in normal style in different fonts and design, bold or italics to separate them with each other. The name of the character is mentioned before their dialogue to separate them with other characters in a conversation scene. After the vital information as mentioned earlier, the visual action is written and thereafter the dialogues corresponding to the action. Care should be taken to ensure that visuals are not distracted by the dialogues. Some writers write the entire visuals of the scene continuously thereafter they mention the dialogues of the scene .Though this may give an idea of visuals and dialogue separately but they miss out the action continuity. The reader has to make efforts to relate visuals with the corresponding dialogues therefore the best way is to write visuals and insert the dialogues of the characters in between in the continuity of action as and when they come in the scene. This makes the reader *'see'* the visual action while *'hearing'* the dialogues. This style also gives a different look to the page due to variations in the font size and style. A new scene should always be started from the next page for separation.

Film- Race   **Page No.**

Scene No.

Name of the scene: Marriage Registrar Introduction scene

Location: Marriage Registrars office,Day

Characters: Anil, Johnny and Lara

C.U. Display board of 'Registrar of Marriage'.Anil and Lara enter in the office of the registrar and move to the reception. Anil looks to his left.

Anil-'Mr. Max'

Receptionist- 'Please have seat. He will be here in five minutes'.

Anil- 'Thank you'

Johnny-(overheard) 'I am not a slave of your father. You have not obliged me if you have delivered children. I told you not to disturb me in my office. Ihave some reputation here, understand?'

Anil and Lara come towards the camera. Both of them come and stands near a table .Johnny enters from the back of the wall talking on his mobile.

Johnny-'will you complain to my father? You are my wife and remain like that. Shut up.'

Anil and Lara sit on the chairs. Johnny stops near his table talking on his phone.Johnny towards the camera. Back Shot-Anil and Lara are on their chairs. Anil and Lara sit in front.

Anil- 'sir, we....'

Johnny- (cuts in between) 'Have to marry...?'

Anil and Lara look at Johnny, Johnny is still talking on other phone, 'see these days boys and boys, girls and girls are getting married. What happened to you and which bug has bitten you?'

Johnny- 'I say instead of bringing a wife by marriage.... See don't mind...'

Anil and Lara look at Johnny

Johnny- 'instead of bringing a wife by marriage.'

Johnny- 'Buy a mobile and talk.'

Johnny- 'Mobile will not be angry. Don't mind sister...'

Johnny- 'You can keep it in silence but how will you silence your wife?'

Anil and Lara looks at him in desperation.

Johnny-'You can change its ring tone. I say, don't mind sister. Wife cannot be controlled, mobile can be in your grip.'

Anil and Lara look at him.

Johnny- 'you can keep it in your pocket... you can exchange it too, give the old and take the new one. wife is a chewing gum... wife is a chewing gum.'

Johnny offers them chewing gum , they pick one each.

Johnny- 'wife is a chewing gum... wife is a chewing gum.' **He too picks one and start chewing,**'Thank you. It is sweet in the beginning than continue masticating.'

Anil and Lara chew gum. Johnny gives them a form.

Johnny-' if you also want to chew for life time then fill up this form.'

Anil- 'sir, myself R.D.....'

Johnny- (cuts him) 'RD Burman, music director.'

Johnny- 'oh, I am a big fan of you. I love your music.

Anil- I am not that RD.'

Johnny is disturbed.

Johnny- 'Annnn...'

Anil- 'RD means Robert de Costa. Inspector Robert de Costa.'

Johnny is now afraid of him. He defends himself.

Johnny- 'My wife has sent you sir? We only have quarrels. I am not a criminal. I am a good man sometimes there is a misunderstanding.'

Anil and Lara are sitting in front of him.

Anil- 'I have come here for a case.'

2.While writing the screenplay for Non-fiction films the visuals and corresponding sounds/Narration should be clearly separated by vertically dividing the page in two columns, one for the visuals and other for the sounds or words (dialogues, monologue, narration or commentary). words should be written parallel to the visuals of the scene. ***Parallel formatting*** avoids confusion or ambiguity as the reader reads the visuals along with the words. This gives him fairly clear idea of what is coming on the screen with its corresponding sounds/words however there is no compulsion on the writer to write in similar fashion but he should make sure that whatever format he chooses, it should clearly define the visuals and the corresponding sounds. Unlike in fiction films, there is no clear demarcation of scenes in non fiction films so it is not necessary to change to a new page with a scene therefore they can be written one after another in numerical order.. Generally visuals on a particular location may be separated with chronological numbers in the description of scene column with corresponding 'words' in the parallel space in other half of the page .

In **parallel formatting** it is appropriate to write visuals and dialogues parallel to each other. In case of visuals taking more page space than the dialogues or vice versa, the place may be left empty and write next relevant visual or dialogue exactly opposite to it. This may provide some page relief even if the visuals or dialogues are longer, they would not look congested. It also makes it easy for the reader to relate particular visuals with relevant narration effortlessly. A proper page design and the look reflect writer's creativity, clarity of thoughts and imagination.

Some film makers of Nonfiction films in order to impress others by the thickness of the script, separate pages according to locations in chronological order. This leaves lot of undesired page space empty as there is nothing much to say about the scene at this stage. It also makes it bit uncomfortable for the reader to relate visuals and sound written/carried forward to the next page. As it is explained earlier, nonfiction in all respect is a short film in comparison to a fiction film so it is futile to prepare a script as thick as that of a fiction film. Such thickness caused by more number of pages may drive the reader away to read the full script due to the motion of *'one page one minute.'*

Generally a screenplay is a mix of prose and poetry that is combined with easy language and a poetry of visuals and emotions. The scene includes important information and fact about it along with emotional and visual action and reactions that's why a *screenplay* is called a combination of prose and poetry. A writer writes visual images in words to communicate and express emotions. The art of expressing through *words* does not come by birth but it is developed by practice and reading stories, novels, screenplays, plays, poetry and other literary works. This knowledge is acquired by the use of different *words* with different *meaning*, collection and recall of from the vocabulary stored in the memory. The writer must pick up most appropriate words to express his vision, imagination and emotions most effectively to recreate an effective response. The expressions should be received by others with the same interpretation and not otherwise.

Dos and Don'ts:

The screenplay is an experience for a writer and the reader to live the action and feel the emotions of the characters along with the images, locations and the sounds presented on the film screen therefore only those things should be included in the screenplay which do not dilute in this experience. Generally camera angles, special lighting for some special effects, back ground set, costumes etc are decided before the shoots in consultation with the writer, director, cameraman, art director and other concerned crew members so such details are not required in the screenplay however if it is specifically required to create a particular effect by giving details of camera angles, special lighting, color scheme, special sound effects, movement of characters and property in the scene, may be provided but they should not disturb the flow of reading.

The development of a Screenplay is undertaken in following steps such as-

1. *The Beginning: Introduction-* In the first step, the problem and the characters are introduced in which various dimensions and contradictions of the issues are brought to the notice of the audience. The objective of this introduction is to make people start thinking about the solution but it is neither to make them aware of the issue or bring them on the same wavelength as that of the characters nor to instigate them to chase for an answer. The resolution of the problem should be peeled out in layers gradually and not at a time. The *beginning* and the *built up* should not take more than 1/6th of the total time.

Pakeeza is one of many mile stones in the history of Indian cinema. Directed by *Kamal Amrohi* the film has been widely appreciated for its poetic and punchy dialogues, emotional performances, cinematography and the screenplay in which special attention had been paid to the Period, situations, country, Physical and panoramic locations.

Scene no: 1

Name of the scene: Introduction scene

Time: Night

Location: Nargis's brothel, Road.

Crane shot, Nargis is dancing in her dance hall. Shahab enters from the main entrance in to the hall.

Monologue: 'This is Nargis, younger sister of Nawab Jaan whose husky voice and ankle bells have made the world crazy. Many hearts fall on her feet but she continues to dance without caring for them.'   (Flash back)

'Who is this who made her stop for a moment and pale? Her soul cries for mercy saying, *'Shahab, take me away from here.'*

This roaring passion of love is expressed through his eyes ensures her to trust him, ' *Yes Nargis, I will not let this candle melt in these infamous gatherings. I will come soon to take you away from this hell.'(Flash back ends)*

Scene 2.-

Crane shot, a horse cart is moving on a lonely road. Shahab sits inside. The horse cart stops beneath the balcony of a mansion where Nargis waits for him. She steps down from her balcony to meet him and both of them return back in the horse cart.

Monologue continues- At last the promised night that was long awaited by Nargis standing on the windows of her dreams, has arrived.

Cut to..

Scene 3-

Nargis is in the arms of Shahab. They move in the tonga.

Shahab: 'Nargis....Najjo , say something.'

Nargis: 'Shahab, are you really there?'

Shahab: 'Of course Najjo.'

Nargis: ' and I am there with you?'

Shahab: 'Yes Najjo. You are with me.'

Nargis: 'and you are taking me to your home? Your perfect white house is on a hill and I am wearing red wedding dress, getting out of the closed litter to step in the verandah of your house.'

The cart stops and Shahab and Nargis get down in front of a palatial house.

Cut to...

Scene No.: 4

Name of the scene: Reprimand scene

Time: Night

Location: Palatial House of Jalaluddine.

Shahab's father Jalaluddine stands with his family. His younger son Salim runs towards Shahab but is stopped by Jalaluddine.

Salim: 'Chacha jani...chacha jani.'

Jalal: 'stop'

Shahab and Nargis are scared . Jalal moves towards them. They step back a little. Jalal chides him .

Jalal: 'How did you dare to marry and bring a prostitute to this house?'

Shahab: 'Baba, you cannot use such indignified words for her. She is my love and now is the daughter in law of this family.'

Jalal: 'Shut up, you cannot give such common abuse to my family. She is not our daughter in law but she is your crime.'

Hearing Jalal's acrimonious words Nargis runs out with her ears closed. Shahab stands stunned. Nargis stops the Horse cart that is about to return.

Nargis: 'Allah: The cart wait... Wait.'

The cart man: 'where you go, Bibiji?'

Nargis: 'Take me to some cremation ground.'

She gets in to it to be lost in the dark.

Cut to...

Scene No.: 5

Name of the scene: Nargis in crematorium.

Time : Night

Location: Cremation ground

The cart stops at the entrance of a crematorium. Nargis gets down and asks the cart to return. The cart turns back and she looks at it moving away.

Monologue: 'Poor Nargis now stands alone in a terrible forest. Her wishes and dreams leave her helpless.'

There cannot be a better introduction of a story , a film or a character than this one. Dancing on the classical beats of a 'Thumri', Nargis, the main female protagonist, hypnotizes her audience hiding a tempest within. The introduction reflects her background, profession and her emotional state. She is never tired of waiting for her love Shahab. When her wait comes to an end and he actually arrives to take her, she is not able to believe her senses. She continues to feel as if she is in a trance that's why being in his arms, she repeats her questions to ensure that it is indeed he who has taken her in arms on the way to his home. .After being convinced, she gets another shock when she is insulted and humiliated by his father Jalaluddin who denies her an identity. Nargis, who left her profession for a dignified life, is almost dead on this insult therefore what a better place could be there for a dead than a cremation ground so she leaves to die a living death. Ordinarily this could only be an end but this is the beginning of the tale of Nargis. This leaves the audience struggling till end to find a culmination of the story.

The introduction in the monologues gets her sympathy from the audience from the beginning and their endorsement of her relationship with Shahab. When Jalal refuses to accept her and calls her a prostitute instead of his daughter in law , her dreams are shattered. This shock is no less painful to the audience as it is to her. While this pain and sympathy makes her a martyr, the rejection by Jalal builds up anger for him. Her trauma brings her close to audience from where her story moves further.

A mix of commentary and dialogues is a unique experiment in communication. With so much of variation in the story and the screen play, one is floored by an extraordinary beginning of the film. This gives impetus for more sensitive and emotional entertainment that continues till the end. The time of the event i.e. the night combined with effects of horse hoofing and cart moving, chiming of ankle bells on the Thumri music and the location creates an unenviable ambience of a red light area with back ground narration introducing the character escalates the interest in the beginning itself. The imaginative choice of place of event, location and the cremation ground is an example of innovation.

The Middle:

Once an interesting beginning is written, the writer moves towards the *middle* of the story. The characters in the story are interlinked to pave the way for different incidents, events and the experiences to create different emotions, conflicts and confrontation, curiosity while giving an identity to each of them. They behave differently in different situations to endorse their identity. Their behavior is a tool to create twists and turns in the events providing entertainment, emotional response and romanticism to keep viewers engrossed throughout the film. In the *middle* it is not important that a specific character always remains a protagonist or an antagonist. They behave differently in different situations as we do in different circumstances. In a particular situation an antagonist may behave like a puritan or a protagonist or a hero may behave negatively. The opinion of a character undergoes variations and modification in his behavioral that results in conflicts and twists, change in relationship, events and circumstances etc make the story interesting and engrossing however they all move towards a predefined goal of the story.

The Goal:

Most of the space in a screen play is consumed by the *middle* of the story that is about 60% in terms of total screen time therefore it is writer's responsibility to develop this segment as interesting as possible. In this pursuit, the characterization of the main characters should be very powerful in terms of their struggle, the clarity of *goal* to be accomplished. We have discussed in **setting of Goals** earlier, every character must have a purpose and an objective to achieve in the end.

Every character has two objectives-

1. **Plot Objective:** These are the goals set in story that are to be achieved by the characters in material form by their hard work such as becoming a doctor or an engineer, winning a race, getting married, serving the parents or be an antagonist, commit crimes, rape and torturing others etc.

2. **Personal objective:** It is decided by the character's courage, merits and physical strength to achieve them. These goals may also be termed as *'ambitions'* or *'desires'*. He stakes his mental, physical and monetary powers to accomplish them. His desires and ambitions can vary from being rich to becoming a leader, to be famous or winning Olympics, receiving national or international honors etc. such ambitions are the *inner voices* coming from the soul/conscience that decide *personal objective* of an individual.

The Goals in a scene:
1. *The transition (Total or partial)*
2. *Information or introduction of the story or characters*
3. *Mental state, psychological or emotional response*
4. *The change*
5. *Any co incidence.*

Scene No.
Time: Day
Location: Prison
Characters: Jai, Veeru, Two Jailers, constable , Thakur Baldev Singh

1. Jai and Veeru are breaking stones inside the prison. Two Jailors talk about them.
First jailor: 'I was searching for these two. When will their conviction be over?'
Second Jailor: Next month on 18th.

Time Lapse

Location: Exterior prison.

2.Jai and Veeru come out of the prison gate. Veeru demands a Bidi from the constable. He gives him a cigarette and points him towards Thakur who stands to wait for them. Jai and Veeru come to him.
Veeru: 'Oh Inspector, who is that you came to see him off today to jail?'
Thakur: 'Now I am not an inspector . I am only Thakur Baldev Singh.'
Jai: 'Have you denounced playing with dangers, Thakur?'
Thakur: 'If you are so proud of your strength and bravery, will you do a job for me?'
Veeru: 'We work only for money.'
Thakur: 'How much money do you want...twenty thousand rupees....?'
Jai: 'What is the job?'

Thakur: 'If you are brave, why should it bother you. Money-whatever you want and work –whatever I say. You have to nab Gabbar Singh.'

Jai and Veeru sit on the ground while Thakur stands nearby. Veeru is shocked to hear about catching Gabbar.

Veeru: 'Gabber Singh that dreaded dacoit? I have heard that Police has announced some reward on his head.'

Thakur: 'It is fifty thousand rupees...dead or alive. You have to catch him for me alive.'

Veeru: 'We have to catch him that too alive. Thakur sahib, Gabbar Singh is not a lamb to just hold him.'

Thakur: 'I know that job is difficult but no one will give you this much of money for a simple job.'

Veeru: 'Ok, if somehow we catch him with a stake of our life. You want us to hand him over to you only for twenty thousand rupees and you earn fifty thousand for nothing that too sitting at home?'

Thakur: 'You will be paid that reward too. I only need Gabbar

Jai: 'Is it an old enmity?'

Thakur: 'It is not your business.'

Jai: 'then do we ask something else? You consider us as thieves and criminals then why did you select us to grab a dacoit.?'

Thakur: 'Because only iron can cut another iron.' **Thakur asks Ramlal to pay five thousand rupees to them. Ramlal takes out the money and gives it to Thakur.** 'Take this five thousand now, next five when you come to Ramgarh. Rest after you finish the job.'

Jai and Veeru look at the money.Jai takes out a coin from his pocket to toss. Jai removes his hand from the coin , it is head.

Veeru: 'Partner, what does it say...?'

Jai: 'Head we go.'

Thakur Baldev Singh of the film *'Sholey'* looks out for Gabbar Singh, a dreaded and insensitive dacoit or one can say that he is a wolf in the garb of a man. It is very difficult to catch him as he always hides in terrains. He is confronted by convicted criminals Jai and Veeru when he attacks a goods train that carries them after arrest by Police Inspector Thakur Baldev Singh. Taking advantage of the situation, they could have easily escaped but Jai and Veeru fight with Gabbar gang to the hilt to save Thakur. The Gabbar gang runs away. Thakur, impressed by their honesty and bravery, is never able to forget them. When the time comes to nab or take revenge with Gabbar, Thakur remembers these brave hearts. He believes only an iron can cut another iron so Jai and Veeru only could nab him. Thakur he has only one *desire,* to take revenge with Gabbar after he leaves his job in police,. He roams around many jails to find out whereabouts of Jai and Veeru. He ultimately he gets them and decides a *goal* for them that is *'Nab Gabbar Singh…that too alive.'* It is not only a goal but a problem too because even the police failed to arrest him so far even after declaration of a reward of fifty thousand rupees on his head. It is a vicious circle and they don't know how to get in and out of it safely. It is a challenge for Jai and Veeru which they accept thus the *goal* of the story is decided in this scene. *'Sholey'* narrates the struggle of Jai and Veeru to nab Gabbar for Thakur braving many challenges, failures and traumatic experiences but in the end they are successful to nab him and Thakur intimidates him for all his sins thus achieving objective that has been set for them in the story.. In this process Jai and Veeru adapt to transform from their criminal past.

It is explained earlier that the audience continue to relate with the characters and the events in search of a possible resolution. This sometimes comes in conflict with writer's vision. If they meet at a point, there is a risk of diminishing interest and if there is too much of conflict between them, it may be disturbing. Walking on this tight rope between him and the audience, the writer has to create a fine balance between his imagination and audience's expectation without losing element of *curiosity and entertainment.* This is a challenge that seems to be simple to surmount but it is not so. Writer must know that his unbridled flight of imagination without conviction, may not go down the throat of people therefore his success depends on his successful accomplishment of the' *middle'* that has a very important place in the story.

One of the most memorable examples the *middle* is extracted from Vijay Anand's film *'Guide'* that is an adaptation of a novel of the same name authored by *RK Narain.* Raju, the protagonist of the film is released from the prison after completion of his conviction in a criminal case. He takes shelter in a temple where people mistake him as a *Saint'.* This mistaken identity forces him to become a saint in reality.

Scene No.

Time:

Location: Temple

Characters: Raju, Makkhan, crowd

Raju comes out of the temple where people and his friend Makkhan stand with folded hands They throw their sticks. .

People with their heads down chant for 'swami..swami...'

Crowd : (chanting)'Swamy ji...swami ji...swamiji.

Makhan: (to Raju) swami ji, riots have stopped after you talked to them.

Raju: 'what did you tell them?'

Makkhan:'what ever you told me to tell them.'

Raju: 'what did I say?'

Makkhan: 'That you will sacrifice your life.'

Raju: 'yah..'

Makkhan: 'and you will stop eating...'

Raju: 'till when?'

Makkhan:' for twelve days'.

Raju: 'I said it?'

Makkhan: 'no.. not you... no... me...They have interpreted as, if you fast, there will be rain.'

Raju: 'Bhola, come with me.'

Raju, Makkhan and Bhola move inside the temple..

Bhola: 'Raju, what is it happening?'

Raju thinks for a while. People outside the temple make a noise for swami.

Bhola: 'swamiji…'

Raju: 'you all have some misunderstanding. I never said that I am a swami or a saint. Even if I would have been a swami, do you think it will rain if I fast.?'

Bhola: ' yes.'

Raju: 'No. It all happens only is fiction that too in children's' stories. Talk to these   villagers and try to make them understand. I only threatened th**Bhola:** 'Yah…'

Raju: 'since now it is over, you return back to your homes and send something for me to eat. I am dying with hunger.' **Bhola looks at him with eyes wide opened.** 'Why are you staring me with wide eyes?'

Bhola realizing his mistake falls down to his feet.

Bhola: 'swamiji…swamiji, please have pity on us. accept that I have committed a crime but what a man cannot do when there is hunger. Nothing has been cooked in my house for two days. Children are crying for food. My wife has high fever. Our cow too lost her breath last night every home in the village has the same situation swamiji. Now you can only do something.'

Bhola is begging to help them on his feet. Raju looks at him.

Raju: 'are you mad? What can I do/'

Bhola: 'swamiji…swamiji, our voice cannot reach there but your prayers will not be unrewarded by God. If you fast, I am sure,everybody in the village will be with you. It has been decided that people will go on relay fasting . somebody for two days and some one for four days. Some people will stop eating once in a daySwami ji ...please help us ... we will be doomed.'

Raju helps Bhola to get up from his feet. He is in tears.

Raju: 'why only twelve days... I will last forever if it helps you but I am not the person you understand me to be. I am a simple Guide. I have been to jail in connection with a girl.'

Bhola: 'Raju...'

Raju: 'Yes.. Jail. If you hear my past story you will know that there is no difference between you and me. I too have weaknesses... I too have troubled people... spoken lies... behaved shrewdly...I have invited bad luck for me and other people.'

Outside of the temple two of the villagers are interacting with each other.

First: 'Its long brother is inside.'

Second: 'Don't know.. what is happening there.' **Raju and Bhola are talking inside the temple.**

Raju: 'I have been on the run for more than a year hiding myself from others. When I took shelter in this temple, you mistook me as a swami. It is true that I denounced everything. You may think that I am a fraud... you may hate me but it is very important for me to tell you the truth.'

People wait for Raju outside the temple. Bhola bows down his head again to his feet.

Bhola: 'swamiji...swamiji...'another man calls him ,'Swami ji...' **villagers barge in the temple and surround him.**

Bhola: 'The path of knowledge is very tardy and difficult. Balmiki became a great saint after indulging in robbery. Tulsidas became a Godman after the rebuff from his wife. Now my faith has become stronger and I am sure that after twelve days of your prayers and meditation , the voice that will come out of your soul will tear the sky and Gods will be compelled to quench the thirst of the earth by shedding tears.'

Raju starts fasting for twelve days. Villagers continue to pray and sing spiritual discourses. Raju is strangled with hunger. He feels greedy when sees eatables and fruits but he cannot eat anything in the presence of villagers.

In the above mentioned scene from the film *'Guide',* it is observed how a person has to accept and adapt certain situations. He has to become something which he is not; he has to do something which he does not want to do. It happens many times in our life when we are victim of circumstances. Raju has faced the similar situations, he has been a convicted criminal who while takes shelter in a temple of a remote village which is facing conditions of a severe draught. People start dying with no trace of rain in the near future. The draught results in accute shortage of eatables and other essentials. Hoarding of essential commodities leads to riots and loots. Raju cannot tolerate such chaos so he threatens people that he will kill himself if riots do not stop. The news spreads like wild fire in the village, riots stop. Consequently people start worshipping Raju as a **saint.** They wish him to go for a twelve day's fast to bring rains in the area. It is an unexpected twist of the events he is not prepared for. People make him what he is not. They develop faith in his divine powers which he never possessed. In such a critical situation, betraying faith of innocent people would not have been proper. The conflict between him and the villagers poses a great challenge. It is not possible for him to fast for twelve days . Even if he does it and it does not rain, people would lose faith in spirituality and the God. Raju swings between the his life and people's faith on him. He sees an end of his life in both the circumstances, he could die during a long fast or he would be beaten to death if it does not rain after the fast. Caught in a cobweb, he is forced to take a decision either way. He has only two options either he runs away from this situation or he accepts what people want him to do. Ultimately he takes a chance to accept the later and go for fasting.

In the *middle* such critical moments and catharsis of a character that completely changes his personality, his faith and beliefs and his ideology provides an unexpected twist in the story that is not only convincing but natural that people can relate with them. It creates a situation that keeps the audience in toes till the end. Similar situations are faced by us very often that prompt us to change our ideology and the decisions.

Change and the growth:

Change is the only thing that is constant and with every change life moves on. It is also true in a story where situations and the characters keep on changing during the course of time. Any event and the growth of a character cannot take place instantly but it comes in a systematic manner in a definite chronology such as a seed is sown, it becomes a plant, then sprouting, petals come out and the flowers bloom. A flower cannot bloom instantly after the seeding. Similarly the development of a situation , character and the object cannot be instant. This change has to come gradually to pave the way for their automatic development . The change take place in physical, mental, natural and also social planes when relationships between the characters are also affected and take a new shape. The *time* too has its contribution and the importance. The time that involves these changes on screen is called *'screen time'*. It can be reduced or increased as required in the story to affect the speed of the events or the actions on the screen.

Normal movement of a story is generally *forward* one. It is important to maintain the interest in the narration. Audience should always be engaged to presume about **what next** however every event or development should take place only after establishing its cause, the purpose and its relevance with previous and the subsequent scene to avoid it appearing suddenly. No event or development should be in isolation otherwise it will break the smooth flow of the narration.

Following training scene from a very successful film *'Aankhen'*, is one of the best examples of change and the development of the story. Rajput , a banker who has been terminated from his job, decides to take revenge with his bank without being seen and held responsible for his action or the plan. He plans to loot a bank with the support of blinds to make it unbelievable. He compels Neha, a teacher for blinds, to train three blind men Vishwas, Arjun and Illiyas to execute his plan. He kidnaps her brother Rahul to blackmail her to accept the job. Neha agrees to comply with his orders. From this point the process of change and the development of various characters and events unfolds to accomplish an unbelievable task.

Scene No.

Time:

Location: Rajput's Mansion

Characters: Rajput, Vishwas, Illiyas, Arjun, Neha.

Neha demonstrates the layout of the bank through a model to the three blinds Arjun, Vishwas and Illiyas. Rajput enters in the room to observe.

Neha : 'you are seeing an almost identical model of the head office of the bank. It has lot of similarities with the original bank. I will explain the details of this lay out to you and....'

Arjun: 'But how it is possible Neha?'

Illiyas: ' Interruption...a bad omen...'

Arjun: 'The moment they come to know that we are blind, they....'

Neha: 'if only they know at all. Arjun, you will behave like a normal man and not like a blind man. After the robbery only you will know that you can't see. Other will think that you can see well.'

Arjun: 'then why you don't get it done through normal men?'

Illiyas: ' Interuupted again, this bad omen... Neha, why don't you kill him?'

Vishwas: 'Arjun is right Neha. Why have you selected us for this work...why we?'

Neha: 'because what you have, those who can see, don't have, that is your blindness Vishwas. You are perfect. If anyone, by chance suspects you after the robbery, you just have to prove that you are completely blind. Who will believe that three blinds can rob a bank in broad day light? Believe me, your weakness is your biggest strength. Now let us go through the layout of the bank with its geography, I mean chairs, dimensions, angles, placement of things. You have to touch and feel everything and make a sketch in you mind. Shall we start?'

Arjun, Vishwas and illiyas come forward. Neha and Rajput look at them. Illiyas fall down.

Arjun: 'who has fallen...?'

Illiyas: 'Basterd it's my teeth... blind and fool... two in one. Are you playing balls on the floor?'

Arjun: 'No I was checking the floor.'

Illiyas: 'are you going to walk on your hands or your legs?' **Neha and Rajput enjoy their conversation.**

Arjun: 'I will strangulate you and say sorry.'

Illiyas: 'You will strangulate me..me?'

Arjun: 'single handedly."

Illiyas: 'Ok well that too single handedly?'

Arjun: 'Do I show you how I will do it?'

Illiyas: 'Hey…hey.. go away. who will kiss your wife. I will kiss my coca cola that too after taking a chewing gum. Once I get fifty lakh, I will marry my coca cola.'

Arjun: 'Then do it…'

Illiyas: 'O Neha …leave this blind man and give me training.'

Dissolve

Neha is busy training the blinds.

Illiyas: 'stop… stop. What is this. Daily you want me to do left right left right after tying my legs with a rope.''

Arjun: 'in fact you mouth should also be tied up with a rope. Get up and practice.'

Illiyas: 'that's what I am doing for four days. My legs are stiff even when I untie the rope in the night. It hangs like a flying machine when I sleep, what is the use yaar.?'

Vishwas: 'If we can not match our steps how the plan will work. Neha will say-move three steps forward' and I will be here, Arjun there and you god knows, where will you be. Now Listen, our steps will work as our eyes in the bank therefore the distance between our steps has to be the same …understand?'

Arjun, Vishwas and Iliiyas are busy practicing their steps.

Arjun: 'I understood the wise man that's why Neha has told us to walk with tied up legs.'

Illiyas: 'yes I know. Neha has told ."

Arjun: 'Now get up soon.'

Illiyas: 'Neha has said. Neha...Neha...Neha...yes to her and no to me...Neha..."

Every character is given a distinct identity In this scene. Illiyas is a happy go lucky careless person. He wants to live every moment lively and creates the same atmosphere for his friends too while the issue they are working for is a serious one. He knows that it is not easy to live the life of blind so he tries to make it as enjoyable as he can. His interaction with his friends makes the scene very interesting. On the other hand, Vishwas is a serious person who talks less and takes everything seriously. Arjun is young man who behaves rashly like any person of his age. Neha's presence in the scene creates a romantic angle for Arjun who loves her silently. All these characters determine the direction of the further development and change in their behavior that will decide if the robbery plan will be successful or not. Every character takes shape in the forth coming scenes on this premise.

Action and Reaction:

We are taught in our schools that when a ball is hit on a wall, it bounces back with the same force. There is always a reaction of an action and same is important to dramatize a scene. The reaction generates confrontation, conflict and hurdles. If there is no reaction, the action will be simple and ineffective that may fail to invite attention. During a conflict and confrontation, the powerful will be a victor and achieve his goal while the weak will break out but still may continue to fight for the cause till he is rendered completely helpless.

Dramatization:

It is not necessary to have *dramatic moments* in every action and reaction however it depends on the importance of the event or the character that brings some twists in the story. If there is more confrontation there will be more drama. If there are few dramatic moments in routine activities, there will be less confrontation. Short and common actions help the story move forward as every scene may not be powerful and dramatic. The writer should create as many hurdles and conflicts between situations and the characters as he can. Such conflicts display and highlight personal strength, mental state, psychological attitudes, the sincerity and objective of the characters. Nothing should happen easily on its own , by luck or miraculously. The scene construction must be based on the actions and reactions, events and accidents in the situations carefully crafted by the writer.

Dramatization is not meant to be starting from the beginning to the middle and the end of the scene. The writer may include some *'information'* regarding a situation or a confrontation, passed on by someone at any point of time during the scene that is sufficient to create further conflicts of interest. A new character in relationship with others can also be introduced anytime if situation so demands. This new character provides links and alerts about forthcoming conflicts. A scene in a screen play is like heart in a body that has emotions and sentiments to move people further along with the story.

In the development of scenes there is lot of importance given to the *'reason'* or the *'cause'*. It can also be called *'the purpose'*. Every action or the event in a scene should have some purpose. A scene included without purpose is not only week but is also a hindrance in the flow. There is no formula to determine the objective therefore writer must work on the scene with proper logic, reasons and the purpose when he divides and devises a scene . Every scene in a script functions like a staircase where the story should move upward step by step heightening the anxiety and interest of the audience in every next scene. Any step that is week or unwanted may pose a danger of diminishing interest .

A scene or an event that takes place in a simple and straight manner without upheavals may not generate an interest but if it is accomplished with lot of sufferings and struggles, hurdles and hopes, it not only achieve its purpose interestingly but also dramatizes the whole action. It creates more interest and anxiety in the audience to be more involved in actions and events as a whole. Such dramatization makes a scene far more effective and entertaining than its simple and easy outcome. *Example*:

Film- 'Ankhen'

Scene No.. ..　　　　　　**Time: Day**

Location: Bank

Characters:　　Rajput, Iliyas, Vishwas, Delnaaz, Prem, Sailesh, Arjun　and others.

People step down on the stairs to gather in a hall. Arjun stands with his gun pointing at others. Iliyas also holds a gun. People are scared. The bank is being robbed. Vishwas stops someone running away breaking the alarm circuit to close

the doors. Delnaaz and Prem too join him. Sailesh tries to abscond when Arjun and Vishwas fire at him.

Rajput: Don't fire please don't fire.

Vishwas: 'Number one, kill everyone.

Iliyas: 'Yes, if anyone dares to move I will take out his eyeballs and her too.'

Vishwas: 'will you...?'

Delnaaz: 'who... me...?'

Vishwas: 'Yes, you.. You do it. I will count up to ten. You go down and return with the jeweler box. Keep that on this red handkerchief.

Delnaaz: Please count up to twenty. The box is very heavy.'

Rajput: 'Do as I say. Hurry up.'

Prem: 'Sir, If Delnaaz says it is heavy it must be true."

Viswas: 'Then you to go with her . One...two...three...fore.. five.. six....'

Rajput: Sailesh, what are you doing. Don't run in front of enquiry counters.'
Sailesh comes to Iliyas and points his gun to his mouth. Vishwas and Arjun too point their gun at him.

Sailesh: 'a...a...a...'

Vishwas: ' No one will move. We have told you .'

Sailesh: 'sorry... sorry.'

Iliyas: 'Do you think yourself too wise...?'

Sailesh: Sorry. It is done by mistake.'

Iliyas: 'Ok, what were you doing here bastered?'

Sailesh: I was going to check the vehicle.'

Iliyas: 'Vehicle... do I clear the waist from your carburetor?'

Sailesh: 'I am the only son of my father.'

Iliyas: 'What? Do you have only one father.? Tell me.'

Sailesh: ' Only one mother and only one father.'

Iliyas: ' only one father and one mother. Behaving wise to me. Come open your mouth.'

Sailesh: 'a...a...'.

Iliyas: 'open your mouth.'

Sailesh: 'aaa.aaa.'

Iliyas: ' Yes, now keep it in your mouth like a tooth brush. (The gun drops out of his mouth but Iliyas could not see it. He hears Sailesh and looks at the gun. Now what has dropped down.. what is it. He tells Sailesh to put the gun in his mouth again.)

Sailesh: ' Gun.'

Iliyas asks him to open his mouth threatening.

Iliyas: 'Pick it up and put it back in to the mouth.'

Sailesh : 'Open your mouth.'

Iliyas: ' oh keep it in your mouth and not mine. (Sailesh keep the gun in to his mouth)Correct. Now keep standing here like this. People are looking at you and your new tooth brush.'Veiko vajradanti.'

Vishwas counts: 'Fourteen...fifteen...sixteen..seventeen..

Delnaaz and Prem return back with the jeweler box. Vishwas and Iliyas move Rajput and Sailesh at gun point. Vishwas pushes Rajput and the trio closes the shutter. Rajput and others come to the shutter. Keep it there on the red cloth.

Rajput begs him: 'see this is our customers' jeweler. Please don't take it.'

Vishwas: 'Number three. Take this box and go out.'

Rajput: 'See. Listen to me. You cannot sell this jewelry in the market.'

Vishwas: ' You shut up and keep quiet.'

Rajput: 'Please accept what I say.'

Iliyas: You shut up.'

Rajput: 'we can sit to gather and negotiate quietly.'

Vishwas :' You will not say anything.'

Rajput : we can talk.... Talk reasonably...we can. Please listen to me...You can't...'

Vishwas: 'I say you shut your mouth.'

Rajput: 'You are committing a crime. This jewelry...'

Vishwas shouts: 'shut up.'

Rajput: ' where are you taking it/ see. Just look at me.'

Vishwas: Number three...'

Rajput: 'See, you can't escape. I am telling you please...'

Vishwas: Number one....'

Rajput: 'yes... yes...'

Iliyas: ok...ok...'

Vishwas: 'are you ready...?'

Rajput: Yes...

Iliyas: yaa...uuu...'

Rajput: oye...'

Vishwas: 'where is the car?'

Sailesh: 'It is there... there.' Vishwas,

Arjun and Iliyas get in to the jeep. There comes a security van. Iliyas tells the driver to take the vehicle to Byculla station.

Iliyas: take the car to the Byculla station quickly.'

Arjun: 'Who is it....'

Vishwas :sit down   first. I will tell you everything. Now do it and move.'(everyone looks at them from the other side of the shutter.)

Sailesh: 'Ok sir.'

Iliyas: 'are you blind. Do you drive the car with jerks?

Arjun: 'Ooh…'

Iliyas: 'Put the gear…'

The jeep runs on the road to Byculla.

The plan to rob a bank by a trio of blind persons Arjun, Vishwas and Iliyas keeps the audience in tenterhooks till the end of the film. It keeps the curiosity factor alive in every passing frame. The plan to execute a bank robbery by a group of three blind men without letting anyone know of their blindness is not only inconceivable but also unbelievable. It is sufficient to keep their interest ever rising. People know that robbers are blind and this fact is intermittently brought to the notice by emphasizing their mistaken actions such as mouth opening by Sailesh and falling of the gun without being seen by Iliyas and others as a reminder of their disability. Similarly Vishwas and Arjun continue committing silly mistakes which are noticed by the audience but not by those present in the Bank. The confusion created by tiny mistakes of these blind men keep audience entangled with the robbery plan for which they are not sure that would really be successful.

Rajput is the main anchor who double crosses and pretends to be with the bank staff in their critical hours as well as coordinates bank robbery with the trio. He is motivated to execute it to take revenge with the Bank. He conceives a unique and foolproof plan to execute it with the help of blind people to keep everyone guessing. No one would ever think of a robbery by blind men who are his main accomplices. The film contains variety of actions to create curious moments throughout the film moving inch by inch to its climax. During the act of robbery the trio does not lose its originality and its normal behavior. Humorous dispositions of Iliyas help release some stressful moments. The struggle of bank officials to prevent this robbery and brutal confrontation of robbers create some trying situations, helplessness and scare among bankers and the audience with their realistic performances. At no point of time it gives an impression except to the audience that the robbery is carried out by blind people and being coordinated by Rajput. The film in general and this scene in particular is a fine example of the dramatization of an action. The imaginative transformation to a dramatic action looks far more real than contrived one.

The outcome of a real action like a cricket , football match or a chase scene itself is enough to create curiosity as it is not planned nor executed in a planned manner. The same is maintained in the film though the unbelievable act that looks real when executed. so people are unable to guess it's outcome, similar to that of a police chasing a thief where nobody knows if the thief would be caught. With this logic, it can be surmised that there are two types of action sequences one which are planned and other which are not therefore the writer must take care to see that an unplanned action scene does not look planned one or vice versa because the behavior of the characters in both the case will be different and the outcome uncertain. This keeps the curiosity mounting till the end that leads to climax.

Action Scene:

If there is an action there is bound to be a reaction. This reaction is an important element of dramatization. The reaction can result in the form of a conflict, confrontation and hurdles in meeting an objective. If there is no reaction the action will be completed unchallenged and the action may pass on unnoticed. In the event of confrontation the person who is more powerful will be a winner, the week may surrender however he may still continue with his efforts to meet his objective. It is not important that every action and reaction has a dramatic movement, it depends on the character or a specific situation that causes the tightening of a knot in the story. If struggle is intense it will be more dramatic but small incidences may not result in intense reaction to dramatize a scene. Such small incidents push up the scene forward. The writer may have to create many hurdles and hindrances for an intense confrontation. Such situations and the characters display their mental, physical, personal traits, their objective and their dedication to their cause. Nothing happens in a scene automatically or by destiny. The writer has to create such actions, reactions, events and accidents with his vision and imagination.

It is also not necessary that every beginning, middle or the end of a scene is dramatic. Some characters and situations are created to provide certain information which can be included anywhere in the scene as required . A new character should be properly introduced to determine his relevance, relations with other characters and his role to affect future events. He works as a warning signal or an indicator of further incidents. A scene in the screenplay conveys emotions, characters and the content of the story to the audience in totality; missing out something important during the course may creates a break.

Comedy scene:

Comedy is one of the most entertaining parts in the *middle* of the story. It gives relief to the viewers after an intense emotional outburst or after a fierce confrontation. The comedy so far has been treated in isolation where comedy generally has no direct relevance with the story. The comedy scenes are conceived as additional anecdotes in the film to give relief to the audience when the tension has been at its peak. There are professional comedy actors who have specialization in the antics and entertaining mannerism. *Charlie Chaplin* is considered to be the *king of comedy*. Some characters and actions have inherent quality to entertain and make people laugh but they may not have any relevance to the story. Such scenes are inserted to entertain the audience and sell the film. With the international expose of cinema and television programs the audience now has not only become wiser but also enlightened therefore such comic inserts don't entice them. The writer therefore must integrate the comedy in the screenplay in such a way that it becomes part of the story. He should create comedy characters and the situations that bring relief after a heightened tension but also such situations don't break the flow of the narrative.

It is normal practice for comedy actors to conceive their own dialogues and actions in consultation with director. The comedy actors know what mannerism and dialogue would make their audience burst in to peel of laughter. Similar is the case with those who play negative characters who conceive their own acts to give a new dimension to their role. The comedy scene of the film *'Sholey'* (1973) directed by *Ramesh Sippy* is still fresh in the memories of cinema lovers whether it is the prison scene in which Jailor repeats his dialogues, **'I am a jailor of colonial times'** or **'My name is Soorma Bhopali'** still make people jump on their seats with laughter.

Film –Sholey
Scene No.
Location: Outdoor, Prison, Time: Day
Characters: Jai, Veeru, Jailor, Warden, Police and other prisoners.

In the open space of the prison Jai and Veeru with prisoners stand in queue for a routine parade. Jailor enters with his police constables for an inspection.

Warden: 'Attention'.
Veeru: 'Chacha, when the parade will start...?'
Chacha: It is your first day today. You will come to know everything. The jailor is an obnoxious man.
Jai: 'He is coming.'
Jailor: 'Attention...'. **Jai and Veeru don't care for his order. Jailor gets annoyed.**
Jailor: 'I said –attention.'
Police: 'Sir, they are already in attention.'
Jailor: 'I know... I know... I know. Everybody listen me with open ears. Whatever has been happening in this jail will not happen till I am here... will never happen, No...no...no. I am a jailor of colonial times. I am not like other jailors of today who worry to reform prisoners. Ha...ha...ha...' **Jailor looks at Jai and Veeru and continues,** 'I know very well that you can never

improve. If I could not change how you can change...ayn? I know people don't like me that's why I am transferred within few days from everywhere but in spite of so many transfers I have not improved, so remember and don't think that whatever you do, I will have no inkling about it. My spies are spread all over the premises. I get the report of every moment. Even a pigeon cannot enter here.' **A pigeon hits the eyes of the jailor and flies away. Jailor is shocked,**' o..o...o. what is it?'

Police: 'Sir. The pigeon.'

Jailor: 'What...?

Police: 'Pigeon...'

Jailor: 'something has fallen in my eyes. Take it out... leave it. It is enough for the day.. Now you all can go. Leave...leave.'

In this scene the comedy is not created by cheap antics but a comic situation is created by dialogues, personality of the character, his costumes, unique dialogue delivery, and mannerism. The clone of Hitler reflects the toughness of the jailor on one hand but on the other his careless persona, dialogues and actions reflect hollowness of this character. This contrast creates a situational comedy. Jailor is one of the main characters integrated in the story thus he becomes an integral part of the scene .The scene is not enforced but has an important place in the script.

The Climax:

It is the responsibility of a writer to create situations and circumstances in such a way that audience is constantly engaged in twists one after another till the end. There are many critical points in the course which are resolved in due course. more complexities generate more curiosity leading to final crisis or the climax. The climax has to be resolved by main characters. This resolution generally consists of the victory of the protagonist, change of heart of the antagonist or the death of the main character or the antagonist who has very intimate relations with its climax. More complex climax means more complex resolution. An easy resolution of a complex situation will become a laughing stock and the impact of the climax will be diluted. Therefore it is quite difficult to develop a complex end of a complex conflict. Example:

Film: Zubaida
Scene No.:
Time; Day
Location: Airport
Characters: Victor, Mandira, Zubaida, Girivar and others.

A chopper is parked to take Victor and Mandira, Victor is seeing off people when Zubaida enters this scene. Victor is shocked to see her there.

Victor: 'Zubaida what are you doing here?'
Zubaida: 'I am going to Delhi with you.'
Victor: 'Zubaida, I will be busy in the meeting whole day and nights, what will you do there? Go back home with children.'
Zubaida:' so what I will be there too. I am not going to stay here anymore.'
Victor: 'but only two persons can sit in this chopper.Mandi is going with me.'
Zubaida: 'Mandy did, I will go this time. Not you.'
Victor: 'Zubi please. Why are you increasing my problems?'

Zubaida: 'whatever you say I am coming with you. Let's go . we are late.'

Zubaida insists to go with him. When refused she herself gets in to the plane. Victor, Mandira and others look at her. After some time Victor too sits there. The chopper takes off after some time. Everyone looks at it flying.

Cut to-

Scene No.
Time: Evening
Location: Basanti Mahal Hotel
Characters: Riyaz, Uday Singh,Girivar, Udham Singh

Riyaz enjoys drinks in a Hotel. Uday Singh enters from the rear and sits beside him. Uday Singh is serving in the Bar. Uday singh enquires about Riyaz's drink. Riyaz looks at him.

Uday: 'Hey young man... Udham Singh.'
Udham:' order sir.'
Uday: ' what this man is taking?'
Udham: 'Old monk sir.'
Uday: 'old monk..Rum.../'
Udham: ' yes sir.'
Uday: 'It is not a masculine drink.. whisky is the male drink. Bring two 'Black label' large.'
Riyaz: ' one small for me."
When the drink is brought Uday Singh serves it to Riyaz. They say cheers and start drinking.
Uday Singh: 'people call me Raja Uday Singh.'
Riyaz: 'and I am Riyaz Massod. Thank you.'

Uday: 'cheers here wishing you health, wealth and happiness. So tell me what brought you to my side?'

Riyaz: 'I am a journalist. I am here in search of a story.'

Uday Singh:' then write well about me and the hotel.'

Riyaz: 'can you clarify something? I have heard that Raja Vijendra Singh and his wife died in very mysterious circumstances?'

Uday Singh: 'No, there has been no mystery. His plane lost its control and crashed and he was alone. There was no one with him.'

Riyaz: 'you mean to say that his younger wife was not going to Delhi/'

Uday Singh: 'younger queen? My brother had only one queen and that is Queen Mandira Devi. Yes there were few women as keep, I don't remember much about them. Ok I will make a move now. Nice meeting you. I hope you young man..."

Riyaz: 'Thank you."

Uday Singh leaves the place after his drink. Waiter and Giriraj come to Riyaz. Girivar hands over a packet sent by Rajmata for Riyaz and invite to visit again.

Girivar: 'Riyaz sahib, I told you to be careful with Raja Saheb. See, this has been sent by Rajmata only for you and conveyed-all the best of your journey. Please do come again Riyaz Saheb. It will be a pleasure. Good bye.'

Riyaz unpacks the packet to see some prints wrapped in a paper. There is a diary. It is a personal diary of Zubaida. We hear voice of Zubaida coming out from the pages.

Words: *'in living memories on M'*

Riyaz: 'The heaven is slipping from my hands...

Zubaida: 'I know there is nothing permanent but still I will never let Victor change. I will not be able to accept him change. Perhaps we will be happy only after our death. If we depart now we may perhaps meet in our dreams like dry petals of a flower in a book.'

Riyaz remembers chopper taking off and caught in fire after few moments. It falls down. A red scarf flies down. There is a blast in the chopper. The flames engulf it. Riyaz looks at the photo in the album.

Cut to –

Scene No.
Time: Day
Location: An auditorium
Characters: Riyaz , Faiyazi.

Riyaz unrolls the roll of a film; the vagabond girl 'Riyaz and Faiyazi are in the theatre.'

Riyaz: 'The vagabond girl?' I fail to understand after what Mom wanted? Did she not deliberately crash the plane?'
Faiyazi: ' God forbid Rijju , My Zubaida was not like this. She knew it was a crime. You don't know if it was a conspiracy of Raja's enemies. News papers too reported this way only'.
Riyaz: ' I will preserve her memories like a fairy queen."
Faiyaz: ' yes of course. She was a fairy queen...very beautiful.'

The film *'Zubaida'* is based on the life of an actor *Zubaida* who remained a mystery till her death. Her son Riyaz consumes all his efforts to unearth the secrets but fails to solve the Jigsaw of her life and death. She created trouble for Rajmata Mandira by her presence in Victor's life, his brother Uday Singh even denounces her existence by saying that victor has only one wife Rajmata Mandira, rest are his keeps. It is presumed that Zubaida herself has orchestrated her death in the chopper accident, others don't rule out a conspiracy by his detractors. Swinging between suspicion and possibilities not only her life remains under clouds but her death too is suspense. Riyaz's journey to reveal the truth too meets the same fate. He is not alone but audiences along with her sympathizers too are associated with his struggle and feel the turmoil of her life. Audiences keep waiting to solve the mystery till the end. There are many critical moments in between till the climax. People expect the mystery to be solved with the diary gifted by Rajmata to Riyaz but it again complicates the suspense when it is known that he is her son and Faiyaz is her father. In fact nobody knows much about Zubaida. This keeps audience counting many probabilities till the end but when the film ends without the mystery being solved, audience exit from the theatre unsatisfied and more sympathetic towards her. Zubaida leaves an imprint of her presence in their minds for longer time than expected that makes the film a grand success.

Inspiration and adaptation:

Many film makers believe that the success of a film can be ensured if it is based on a successful play, Novel or inspired from an earlier successful film. It is true that originality of the work is not necessary either for making or the success of a film. Story can be adapted or inspired from any event, individual, literary work, Novel, play or a film made earlier. It is called *'Adaptation'*. Those directors who don't want to tread on a risky path with an original story prefer to go for an adaptation hoping for a sure success but it is not so.

Adaptation- Novel:

When a story is adapted from a novel or a play the screen writer should try to visualize the film with least deviation from the original vision and concept of the author however creative liberties can be availed for the medium taking him in to confidence. This helps to establish a better understanding and coordination between the author, screen play writer and director. Adaptation of other's work also requires a great deal of imagination and creative merits of screen play writer. Generally, reading of a novel or other literary work dominated by *'words'* cannot be accomplished in one sitting therefore every *word* has its own effect and influence on the reader while a film, that is watched in one sitting from beginning to end, is expressed by its *'visuals',* has more impact than written words so any adaptation should predominantly consist of *'visualization'* without hurting the sentiments of the original imagination of the author within the screen time restrictions for a film.

It is always not true that every adaptation can lead to a successful film. If it would be so then every adaptation could rake mullahs for its producer and no film could be made on an original story. The success of any creative work that includes a play, novel or any other form depends on many factors such as period, socio economic situation, atmosphere, culture values and above all the generation of people therefore it is not necessary that if something was successful earlier will be so even today. Similar is the case with remakes of earlier successful films . All remakes may not be so appealing and convincing. This can be proved by the success and failure of many films based on the Novel *'Devdas'* of the same name authored by *Sharat Chandra* first written in the year 1907.The story reflected the social discrimination, economic deprivation, unacceptability of love marriages and social status of women who struggles to find her place in the society. The first film in *'Devdas'* series was made in the year 1935 which was highly successful as people could identify with the content and its characters. After Indian independence, another film with the similar name was produced by octogenarian film maker *Bimal Roy* in the year 1952 with Dilip Kumar as Devdas. Dilip Kumar has re-lived the same magic with his histrionic performance. It is said that this is the best film of over a dozen films made on the novel till date. The recent film 'Devdas' made with an astronomical budget with Shahrukh Khan in the main lead failed to entice people due to its poor casting and characterization, distortion of period, socio economic situation of the characters and an attempt to modernize the content that altered the basic sentiments and emotions of the story. It made the film a cocktail that could neither become a modern tale nor preserved its original flavor. The film was a great disappointment for the cinegoers. Therefore one should never make an effort for whatever creative or professional reasons to distort the original concept of the author when ever such adaptations are made in to a film. Any deviation or distortion in its period and socio economic conditions of the characters that have permanent imprints in the memory challenges the audience's knowledge, intelligence and thoughts which is normally not appreciated. Creative modifications in the work should be carried out within the limits of the original vision and sensitivities.

The enormous challenge is faced by a screen play writer when he works on an adaptation of a literary form that is more 'verbose'. It cannot be effectively translated to a film form. This *verbal form* has to be transformed in to *visual form* in which a shot conveys many things that takes one or more paragraphs in a novel. This cannot be done by reducing dialogues but the entire verbal scene has to be recreated in visual form with special attention given to maintain *'filmic time'*. Adaptation of a written form in to visual form is an extensive exercise where every scene from the beginning to end is recreated, generally to the dislike of the original author.

Adaptation-Play:

If someone is inspired by a story or adapts a play for a film it is better for him to pick up the essence or the main idea of the story and conceive a screen play with an entirely new vision and concept instead of translating the play itself. A mere translation will devoid the film of its basic elements of cinema and the film will just be a visual presentation of the play as captured by a camera. So, one should desist from literal translation of a play while writing a screen play as it would be a waste of time and money. It does not mean that a film cannot be made on the successful plays. A well known Marathi play *'Toh me navech'* was adopted for its successful Hindi film *'Woh main Nahin'* and recently another very successful film *'Aankhen'* and *'Oh my God'* were adaptations of renowned Gujrati plays however more care should be taken when adapting and visualizing a play for a film. Those play writers who decide to make film on their work themselves face a bumpy ride ahead due to their lack of film sense and knowledge of technology which is essential for writing screen play.

The basic difference between a novel and the play can be explained by their structure. A novel expresses an opinion with more creative freedom in which author's unbridled imagination allows him unlimited opportunities to develop his characters, situations and emotions more extensively than a play where the characters are restricted to display their emotions in limited actions in a limited space of a stage thus reducing the scope of expressions and performance.

In the adaptation of a novel, there is also a problem to select a story and contracting its content to the limited screen time. In case of a play, adaptation does not only require a complete visual restructuring of scenes but also needs to introduce new characters and new situations. It cannot be restricted to the limited vision and space of a theatrical production. The success of a play largely depends on the performance of its actors and the sleekness of stage management; it is not possible and also not required for a film like shouting of dialogues and moving fast on the stage for a loud acting.

The Documentary Script:

It is bit uncomfortable to call it 'screenplay' for a documentary film. Everyone is aware that there is no story content in a documentary or a nonfiction film than how there could be a 'screenplay' therefore the format for a nonfiction is rightly nomenclature as **'Script'**. In journalistic jargons any written content is called a *'Script'*.

When *Lumiere Brothers* pioneered film making, it was based on realistic content. In fact it was coverage of reality as captured by camera without cuts that's why these films are known as *'single shot films'*. Subsequently the same style was extended to the coverage of news events that did not require a written script. In fact the word *'screenplay'* was not coined then and was unknown to everyone. Those were the early years of experiments in making films which gradually included individual imagination in the reality coverage. With the lapse of time and many innovations taking place in film technology, film makers also experimented with *documentary* on issues of social and national importance in addition to the coverage of news reels and reality films. In the initial years of cinema due to the absence of a written script the consumption of raw film material was too high and expensive which not many could afford. Since there was no element of entertainment in documentary like its later incarnation of fiction films, it was difficult and it is still so to arrange money for making nonfiction films. Even then awakened film makers consider production of documentary films very important and challenging. The lack of money and enthusiasm of financiers makes it more important that the director of a documentary works on his subject with in-depth research. Without in-depth study of the subject matter, the documentary will only be superficial and fail to impress its target audience.

In-depth research of the content related to the place, the personality, the issues and their resolutions makes a documentary maker more confident and sensitive about the outcome. While doing so the director is also informed about the local needs required for the shoots like availability of electrical power, transportation and local contacts that could be of immense help to him at the time of shooting.

Once the research is complete, director with his imagination and the vision of the film proceeds with writing probable visuals and tentative supporting/corresponding words like dialogues, narration or commentary, content of possible interviews and interaction with people related to the subject matter. Unlike the screen play, a documentary script can only be accepted as a *'Guide line'* for the film that can be altered anytime before, during and after the shoots. A documentary script is generally more flexible than its counterpart in fiction film. These are the advantages of working on *draft script* for a nonfiction film-

1. It provides clarity of purpose and concept of the subject matter.

2. It helps director to research and plan every visual and its corresponding sounds including commentary. If there is less information, the scene will be shorter and in contrast if there is more to say in the commentary, the scene will be longer, then he will require to shoot more visual material with more number of shots. Some scenes can also be planned to have music and the sound effects prominently.

3. The script is a *'guide'* to the film maker to remind him of every important scene or information to avoid missing out any of them.

4. It brings clarity about the content, specific *'time'* and *'Location'* of the shoots.

In a documentary film script there is nothing permanent or fixed that cannot be modified including visuals, sound and narration. That's the reason that a final version of a documentary may be completely different than what is conceived. These modifications during the production take place in the form of new information that keeps on pouring and are included or something found redundant are deleted. It may so happen that something is not available /possible to shoot in a preconceived location or something may not be available at all. It is managed with the use of still photographs, graphics or animation, stock shots, paper clippings etc. Finally the commentary is rewritten complementing the visuals to include fresh information by a professional writer. This commentary and narration is different than that is written by the director himself in the draft script before shoots..

Documentary film: Khadi and Village Industries Commission

The film example from the documentary on 'Khadi and Village Industries Commission' promotes the activities of the institution. Like advertisement films it does not promote a product but the dedication of KVIC to the cause of social service to the people of rural India. KVIC is an autonomous organization of the Indian government which was primarily established to realize the dreams of Mahatma Gandhi for the development and growth of rural society.

Scene 1:

1. L.S. Tilt down from sky to the courtyard of a house where many people are busy weaving cloth on looms.
2. M.C.S. two children fall on the heap of cloth.
3. C.U. The supervisor looks at them with anger.
   Supervisor- what have you done...scattered all the material.
4. As in shot 2. A lady the children's mother, lifts them up from the heap.
   Lady-- Get up...get up.

5. C.U. The supervisor as in shot 3.

   Supervisor- why don't you take care of them?

6. M.C.S. Mother beats her children.

7. L.S. Trolley. A boy is reading some files on a table. A girl is doing something nearby. The boy gets up to set the children free.

   Girl- why are you beating them, Mamta ben?

   Boy- why don't you send them to school? Often I find them loitering here.

8. M.C.S. Mother and children

   Lady-- How do I send them to school? Their father does not pay their fee.

9. C.S. the boy convinces the lady.

   Boy- you should have told me earlier. You can do so. All the children of our institution staff study in 8th, 9th and 11th standard or they are in ITI. They also get scholarship under workers welfare scheme.

10. Some people listen to the boy standing nearby.

    Lady-I don't know anything about it.

11. C.S. the girl too starts talking-

    Girl- Now you know. Go and get your children admitted in school and I will try for their scholarship.

12. L.S. Men and women

13. .C.S. A lady removes thread from the loom.

Scene 2.

14. L.S.A senior officer is on the stage. A boy works on a spinning wheel.

15. M.C.S. some people stand near the stage.

16. C.S. Of a hand spinning on wheel.

17. C.S. of a hand pushing a button.

18. C.U. the light is on.
19. L.S. all the workers clap.
20. L.S.Tilt up.officer.

Officer-Brothers and sisters, you see a miracle on spindle wheel. You see, how fast it works. Now Khadi and village industries commission has manufactured a new type of spinning wheel. With this you can produce electricity while spinning. You can light up your home with this electricity.

21. L.S. Top angel. People clap.
22. L.S. A boy Madhav stands up on the stage.

Madhav-'Gandhi ji used to say, Khadi is a mission.' Khadi is an employment of millions of unemployed people. It gives them to work with dignity. More over it pays them money and respect. Khadi gives them equal opportunity to grow and be equal.

23. M.L.S. People are clapping

'Khadi and Village Industries commission' is not an institution but an opportunity to underprivileged to learn new skills. It is involved in preserving the traditional past and innovating technology for the future. The innovative spinning wheel which also produces electricity to light up the darkness in the lives of rural folks is an evidence of KVIC's passion for the poor.

Criticism:

Everybody craves for appreciation for his work and writers are no exception as any appreciation works like a booster for developing his confidence and creativity however it may not be possible and practical to have it instantly. It requires a great deal of efforts, practice , maturity , command and knowledge before he is given a certificate of merit therefore the writer must be prepared to face a little amount of criticism and disappointments. He should welcome creative criticism to improve his skill. For this purpose he should move around in a group of experienced people who are experts in the field and who can render neutral appreciation and criticism to the writer. Anyway writer should also be careful of those who are either critics or appreciators of his work with a biased attitude as they can never give the right feedback to him. Self criticism with an objective outlook is also an important factor for a writer who should be his own critic first before others however an excess to it may block his creativity. The writer must read his scenes again and again to find out flaws if any and in totality afterwards. The final reading must be undertaken continuously after some time lapse to assess its continuity and emotional effects in complete disassociation with his work in accordance with the story. It will provide him a pre view of his screenplay as if he is watching his film on paper.

XXXXX

Glossary:

Accelerated Motion: The natural speed of an action in the shot is fastened. It is opposite to 'slow motion'.

Actual Sound: This is the sound which occurs from the actual actions in the scene as actors delivering dialogues, telephone bell, footsteps etc.

Back Projection: When shooting in a studio there is a moving background behind the actors which is projected from a projector kept behind a screen.

Bloop: The triangular shaped Bloop is pasted on the joints to stop unnecessary and irritating 'thud' sound coming from the joints of negative or positive film material.

Bridging Shots: when a continuity jerk is observed between the joints and juxtaposition of two shots, Bridging shots are joined in between the two.

Close Shots: a shot is taken by a camera kept near to the subject or object. Zoom lens is also used to take close shots or medium shots when a subject or object is at a distance.

Camera Angle: an angle to place a camera by which a visual is proposed to be seen.

Cheat Shots: Splitting shots of a dangerous act from a miraculous distance or danger to give a feeling of complete action.

Clap board: A wooden clap board used before a take to give details of the scene, shots and number of takes and clap to synchronize the visual and sound in editing.

Clapper Boy: The person who speaks the details of the scene written on the board and claps before the take.

Close Medium Shot: The shot between close and medium distance generally from knee to head.

Close up: very close to the subject or object to show the details. Generally it is only the face of a person.

Commentary: Explanation or comments running parallel to the visuals.

Commentative sound: The sounds like Back ground music, general atmospheric sounds etc. which are not produced by an action but are felt psychologically along with the scene. Opposite to 'Actual sounds'.

Continuity sheet: A prescribed format which has various columns to be filled with the details of scenes/shots.

Continuity man: The technician who writes about the details of a scene /shot in a prescribed form.

Continuity Title: The caption to link two disconnected scenes for continuity.

Crane shot: Specially designed crane for shooting purposes where a camera is placed to take a shot.

Cross cutting: showing of parallel actions taking place in different locations at the same time to enable the viewers to see both the actions simultaneously one after another without missing the other.

Cutter: The technician who does the physical part of editing.

Cutting Print: The positive print which is used for editing the film. This print is also called the 'Rush print' or 'Rushes'.

Dissolve: Emergence of a shot from the dark with parallel fade out of another one with in the same duration and length gradually. It is decided by parallel markings of fade in and fade out on both the shots on a synchrometer.

Dubbing: It is re recording of dialogues originally recorded on location during shooting. The actors reproduce their dialogues in the basic or any other language in a recording studio.

Dupe Negative: The Duplicate negative which is different from the original negative is made from inter- positive print. This is used to make multiple prints of the film for release purpose.

Duplicate Print: The print made out of the dupe negative.

Establishing shot: It is generally a Long shot used in the beginning to establish the location of the scene.

Effect track: A separate sound track for sound effects in addition to dialogue and music tracks.

Extra shot: The additional shots taken during the shoot.

Fade in: The shot emerge slowly from the dark to full illumination.

Fade out; The fully visible or illuminated shot gradually vanishes in to dark.

Flash back: the scene that takes the viewers to the past. It is used to show a past event or experiences.

Footage: the length of film stripe or a scene measured in feet.

Frame: one of the transparent (Transparency) pictures in the series on the celluloid stripe.

Full shot: Full visual of a subject or object seen in the frame. From head to toe.

Joint: A joint of two celluloid pieces.

Jump: Breaking of the continuity of time and action to proceed to another time and action.

Leader: An ordinary film stripe added before the first frame of the film (Positive or Negative) to thread in the projector/printing machine. Generally it is a negative film exposed in the sun. There are special leaders for the final film prints and the negatives.

Library shot: the film material not shot for the purpose of a film and preserved separately in the archive or a film library.

Long shot: it is like full shot from head to toe with some additional head space. Long shots also denote wider visual perspective. It is generally used to establish a location or a place.

Married Print: A film print combined with visuals and sound in the same stripe.

Mask: Hiding a portion of a visual seen from the camera. It is done in the camera itself.

Master shot: A shot containing the entire scene in a single shot to guide the editor about the scene. Some directors take master shots for creative purposes.

Medium Shot: Closer than the long shot but away from the range of close shots.

Mixer: An equipment to mix separate sound tracks at the time of rerecording.

Montage: Juxtapositions of disconnected shots to construct a scene with a new meaning.

Multiple exposures: Exposing a frame more than once. It is done to create special visual effects.

Mute Negative: The sound negative which does not contain sound modulations or sound track. It is used to fill the gaps in the sound negative.

Mute print: It is also called 'Silent sound Track (SST) which is used to fill the gaps in the sound positive or 'cutting print' during the editing.

Narrator: A character who explains story or event in a fiction film or a commentator who explains about the scene in non-fiction films.

Optical: Visual effects like dissolve, fades and wipes, super impositions etc. created on a special machine in a film laboratory.

Optical printer: A special machine which creates a scene with the help of a lens and also to make reduction print, special or trick effects.

Over the shoulder: The Camera on the back of the shoulder of a character.

Pan: Moving the camera from left to right or right to left from a fixed position.

Pan Shot: A shot taken by moving camera left and right.

Parallel action: Showing different events occurring at the same time one after another.

Play back: Re play of a pre recorded music track at the time of shooting to synchronize the action with the sound. Play back is generally used for shooting songs and dance sequences.

Post synchronization: Matching of pre recorded sound effects and other sounds with the visuals after the shooting.

Print: Final copy of a film.

Relational Editing: Creating a relationship between the shots during the editing.

Re-recording: Mixing of multiple sound tracks.

Retake: Shooting a shot again.

Rewind, Rewinder: Winding the film rolls on a machine called 'rewinder'.

Rough cut: First assembly of selected shots to construct a scene.

Slow cutting: Keeping the shots lengthy or for more duration to slow down the pace of the scene. It is reverse of the 'fast cutting.'

Slow motion: Slower than actual speed of an action.

Sound track: on the sides of film stripe the sound modulations or track run parallel to the visuals.

Stock shot: shots preserved in an archive or a film library.

Super impose: Printing of two or more shots on the similar place and length of the film to see them one over another.

Synchronization, Synch: Matching the visuals and sounds parallel to each other so that visuals are seen and sound is heard simultaneously during the projection as if it is coming from the visuals.

Synchronizer: An equipment to synch visuals and sounds in parallel tracks. It can accommodate up to four or six tracks.

Synchronous sounds: The sounds which are synchronized with the visuals or can be synchronized to show the visuals as source of the sounds in the scene.

Take: Recording a shot in the camera.

Tilt: Moving the camera up and down from a fixed position.

Track, Tracking: Moving the camera straight forward or backward on a trolly or any other device. The word 'track' is also used for sound tracks.

Trolley (straight and round): A cart on wheels on which the cameraman sits to take the shot in whatever direction he wants to move.

Truck shot: Shot taken from a truck, trolley, car or any other vehicle.

Wild shooting: Shooting without sound where no sound is recorded with the action.

Wild sound: Recording without visuals. This sound is matched with the scene later.

Wipe: A device to show the transition of the scene like dissolve and fades.

XXXXX

Bibliography:

- **Kuldeep Sinha** is a Film graduate from Film and Television Institute of India, Pune with an experience of over 30 years.
- International Participation in Film festivals-Slovakia, Sweden, Berlin, Rome, Australia, India etc.
- Written, Produced, Edited & directed more than 200 Short films on variety of subject.

- **Books Authored:**

Cinema:	1 . **'Film & Tv: A Director's guide,**
	2. 'Art of Screen play writing',
	3. 'Elements of 'Film Editing',
	4. Mohammad. Rafi:
	The melody man
Anthology:	**5.Siskiyaan,**
	6. Dastak,
	7.Kashish,
	8.(Rashmin: (Kashish:Marathi)
Personality - Development:	**9..Galion se chaurahe tak.**
English novels:	**10..The Darkness in the Arc,**
	11. Neither ,
	12..Behind the moving Images.
Editor:	**Documentary Today**
	(A magazine on Non-fiction film)

- **International Awards:**
  Non-conventional Energy Resources-Agro Film 84 Slovakia
  Non Conventional Energy Resources- Golden Ear Berlin.1984
  Non Conventional Energy Resources- International consumer film competition-Berlin1985
  Non Conventional Energy Resources- Boris Kidvic Award, International scientific film competition-Belgrade 1985.
  Services of tress-Silver Bunch, International film festival Santarem Portugal 1987
  Watershed Management- F.A.O. Award. slovakia1996
  Poultry Farming- F.A.O. Award, Slovakia 2005.

- **National film Awards:**
  Special Children-Special award 2005
  Hans Akela- Best Biographical film-2008
  Teejan Bai- Best Biographical Film 2002
  Vermiculture-Best Agriculture film 2000
  Tribal Women Artists- Best Art and culture film 2000
  From the land of Buddha to the land of Buddha-Best Historical Reconstruction film 2000
  In search of Excellence - Best Adventure and exploration film. 1998
  Tara Nath Shenoy-Best News Film 1986

- **Other Awards:**
  Police –your friend: Best documentary film, Maharashtra State Award 2002
  Anmol Patthar Bemole Zindagi: Best Documentary film-R.A.P.A. Award 2001

- **Special Honours:**
  - **Scroll of Honours:** for contribution in Indian cinema by Indian organization of mass communication and Institute of Broadcasting Mumbai.
  - **Life Time Achievement Award:** International centre for Cultural Relations, Mumbai.
  - **Hindi Sahitya Samman-** Ministry of Information & Broadcasting, Govt. Of India.
  - **Rajbhasha Shree-** Prasar Bharti (Govt. Of India) & Ashirwad Award Mumbai.
  - **Saraswat Samman-** Ashirwad Award, Mumbai.

- **Notable Films-**
  - **Rafi: We Remember you**
  - **Toote Pankh**
  - **Gandhi- an emerging reality**
  - **Through a lens starkly**
  - **No Room for fear.**
  - **Druzhba**
  - **India-Bhutan Friends forever.**

XXXXX